Joseph Baldwin

Psychology Applied to the Art of Teaching

Joseph Baldwin

Psychology Applied to the Art of Teaching

ISBN/EAN: 9783337003685

Printed in Europe, USA, Canada, Australia, Japan

Cover: Foto ©Paul-Georg Meister /pixelio.de

More available books at **www.hansebooks.com**

International Education Series

EDITED BY

WILLIAM T. HARRIS, A. M., LL. D.

VOLUME XIX.

ELEMENTARY PEDAGOGY.

CONTRIBUTIONS BY JOSEPH BALDWIN, A. M., LL. D.

VOLUME I.
ART OF SCHOOL MANAGEMENT.
Kirksville.
Missouri State Normal School.

I. Educational Instrumentalities and School Hygiene.
II. School Organization and Classification.
III. School Government and Educative Punishments.
IV. Courses of Study and Programmes.
V. Class Management and Methods of Teaching.
VI. Examination, Marking, Records, Promotion, and Graduation.
VII. Professional Education, School Supervision, and Educational Progress.

VOLUME II.
ELEMENTARY PSYCHOLOGY.
Vol. VI, Int. Ed. Ser.
Huntsville.
Texas State Normal School.

I. Instinct, Sensorium, Sensation, and Attention.
II. Sense Perception, Self Perception, and Necessary Perception.
III. Memory, Fancy, and Imagination.
IV. Conception, Judgment, and Reason.
V. Egoistic Emotions, Altruistic Emotions, and Cosmic Emotions.
VI. Will—Attention, Choice, and Action.
VII. Physiological Psychology and Education.

VOLUME III.
PSYCHOLOGY APPLIED TO THE ART OF TEACHING.
Vol. XIX, Int. Ed. Ser.
Austin.
University of Texas.

I. Education of the Perceptive Activities.
II. Education of the Representative Activities.
III. Education of the Reflective Activities.
IV. Education of the Emotional Activities.
V. Education of the Will Activities.
VI. The Art of Teaching and Teaching Methods.
VII. Application of Psychology to teaching Conduct Studies, Language-Literature Studies, Science Studies, Mathematics Studies, and Art Studies.

VOLUME IV.
SCHOOL MANAGEMENT AND SCHOOL METHODS.
Vol. XI., Int. Ed. Ser.
Austin.
University of Texas.

I. Pupil Betterment through Better Educational Conditions.
II. Pupil Betterment through Better Educational Facilities.
III. Pupil Improvement through Educative School Government.
IV. Pupil Improvement through Educative Correlation of Schools and School Work.
V. Pupil Betterment through Educative Class Management and Class Methods.
VI. Pupil Improvement through Efficient Methods of teaching the Conduct Studies, the Language-Literature Studies, the Science Studies, the Mathematics Studies, and the Art Studies.
VII. Pupil Betterment through Educative School Unification and Supervision.

INTERNATIONAL EDUCATION SERIES.

12mo, cloth, uniform binding.

THE INTERNATIONAL EDUCATION SERIES was projected for the purpose of bringing together in orderly arrangement the best writings, new and old, upon educational subjects, and presenting a complete course of reading and training for teachers generally. It is edited by WILLIAM T. HARRIS, LL. D., United States Commissioner of Education, who has contributed for the different volumes in the way of introduction, analysis, and commentary. The volumes are tastefully and substantially bound in uniform style.

VOLUMES NOW READY.

1. THE PHILOSOPHY OF EDUCATION. By JOHANN K. F. ROSENKRANZ, Doctor of Theology and Professor of Philosophy, University of Königsberg. Translated by ANNA C. BRACKETT. Second edition, revised, with Commentary and complete Analysis. $1.50.

2. A HISTORY OF EDUCATION. By F. V. N. PAINTER, A. M., Professor of Modern Languages and Literature, Roanoke College, Va. $1.50.

3. THE RISE AND EARLY CONSTITUTION OF UNIVERSITIES. WITH A SURVEY OF MEDIÆVAL EDUCATION. By S. S. LAURIE, LL. D., Professor of the Institutes and History of Education, University of Edinburgh. $1.50.

4. THE VENTILATION AND WARMING OF SCHOOL BUILDINGS. By GILBERT B. MORRISON, Teacher of Physics and Chemistry, Kansas City High School. $1.00.

5. THE EDUCATION OF MAN. By FRIEDRICH FROEBEL. Translated and annotated by W. N. HAILMANN, A. M., Superintendent of Public Schools, La Porte, Ind. $1.50.

6. ELEMENTARY PSYCHOLOGY AND EDUCATION. By JOSEPH BALDWIN, A. M., LL. D., author of "The Art of School Management." $1.50.

7. THE SENSES AND THE WILL. (Part I of "THE MIND OF THE CHILD.") By W. PREYER, Professor of Physiology in Jena. Translated by H. W. BROWN, Teacher in the State Normal School at Worcester, Mass. $1.50.

8. MEMORY: WHAT IT IS AND HOW TO IMPROVE IT. By DAVID KAY, F. R.G.S., author of "Education and Educators," etc. $1.50.

9. THE DEVELOPMENT OF THE INTELLECT. (Part II of "THE MIND OF THE CHILD.") By W. PREYER, Professor of Physiology in Jena. Translated by H. W. BROWN. $1.50.

10. HOW TO STUDY GEOGRAPHY. A Practical Exposition of Methods and Devices in Teaching Geography which apply the Principles and Plans of Ritter and Guyot. By FRANCIS W. PARKER, Principal of the Cook County (Illinois) Normal School. $1.50.

11. EDUCATION IN THE UNITED STATES: ITS HISTORY FROM THE EARLIEST SETTLEMENTS. By RICHARD G. BOONE, A. M., Professor of Pedagogy, Indiana University. $1.50.

12. EUROPEAN SCHOOLS: OR, WHAT I SAW IN THE SCHOOLS OF GERMANY, FRANCE, AUSTRIA, AND SWITZERLAND. By L. R. KLEMM, Ph. D., Principal of the Cincinnati Technical School. Fully illustrated. $2.00.

13. PRACTICAL HINTS FOR THE TEACHERS OF PUBLIC SCHOOLS. By GEORGE HOWLAND, Superintendent of the Chicago Public Schools. $1.00.

14. PESTALOZZI: HIS LIFE AND WORK. By ROGER DE GUIMPS. Authorized Translation from the second French edition, by J. RUSSELL, B. A. With an Introduction by Rev. R. H. QUICK, M. A. $1.50.

15. SCHOOL SUPERVISION. By J. L. PICKARD, LL. D. $1.00.

16. HIGHER EDUCATION OF WOMEN IN EUROPE. By HELENE LANGE, Berlin. Translated and accompanied by comparative statistics by L. R. KLEMM. $1.00.

17. ESSAYS ON EDUCATIONAL REFORMERS. By ROBERT HERBERT QUICK, M. A., Trinity College, Cambridge. Only authorized edition of the work as rewritten in 1890. $1.50.

18. A TEXT-BOOK IN PSYCHOLOGY. By JOHANN FRIEDRICH HERBART. Translated by MARGARET K. SMITH. $1.00.

19. PSYCHOLOGY APPLIED TO THE ART OF TEACHING. By JOSEPH BALDWIN, A. M., LL. D. $1.50.

20. ROUSSEAU'S ÉMILE : OR, TREATISE ON EDUCATION. Translated and annotated by W. H. PAYNE, Ph. D., LL. D., Chancellor of the University of Nashville. $1.50.

21. THE MORAL INSTRUCTION OF CHILDREN. By FELIX ADLER. $1.50.

22. ENGLISH EDUCATION IN THE ELEMENTARY AND SECONDARY SCHOOLS. By ISAAC SHARPLESS, LL. D., President of Haverford College. $1.00.

23. EDUCATION FROM A NATIONAL STANDPOINT. By ALFRED FOUILLÉE. $1.50.

24. MENTAL DEVELOPMENT IN THE CHILD. By W. PREYER, Professor of Physiology in Jena. Translated by H. W. BROWN. $1.00.

25. HOW TO STUDY AND TEACH HISTORY. By B. A. HINSDALE, Ph. D., LL. D., University of Michigan. $1.50.

26. SYMBOLIC EDUCATION : A COMMENTARY ON FROEBEL'S "MOTHER PLAY." By SUSAN E. BLOW. $1.50.

27. SYSTEMATIC SCIENCE TEACHING. By EDWARD GARDNIER HOWE. $1.50.

28. THE EDUCATION OF THE GREEK PEOPLE. By THOMAS DAVIDSON. $1.50.

29. THE EVOLUTION OF THE MASSACHUSETTS PUBLIC-SCHOOL SYSTEM. By G. H. MARTIN, A. M. $1.50.

30. PEDAGOGICS OF THE KINDERGARTEN. By FRIEDRICH FROEBEL. 12mo. $1.50.

31. THE MOTTOES AND COMMENTARIES OF FRIEDRICH FROEBEL'S MOTHER PLAY. By SUSAN E. BLOW and HENRIETTA R. ELIOT. $1.50.

32. THE SONGS AND MUSIC OF FROEBEL'S MOTHER PLAY. By SUSAN E. BLOW. $1.50.

33. THE PSYCHOLOGY OF NUMBER, AND ITS APPLICATIONS TO METHODS OF TEACHING ARITHMETIC. By JAMES A. McLELLAN, A. H., and JOHN DEWEY, Ph. D. $1.50.

34. TEACHING THE LANGUAGE-ARTS. SPEECH, READING, COMPOSITION. By B. A. HINSDALE, Ph. D., LL. D., Professor of Science and the Art of Teaching in the University of Michigan. $1.00.

35. THE INTELLECTUAL AND MORAL DEVELOPMENT OF THE CHILD. PART I. CONTAINING CHAPTERS ON PERCEPTION, EMOTION, MEMORY, IMAGINATION, AND CONSCIOUSNESS. By GABRIEL COMPAYRÉ. Translated from the French by MARY E. WILSON, B. L. Smith College, Member of the Graduate Seminary in Child Study, University of California. $1.50.

36. HERBART'S A B C OF SENSE-PERCEPTION, AND INTRODUCTORY WORKS. By WILLIAM J. ECKOFF, Ph. D., Pd. D., Professor of Pedagogy in the University of Illinois ; Author of "Kant's Inaugural Dissertation." $1.50.

37. PSYCHOLOGIC FOUNDATIONS OF EDUCATION. By WILLIAM T. HARRIS, A. M., LL. D. $1.50.

38. THE SCHOOL SYSTEM OF ONTARIO. By the Hon. GEORGE W. ROSS, LL. D., Minister of Education for the Province of Ontario. $1.00.

39. PRINCIPLES AND PRACTICE OF TEACHING. By JAMES JOHONNOT. $1.50.

40. SCHOOL MANAGEMENT AND SCHOOL METHODS. By JOSEPH BALDWIN. $1.50.

41. FROEBEL'S EDUCATIONAL LAWS FOR ALL TEACHERS. By JAMES L. HUGHES, Inspector of Schools, Toronto. $1.50.

OTHER VOLUMES IN PREPARATION.

Toronto : GEORGE N. MORANG, 63 Yonge St.

PSYCHOLOGY APPLIED

TO THE

ART OF TEACHING

BY

JOSEPH BALDWIN, A. M., LL. D.

PROFESSOR OF PEDAGOGY, UNIVERSITY OF TEXAS; AUTHOR OF "ART OF SCHOOL
MANAGEMENT" AND "ELEMENTARY PSYCHOLOGY"

WITH AN INTRODUCTION BY
JAMES GIBSON HUME, M.A., PH.D.
Professor of Philosophy, University of Toronto.

TORONTO:
GEORGE N. MORANG,
1897.

INTRODUCTION TO CANADIAN EDITION.

It is said that, in some of the engagements in a war lately waged, tons of ammunition were used, and yet only comparatively few of the combatants were killed or wounded. It was not merely an instance of poor marksmanship on a large scale, for a war correspondent reported that the majority never aimed at all, and many had even removed the "sights" from their rifles as inconveniences. In the great educational army, in its campaign against ignorance, do we not find similar conditions and a like waste of the infinitely more valuable ammunition of life forces and life energies, all for want of "aim." This volume is intended to assist the young educational recruits, while they are engaged in target practice in the training institutes. It is written by one experienced in teaching and in training teachers, for the special benefit of untrained and inexperienced beginners in the noble profession of teaching. Instead of giving many rules without reasons, it seeks to lead the young teacher to such a knowledge of the laws of mental growth that he may be able to draw up intelligently his own rules for the successful prosecution of his calling as an educator.

This book is not meant to be "memorized"—the author insists that it is simply intended to suggest and guide the search for self-knowledge, which the educational explorer must conduct for himself.

Many young people have read books such as Smiles' "Self-Help," and Blackie's "Self-Culture." They will find that the best book to direct them in self-help and self-culture is a good work on Psychology properly utilized. Many have consulted phrenologists to discover their capabilities and aptitudes, not knowing that a study of Psychology would enable them to know more about their own powers and disposition than any phrenologist could tell them. Perhaps others have sent for some well-advertised device for memory-strengthening, while the only means of training memory is a judicious conformity to the laws of mental acquisition and reproduction as they are unfolded in Psychology. To attain to this insight no expensive laboratory, no costly apparatus is required.

Psychology while valuable in the education of every one, is of paramount importance to the teacher.

An able thinker writes: "There is no question of importance, which is not comprised in the Science of Man ; and there is none, which can be decided with any certainty, before we become acquainted with that science."*

---

* Hume, "Treatise on Human Nature."

Wundt says: " Psychology is in relation to natural science the *supplementary,* in relation to the mental sciences the *fundamental,* and in relation to philosophy the *propædeutic empirical science.*"†

This is an age of remarkable progress in the natural sciences. For the advancement of natural science itself, psychology is of great service. A scientist with true psychological insight, says that the majority of scientists are teaching their pupils facts, facts, facts, while they should be teaching method, method, method. Let the pupils learn how to discover for themselves. Investigation should not be curtailed; development should not be curtailed; development should not be lopsided. For full knowledge and symmetrical growth the psychical enquiries must be conjoined to the physical.

This is an age of intense interest in the social sciences. All such enquiries rest upon the knowledge of human nature. Philosophical and theological problems maintain their perennial interest and importance. The preparation for the examination and comprehension of these lofty themes is through the antecedent study of Psychology.

The central position of Psychology, and its intimate connection with all lines of human enquiry make it of inestimable value to the teacher who

† Wundt, "Outlines of Psychology."

desires to co-ordinate all his knowledge into a mutually supporting system, thus making his experience a fruitful starting-point for the acquisition and "assimilation" of further knowledge. It helps him to understand the educational significance and value of different studies, and to adopt methods suitable to the subject taught, and adapted to the mental conditions of his pupils. It leads him to acquire an absorbing and intelligent interest in his pupils and in everything that concerns their physical, mental, and moral well-being. It aids him in avoiding many mistakes on his own part. It enables him to assist his pupils in guarding against many dangers that beset them. It leads to at least the beginning of an acquaintanceship with many of the highest and most renowned exponents of the intellectual life of the race.

Although the history of the science of Psychology still remains unwritten, it has nevertheless had a noteworthy growth, extending over many centuries, and gathering up the wisdom of many of the ablest thinkers of every age. Beginning, as every science has done, in the vague generalizations of ordinary experience recorded in language and literature, passing on to more explicit classifications, definitions, and explanations of a descriptive kind, it has at last become exact, definite, experimental and scientific, at least in aim and method, if not in full accomplishment.

A reference to Ward's excellent article on Psychology, in the Encyclopædia Britannica, will shew that he cites frequently from the following, and from many others of similar fame who have contributed to the upbuilding of the science of Psychology: Plato, Aristotle, DesCartes, Bacon, Hobbes, Spinoza, Leibnitz, Locke, Berkeley, Hume, Kant, Fichte, Hegel, Hamilton, Mansel, J. S. Mill, Darwin, Herbart, Lotze, Fechner, Green, Bain, Herbert Spencer, Wundt.

The acquaintanceship thus begun may in time ripen into more complete and intelligent appreciation of the masterpieces of the great leaders of human enlightenment.

JAMES GIBSON HUME,

Professor of Philosophy,
University of Toronto

TORONTO, AUGUST, 1897.

EDITOR'S PREFACE.

In the preface to Prof. Baldwin's Elementary Psychology and Education (Vol. VI of this Education Series) I have dwelt upon the broad distinction that exists between external observation and internal observation, or between sense-perception and introspection. External observation sees things and records their movements, changes, and inorganic properties. Introspection perceives what goes on in the mind— namely, feelings, thoughts, and volitions. There is a wide difference between these two classes of objects. Outside things are all related to environments, and more or less dependent on them The doctrine of relativity holds supremely among them; each is what it is only through the relation it bears to something else; on the contrary, the objects of introspection pertain to independent being, to that which controls and determines itself, to that which is not only an object but also at the same time a subject.

Hence all objects of introspection are double—they are both objects and subjects—they are phenomenal acts or manifestations, belonging to a self—and both are presented in consciousness or introspection. I perceive my feelings, but not isolately or abstractly—I

do not perceive feelings detached from a self or subject
that feels, but in every case I perceive a self that is in
the act or state of feeling.   This is an essential distinction to be borne in mind.   I perceive not isolated and
detached feelings, ideas, or volitions, but the feelings as
I—the self—feel them; the ideas as I think them; the
volitions as I will them.

The feelings, ideas, and volitions are phenomenal or
dependent beings existing in and through a self which
is their substance; but the self is known to be a nou-
menon, an independent being—a being that can originate activity in itself and others; it is a free being and
a moral personality.

We see by this that the act of introspection is worthy
of the most careful study, because of the high character of its object.   But the most important thing to notice here is that external perception has to be re-enforced by introspection in order to enable it to perceive
organic beings and their phenomena.   This is a point
which has escaped the attention of many of the students of physiological psychology.   They speak of objective methods of studying the mind, and take frequent opportunity to disparage introspection as an old
and discarded method of studying the mind.   This all
comes from ignorance of the history of psychology,
and especially from lack of familiarity with the works
of the great thinkers in this field.   If one has mastered
Plato's *Republic, Sophist, Parmenides, The Laws* (especially the tenth book), *Theœtetus*, and *Timœus*, he will
never speak disparagingly of the results of inner experience.   If one has (not a mere grammatical or philo-
logical, but) a scholarly acquaintance with Aristotle's

book on the soul,* he will revere introspection as the
eye of the soul itself, which sees not only the divine
objects of knowledge, but also interprets for us the
vast bulk of our external experience. Such, too, will
be his reverence for introspection if he has studied
those giants of modern philosophy, Kant, Fichte, Schell-
ing, and Hegel. It was well said of these men by a
writer in *The Dial* fifty years ago: "These four philosophers would have been conspicuous in any age, and
will hereafter, we think, be named with Plato, Aristotle, Bacon, Descartes, and Leibnitz, among the great
thinkers of the world. Silently these lights arose and
went up the sky without noise, to take their place
among the fixed stars of genius and shine with them
—names that will not fade out of heaven until some
ages shall have passed away. These men were thinkers all—deep, mighty thinkers. . . . They sat on the
brink of the well of Truth and continued to draw
for themselves and the world. Take Kant alone,
and in the whole compass of thought we scarce know
his superior. From Aristotle to Leibnitz we do not
find his equal. No, nor since Leibnitz. Need we say
it? Was there not many a Lord Bacon in Immanuel
Kant?"

But the beginner in mental science is excusable if
he does not admit the claims of introspection; for it is
a higher faculty which grows slowly with painstaking
culture—of great worth, but costing hard mental work.
Although the weakest mind possesses introspection in
the fact that it is conscious of itself, it does not yet

---

* Let him use the splendid text-book of Edwin Wallace, "Aristotle's
Psychology in Greek and English."

control it as an instrument of scientific discovery. It must discipline itself in order to acquire this power.

The first step in this difficult road is to make an inventory of the three great departments of mental phenomena, and the present volume will afford the student timely aid in this work. It will help the teacher in training his pupils into the second order of observation —the observation of noumena or self-activities.

As I have above intimated, the first order of observation—sense-perception—does not suffice to the perception of organic beings ; it can perceive only mechanical things and movements. The phenomena of plant life, animal life, and human life involve self-activity, and they must be recognized and interpreted through our consciousness of our inner self, its desires and instincts, its ideas and volitions.

We apperceive—to use the new technical word for this act of recognition and interpretation of what is perceived by what is known before—we apperceive plants and animals by referring their actions and manifestations to inward selves analogous to our own.

By no possibility can we perceive through external observation a feeling, a thought, or a volition in any object before us in time and space. The anatomy of the brain does not furnish anything visible or tangible that resembles a thought any more than does a wig-block. There is no known movement in the brain which indicates that any process of feeling or thought or will is going on. By introspection alone we see mind directly, and by its aid we conduct observations on whatever in nature manifests life and mind.

W. T. HARRIS.

WASHINGTON, D. C., *February 1, 1892.*

AUTHOR'S PREFACE.

THE hope of producing a book helpful to the great brotherhood of teachers inspired this volume. During four decades these chapters have been given as lessons to many classes of teachers. The practical results in a thousand schools have been observed with intense interest. From year to year, in the light of experience and study and criticism, these lessons have been remodeled. They are now submitted in the form which seems to the author best calculated to aid teachers in preparing themselves for their great work.

Teacher, if you are far advanced, this book is not meant for you. You feast on a profounder professional literature. But you are earnestly asked to judge this work as a contribution to elementary pedagogy. Each paragraph was written to help the teachers of our ungraded country schools as well as the teachers of our graded schools. These, with their schools, were constantly before the mind of the writer. Chapters were condensed into pages, and pages into paragraphs, that overworked teachers might have the most helpful things in the briefest space. The aim of every page is to stimulate the teachers of our elementary schools to make the most of themselves, and do most for their pupils.

The history of the growth of these chapters, it is thought, will best explain their contents. During my senior year in college I had taken the usual course in mental and moral science, and had written essays on education; but when I assumed the position of a teacher of teachers I began to realize my profound ignorance. Even now I can almost feel the darkness through which I tried to grope my way. I had studied theories, but *spirit* and *soul* and *mental culture*, and my own *mental economy*, were to me inscrutable conundrums. In my world, teachers' institutes, educational journals, and works on pedagogy, were not yet even thought of. For a weary decade I literally groped my way.

First Step.—Aided by a distinguished professor in a medical college, I studied the brain and its connections from the standpoint of the soul. As fast as I learned these lessons I gave them to my classes of teachers. The "laboratory" method had not then been thought of, but through all these years I have continued these studies, and have made these lessons in psychological physiology the basis of my work in pedagogy.

Second Step.—States of consciousness, mental phenomena, mental faculties, and similar expressions, were to me perplexing mysteries. Happily, the expedient of organizing my classes into exploring parties now occurred to me.* I became the leader of expeditions to explore the self-world. *How do we gain sense-ideas?* This was the topic. We became children again, and had many object-lessons, but we critically observed our acts of gaining ideas through each of the senses. We analyzed many of our own acts of sense-perceiving. It became clear to us that self makes his sense-ideas out of his sensations. The capability of self to gain sense-ideas was termed *sense-perception.* Thus, building on our own experiences and insight, we explored as best we could the self-world. We unscrupulously appropriated the discoveries of other explorers, such as Aristotle, Kant, Hamilton, and Herbart. These lessons grew year by year, and are now the chapters of the Elementary Psychology.

Third Step.—Philosophy of education, methods of culture, laws of mental growth, educational principles, and such expressions appeared to me as intangible abstractions. I was benighted and

---

* Whatever success I have had as a teacher I owe very largely to this plan of work. I have all along taken my students into partnership, and we have together investigated all subjects considered.

felt helpless. But my classes waited. They were ready and anxious to enter upon new voyages of discovery. The great unknown world of human education was before us. *How do we educate sense-perception?* This was the momentous question. We observed that infants slowly gained imperfect sense-ideas, while youths quickly gained perfect sense-notions. It became clear to us that education made the difference between the feeble perceiving of the infant and the vigorous perceiving of the youth. It also became evident that this growth, this development, this increase of power, came of *well-directed effort in gaining sense-ideas.* We had discovered the law of effort. The discovery of other laws, and of means and methods of promoting sense-perception growth, followed. Thus we advanced step by step until we had investigated in our imperfect way the education of the intellectual powers, the emotions, and the will. These chapters *were* those lessons. Even in their present form they will doubtless be recognized by several thousand teachers.

Fourth Step.—The great problem, "*the mental economy,*" remained a dark mystery. I grew weary of pondering the solutions of writers who looked at the facts through their theories. I could not understand the *organic soul* of the phrenologist; or the *triangular soul* of writers who represented intellect, sensibility, and will as the three sides of the one energy; or the *composite soul* of Froebel, who taught that the infant soul is composed of *germ faculties* which education develops; or the *faculty-less soul* of Herbart, who had created a new psychology to *fit* his pedagogy. He thought of the infant soul as a simple essence, and of the faculties as acquired facilities. He taught that "the power of self-determination, like the powers of perception and memory and reason, is acquired." Much less could I understand Herbert Spencer's *material soul.* I organized my advanced classes to grapple with this problem of the ages. *What does the mental economy mean to you?* This was now the absorbing question. To assist us in our efforts to grasp the mental economy as a whole, we constructed the psychological pyramid and the psychological tree, and the maps of mental growth. Our brethren ridiculed, but we found these crude devices materially helpful. We had learned to think of a self as having native energies to do acts different in kind, and we had learned to think of these activities as merely the capabilities of the self. But our syntheses now led us to study the relations of these powers. We saw through a glass darkly, but years lengthened into decades before we gained the deeper insight that each capability of self supplements all his other capabilities, and that education comes of co-ordinated and concentrated effort. These simple, far-reaching truths came to us like revelations. We could now understand that while the mental powers are elemental, mental acts are wonderfully complex. We could now better understand Herbart's apperception, and Lewes's assimilation. In the light of these and similar truths we began over again our lessons in psychology and education, and the art of teaching. All possible helps were sought. As each improved telescope compels the astronomer to revise his science of the heavens, so this deeper insight compelled us to revise our work. From the history of education, and from the methods of the world's great educators, we gleaned invaluable lessons. We joyously seized upon truth wherever found. I would gladly credit each discoverer, but this is now impossible. I can only express my deepest gratitude to educators and to the members of my classes. Everything gained was assimilated into these lessons, which have grown into the Applied Psychology and the Art of Teaching.

Sister, brother, you are a *teacher*, or you intend to be one. You will now be my class. Together we will venture anew on these voyages of discovery. Psychology and education are as old as the race and as young as the latest human consciousness. Through a knowledge of self, to a knowledge of others, is the divine law. Each new teacher must create a new psychology and a new education. You are entitled to the thought and experience of the race, but at every step you must build on your own experience and your own insight. I will be happy to lead and to suggest, but that success may attend our efforts you must discern everything, feel everything, do everything. This is no easy task. It will require your best efforts, but you will be rewarded by becoming able to lead others.

JOSEPH BALDWIN.

UNIVERSITY OF TEXAS,
AUSTIN, TEXAS, *March*, 1892.

CONTENTS.

PART I.

EDUCATION OF THE PERCEPTIVE POWERS.

PART II.

EDUCATION OF THE REPRESENTATIVE POWERS

PART III.

EDUCATION OF THE THOUGHT-POWERS.

PART I.

EDUCATION OF THE PERCEPTIVE POWERS.

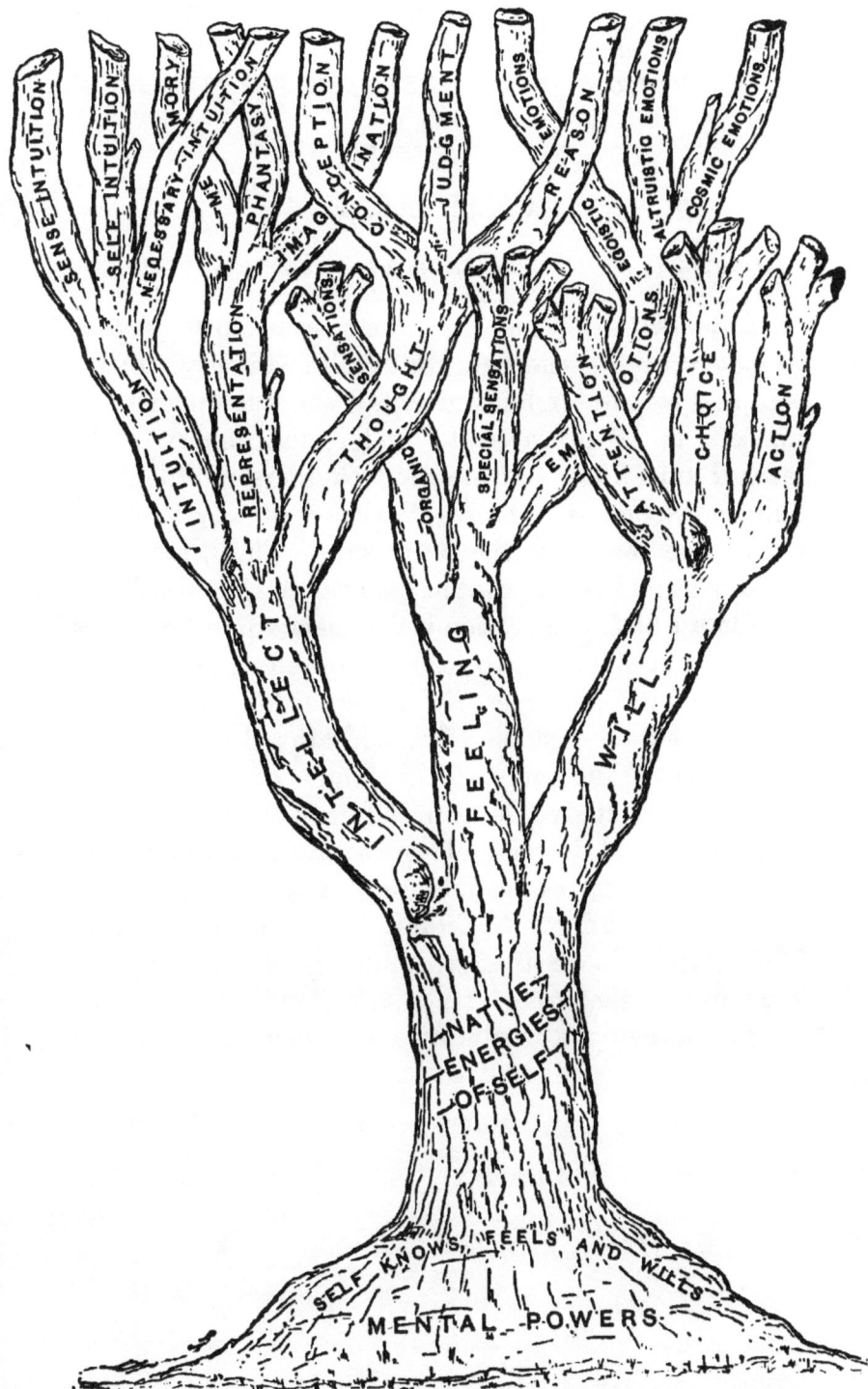

PART FIRST.

EDUCATION OF THE PERCEPTIVE POWERS.

CHAPTER I.

PSYCHOLOGY, APPLIED PSYCHOLOGY, EDUCATION, TEACHING.

Know Self.—Psychology is the science of self (*psycho* + *logy* = soul + science). But each self is a type of the race and stands for humanity. When one understands himself, he is prepared to understand others. The teacher must know self in order to understand the child. Self-knowledge is not only the shortest way to child-knowledge, but it is the only way. This knowledge underlies and makes possible the science of education.

Educate Self.—Education is the science of self-development (*e*, out + *ducere*, to lead). Self-effort made in accordance with law educates. Around this central truth are grouped the results of the educational thought and experience of the race. In the light of the ages the teacher *must* study his own self-growth, that he *may* understand and foster child-growth. This knowledge underlies and makes possible the Art of Teaching.

Guide Self-Effort.—Teaching is the art of promoting self-growth. Self-effort, under guidance, educates. Teaching is the art of stimulating and guiding self-effort. In the light of education as a science, the teacher *must* learn to guide his own efforts, that he *may* wisely guide the efforts of others.

Manage Self.—Management is the art of character-building. Ideas pass over into emotions, and emotions pass over into actions. The teacher controls child ideas and thus controls child emotions and child acts. When wisely managed, the child builds a noble character. The teacher *must* manage himself, that he *may* manage the child.

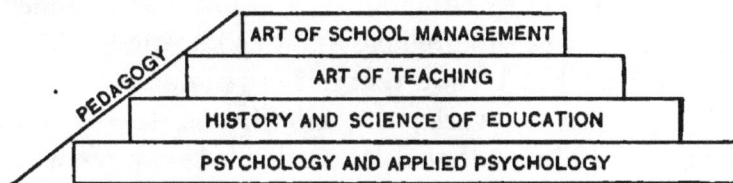

```
         ┌──────────────────────────────────┐
PEDAGOGY │    ART OF SCHOOL MANAGEMENT       │
      ┌──┴──────────────────────────────────┴──┐
      │           ART OF TEACHING               │
   ┌──┴─────────────────────────────────────────┴──┐
   │      HISTORY AND SCIENCE OF EDUCATION          │
┌──┴─────────────────────────────────────────────────┴──┐
│         PSYCHOLOGY AND APPLIED PSYCHOLOGY              │
└───────────────────────────────────────────────────────┘
```

Lead the Child.—Pedagogy includes the professional studies and the training which fit one for an educational leader (*pais* or *paida*, child + *agogos*, leading). A slave in the olden times literally led the boy to school; in our day the teacher leads the child up to a higher and better life, and elevates the individual into the experience of the race.

I. Psychology.

By this is meant the science of self. I find out all I can about myself. I perceive myself knowing, feeling, willing. I discover my native energies and their laws of activity and growth. I systematize this knowledge. I give an account of the ways in which self acts. I have made a science of self—a psychology.

1. **Self**—I know, I feel, I will. I am aware that I thus act, and that I am the same I that thus acted last

week and last year. I am aware that I do these acts spontaneously. I determine; I am free. I am endowed with the capabilities of self-knowing, self-consciousness, self-determination, self-activity. I am a self, a person.

2. **Self works in a Physical Organism.**—My sensorium and motorium give me direct connection with the universe. I have my headquarters for life in my cerebrum. In some unknown way I think, love, and decide in and through my cerebral ganglia and their connections. I can not comprehend it; this knowledge is too high for me; but I know that self is generated with the body, lives in it, works through it, and leaves it at death. I also know that Self can do his best work when his body is in the best condition.

3. **Self has Native Energies called Faculties.**—I find that I have capabilities to know, feel, and will in distinct ways. I learn to call these energies my powers, my faculties, my capabilities. Self is endowed with energies to do acts different in kind. My faculties are simply my capabilities of knowing, feeling, and willing. I learn to call my capabilities to know by the group name, *Intellect*. I find that I know in different ways.

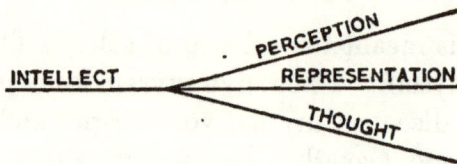

I gain some notions at once; this is immediate or *Perceptive-knowing*. Then I can make present again, in old or new forms, my past acquisitions; this is *Repre-*

sentative-knowing. I can also think my intuitions into higher forms, and gain new truths through the medium of known truths; this is mediate knowing or *Thought-knowing.* I learn to call my capabilities to know, my intellectual powers. Intellect includes *Intuitive*-knowing, *Representative*-knowing, and *Thought*-knowing.

Feeling.—I enjoy and suffer. I experience various feelings differing in kind. Some feelings are occasioned by sensor-excitations caused by organic stimuli; these feelings are *organic sensations.* Some feelings are occasioned by sensor-excitations caused by external stimuli acting through the special senses; these feelings are *special sensations.* Other feelings are occasioned by ideas; these feelings are *emotions.* Feeling includes organic sensations, special sensations, and emotions.

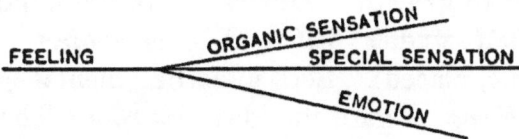

FEELING — ORGANIC SENSATION / SPECIAL SENSATION / EMOTION

Will.—I make voluntary efforts, and I notice that these efforts are distinct in kind. Now I concentrate my efforts; I *attend.* Now I determine in view of motives; I *choose.* Now I execute my determinations;

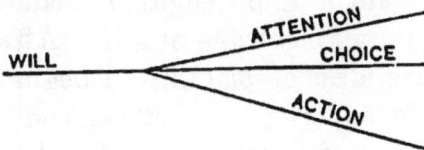

WILL — ATTENTION / CHOICE / ACTION

I *act.* I learn to call my effort-making capabilities my *Will-powers.* Will includes my capabilities to attend, choose, and act.

The native energies of self are termed capabilities, powers, faculties. I do acts different in kind; I perceive, I admire, I determine. I learn to call my energies to do acts different in kind my powers, my faculties, my capabilities. The name by which I learn to designate each of my capabilities indicates its office in my mental economy.

4. **Law reigns in the Self-World.**—Deeper insight satisfies me that self acts spontaneously, but acts in *uniform ways*. I find that the uniform ways in which self acts are the laws of the mental economy. Self is subject to mental laws just as matter is subject to physical laws. Self *must* attend, in order to know. Self *must* ascend through particulars to generals. Self *must* recall the past through the present. Self *must* make effort, in order to growth. Law reigns in the mind-world.

5. **Self studies Self.**—Self is *subject* (*sub*, under + *jactus*, placed). Self underlies mental phenomena, *causes them.* I gain the idea *this rose.* The rose is object, but the self that creates the idea is *subject.* Self may also be *object* (*ob*, before + *jactus*, placed). I perceive myself rejoicing. The I that perceives and rejoices is *subject*, but the self that is perceived is *object.* Self studies self; self is both subject and object. I look without and gain a knowledge of plant-life; I look within and gain a knowledge of self. After I accumulate immediate ideas of plant-life, I begin to be able to appropriate the experiences of others, and little by little I create a science of Botany. So, after I have acquired sufficient direct knowledge of self, I begin to be able to appropriate the experiences of the race, and I thus gradually create a psychology.

6. Psychology is the Science of Self.—Knowledge of self is a key to all knowledge. It opens to us the book of nature, the book of human nature, and the book of Divine nature. One ignorant of self gropes in the dark. A teacher who knows self builds on the rock, but one ignorant of self builds on the sand. The wise physician studies psychology side by side with physiology. The wise minister studies theology in the light of psychology. Everywhere self-knowledge is most valuable, but to the teacher it is the *sine qua non*.

7. Youth is the Golden Time to study Self.—The child and the boy and the girl are busy exploring the great world around them. It is well. But the youth begins to look within, and longs to explore the self-world. Before this, self-lessons have been incidental, but now is the golden time for systematic self-lessons. The study of psychology, until recently, was limited to college seniors and specialists. But educators begin to realize that youth is the time for elementary mind studies, and that introspection and observation are equally essential. Elementary psychology, rightly presented, is found to be as interesting to young people as physiology or botany. Our youth are now trained to look within as well as without, and to explore the mind-world as well as the matter-world. It is well. The third year in the high school, the second year in the Normal school, and the second year in the college, are doubtless fitting periods for the study of elementary psychology. The foundation is now laid in self-experience for profounder psychological study.

8. I study Self directly and indirectly.—I, self, mind, soul, are easy and safe terms. At first we must carefully exclude all confusing and misleading expressions and theories. As the child studies material things, so the youth studies self. The one takes object-lessons, the other subject-lessons. The youth by direct insight gains a knowledge of self just as the child by direct experience gains a knowledge of things. Here and everywhere immediate experience must precede, accompany, and make possible book-work. After one actually studies self and becomes acquainted with his own mental economy, he can re-enforce his own experiences by the experiences of others. An easy elementary psychology will now help the youth to study himself systematically, help him to appropriate the experience of others, help him to study self through his physical organism, help him to study self through products of mind in art and language and literature. But mere book psychology is worse even than mere book botany or book chemistry. It injures and does not help.

II. Applied Psychology.

By this is meant *educational* psychology. We speak of pure and applied mathematics, pure and applied logic, pure and applied psychology. It is true we apply psychology in theology and medicine and law and government and literature and art and business; but when we teachers use the expression *applied psychology* we do not think of its application in these departments, but of its application in the science and art of human development.

1. **The Facts of Psychology are restated in Terms of Education.**—In pure psychology we study self; in applied psychology we restudy self from the standpoint of education, and restate facts of the mind in terms of

education and teaching. *Practical* surveyors, architects, and engineers ask, "How can pure mathematics help us?" The answer comes, "In every way when the facts are restated in terms of your specialty and in the forms of art." The farmer asks, "How can botany help me?" The response is, "In many ways when the facts of plant-life are restated in terms of agriculture and are applied to the art of promoting plant-growth." Many *practical* teachers ask, "How can psychology help us?" The same answer comes, "In every way when restated in terms of education and applied to the art of promoting mind-growth."

2. **In Applied Psychology we study Periods of Growth.**—Pure psychology asks, "What am I—the developed self?" Applied psychology asks, "What is the child? what is the boy or girl? what is the youth? what is the young man or woman?" It furnishes the primary teacher a map of childhood; the intermediate teacher a map of boyhood and girlhood; the high-school teacher a map of youth; and the college professor a map of early manhood. The schoolmaster without it gropes in the dark; but the teacher who is familiar with applied psychology works in the light.

3. **Applied Psychology treats of the Growing Self.**—This is its peculiar province. How does the child become the man? Applied psychology answers in particulars; the science of education in generals. Applied psychology states the nature of each capability of self and its laws of growth, and discusses the means and methods of promoting its growth. The teacher learns to think of a child as a self endowed with feeble native energies, and realizes that it is the work of the educator

to so guide child effort as to develop these powers. As the musician so touches every key as to produce thrilling music, so the touch of the skillful teacher awakens to educational activity each child-capability, producing a grand and noble life.

4. **Pure and Applied Psychology.**—We may restate in brief these distinctions : **Pure Psychology** deals with a self whose native energies are fully active; **Applied Psychology** deals with a growing self. Pure psychology asks, "What am I, the developed self?" Applied psychology asks, "What is the child? what is the boy? what is the youth?" Pure psychology investigates the capabilities of self; applied psychology investigates the growth of these capabilities. Pure psychology ascertains and states the laws of mental activity and mental growth; applied psychology applies these laws to the promotion of human growth. Pure mathematics and applied mathematics, pure logic and applied logic, and pure psychology and applied psychology are corresponding expressions. Applied psychology enters incidentally into logic and philosophy and theology and law and medicine and science, but it enters into the very essence of education, and is called educational psychology. We do not think of logical psychology or legal psychology, but of educational psychology, when we use the expression Applied Psychology.

III. Education.

Education is the science of human development. We cultivate plants, train animals, and educate persons. Education makes the difference between the feeble infant and the strong man. What a change from the

infant Newton uttering its first cry, and Newton the
philosopher trembling with joy as he grasped the problem of the heavens!

1. **Education is Self-Evolution.**—The bud develops
into the rose; the egg develops into the eagle; the
child develops into the man. The process is termed
evolution. All the native energies possessed by the
man Newton were in the child; but the child knew
and felt and willed feebly, the man mightily. The process of the child-self developing into the man-self is
called education and is *self-evolution.* The germ-self
becomes the man-self. This *becoming* is growth, development, evolution, education.

2. **Self-Effort educates.**—Nothing else does. The
germ-tree in the acorn spontaneously appropriates the
elements necessary to its growth and so develops into
a great oak. The child-self spontaneously makes the
efforts necessary to its growth and so develops into a
powerful man. The child makes efforts to remember;
somehow, its memory becomes more and more vigorous. The youth thinks; somehow, his capabilities to
think become more and more powerful. Self-effort
develops power—*educates.*

3. **Lawful Effort educates.**—Well-directed effort develops capability. The uniform ways in which self
must act in order to growth are educational laws.
Self-effort, conforming to the laws of growth, educates.
Applied psychology states the laws of self-growth
concretely, as, "Well-directed effort in gaining sense-
knowledge educates sense-perception." The science
of education states the laws of self-growth in general
terms, as, "Well-directed effort develops faculty."

4. **The Science of Education formulates the Educational Thought and Experience of the Race.**—Development through effort is the central idea. Around this are grouped the facts of mind, the laws of growth, the means of education, the methods of promoting growth, and helpful devices and suggestions.

We study the story of education and learn from the masters. From Moses and Jesus we learn our best lessons. We learn valuable lessons from Socrates and Plato and Aristotle. Athens still teaches us in æsthetic culture. Rome still gives us lessons in heroism and law and government. We gain much from the thought and experience of great German teachers, great British teachers, great French teachers, great American teachers.

We study sociology, and history, and literature, and gain invaluable lessons, for we must educate the child to act well his part in the drama of life. The science of education includes all of man and all of life. Education is complete development for complete living. *This is the science of manhood.*

5. **Applied Psychology and Education.**—In its school sense, education as a science is limited to the development of the capabilities of self. Applied psychology quarries materials for the educational temple. Each capability of self is studied as to its nature, its relations, its stages of growth, its means of growth, its laws of growth, and as to methods of promoting its growth. Education generalizes and systematizes these concrete facts. From other sources much is gained; but applied psychology enters into the very warp and woof of education. It underlies and makes possible the science of education and the art of teaching. To one practically

ignorant of applied psychology, education as a science is unmeaning. Here and everywhere, we must struggle up to generals through particulars, raising ourselves round by round.

IV. ART OF TEACHING.

Teaching is the art of promoting human growth. The efficient teacher understands himself, understands the growing pupil, and understands the subject taught. He completely adapts matter and method, and leads learners to put forth their best efforts in the best ways. To him the physical and mental and moral economy of the child is an open book. He sees in each pupil a self-determining person, free but leadable. As teacher he largely controls the ideas of his pupils; but ideas occasion choices, and choices pass over into actions. Through ideas he awakens in his pupils all ennobling emotions and high resolves, and thus leads them up to a higher and better life. This is the teaching that makes for character. *This is the art of manhood.*

1. **Applied Psychology is a Priceless Boon to the Teacher.**—The teacher works in the light. He studies each mental power and discovers its nature and relations, its periods of growth, its laws of growth, its means of growth, and methods of promoting its growth. Now he forms a map of childhood, a map of youth, a map of manhood. He beholds in one view the entire mental economy of the child, of the boy, of the youth, of the man. Here he discovers three fundamental principles: (1.) *All the mental powers supplement and re-enforce each other*, so that educating one power incidentally educates in some degree all the pow-

ers. (2.) *Each capability is susceptible of and requires distinct and specific culture.* As each stroke of the artist's brush tends to perfect the painting, so each lesson has its specific culture value. Teaching educates. (3.) *The faculties develop in a definite order.* Educational maps attempt to show the order, and the teacher finds that a method of teaching is simply a systematic, persistent, efficient plan of work adapted to a growing mind.

2. **Teaching builds on Science.**—Education as a science states in general terms the laws of human development; teaching restates these laws in specific forms and in the terms of art. Education determines what methods must be; teaching applies these methods in the actual work of promoting growth. Education is abstract and deals with generals; teaching is concrete and deals with particulars and with individuals. Education gives the theory of human growth; teaching embodies the theory in practice. Education is a science; teaching is an art.

3. **Teaching is educating.**—Your head may be full of theories, but somehow when you stand before your class you never think of theories. You, like all artists and masters, intuitively discern the fitness of things. Deeply interested yourself, you make the lesson intensely interesting to your pupils. You remove unnecessary difficulties; you exorcise the demon of confusing details and lead your pupils to learn only what is essential. You may not be able to tell how, but in some way you get your pupils to put forth their full energies; and this is the art that educates.

4. **But Teaching must build on the Rock.** — The

great musician does not think of theory when performing; but without the mastery of theory the performance would be impossible. Wellington at Waterloo did not think of military science; but without a mastery of military science the victory could not have been achieved. "Yes," said one of the masters, "I paint under inspiration, but in the mean time I study hard that I may be able to paint when the inspiration comes." The genuine teacher studies profoundly the *best* things. He feels at home in educational psychology and the science of education and the methods of the masters. When teaching he does not need to think of theories. He is an artist and teaches under inspiration; but he does not forget that the science of education makes the art of teaching possible.

5. **Teaching is the Noblest Art.**—We feel the spell of drawing and painting and sculpture and architecture, for these arts articulate the language of material nature. We are thrilled by eloquence and poetry and song, for these arts express the universal throbbings of the human heart; but we are exalted by teaching, for this is the art of manhood. We are pupils; Plato is our teacher, Arnold is our teacher, Agassiz is our teacher, Horace Mann is our teacher, Christ is our teacher. The inspiration of a great teacher thrills through our entire being. Our intellects become penetrating, broad, commanding; our hearts glow with all lovely and sublime emotions and exalting impulses; our wills become high resolves and noble acts. This is the art of teaching.

CHAPTER II.

THE PERCEPTIVE POWERS.

THESE powers are our capabilities to know immediately. They are called our intuitive powers, because
they are our capabilities to see immediately into things.
In, into + *tueri*, see.) They are also called our perceptive powers, our powers of direct insight. (*Per*, by +
capere, to gain.) With some to perceive means only to
gain ideas by the senses; but it is more common to
make it include all intuitive knowing. I know at once
the rose as sweet-smelling. By direct insight I also
know myself as feeling glad. I likewise know immediately that these parts are equal to this whole. This is
direct knowing, intuitive knowing, perceptive knowing,
immediate knowing. Our capabilities to gain ideas
immediately are our intuitive powers, our perceptive
powers, our presentative powers, our acquisitive powers.

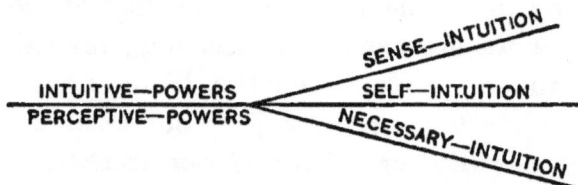

```
                                    SENSE—INTUITION
INTUITIVE—POWERS                    SELF—INTUITION
PERCEPTIVE—POWERS                   NECESSARY—INTUITION
```

Self looks directly into the three worlds—the *matter*
world, the *mind* world, and the world of *necessary
realities*. Our native energies to gain elementary notions of material things, of self, and of necessary realities, are our intuitive powers, our perceptive powers.

Endowed with intuition, self looks directly into these
three worlds. As sense-intuition, self perceives the

2

sense-world; as self-intuition, self perceives the self-world; as necessary-intuition, self perceives the world of necessary realities. This is immediate knowing, perceptive knowing, intuitive knowing.

I. SENSORIUM AND MOTORIUM.*

Self works in and through a physical organism. All soul activity goes on in connection with this organism. It is a great thing in education to make this organism an ally and not an enemy.

The teacher must understand the body that he may understand the mind. Physical improvement makes mental improvement possible. You, as a physiologist, have studied the body simply as an animal organism. As a psychologist, you must restudy the body from the standpoint of self. You will wisely ignore curious conundrums and misleading theories, and simply ask "What are the facts?" "What is the plan of the human body?" "How may it be made the fittest instrument of self?" "How does self receive and send messages through the body?"

I. Cerebrum.—Every cell in the animal body is a standing miracle. Think what it has to do! In addition to its specific functions it must grow and produce other cells like itself. The lowest animal consists of a single cell; but a human brain, it is estimated, contains more than a billion *nerve-cells*.† These are organized into groups called ganglia. A ganglion is a group of nerve-cells with nerve connections. The structure and workings of ganglia and their connections may be illustrated by a telegraphic system. Of all physical mech-

---

* This chapter is an attempt to present the essential facts of the sensor and motor mechanisms, and of perceptive knowing. You are recommended to read also Chapters V, VI, VII, and VIII, Baldwin's Elementary Psychology, or similar chapters in some other Psychology.

† Lubbock.

anisms, the nervous system is the most wonderful. The organisms through which self keeps touch with the outer world are the

SENSORIUM AND MOTORIUM.

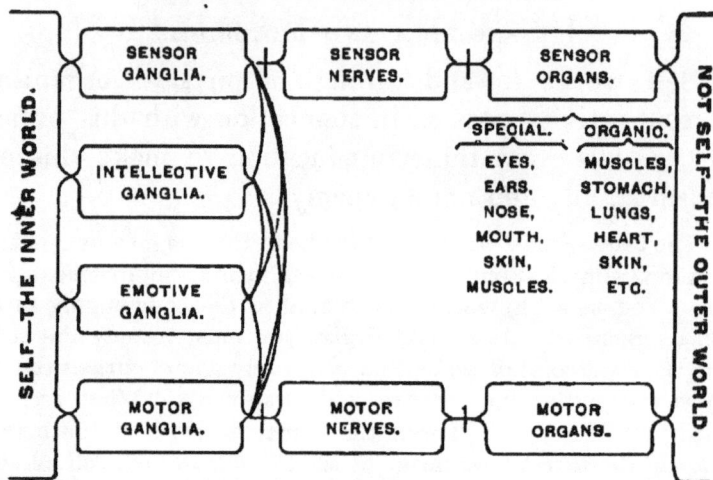

SENSOR GANGLIA.	SENSOR NERVES.	SENSOR ORGANS.

SPECIAL.	ORGANIC.
EYES,	MUSCLES,
EARS,	STOMACH,
NOSE,	LUNGS,
MOUTH.	HEART,
SKIN,	SKIN,
MUSCLES.	ETC.

INTELLECTIVE GANGLIA.

EMOTIVE GANGLIA.

MOTOR GANGLIA.	MOTOR NERVES.	MOTOR ORGANS.

SELF—THE INNER WORLD.

NOT SELF—THE OUTER WORLD.

From the standpoint of self, the cerebral ganglia are roughly grouped as above. The *sensor-ganglia*, sensor-nerves, and sensor-organs constitute a marvelous telegraphic system called the sensorium. Through this system self receives all messages from the outer world.

The *motor-ganglia*, motor-nerves, and motor-organs constitute another wonderful telegraphic system called the motorium. Through this system self transmits all messages and executes all volitions.

Intellective and Emotive Ganglia.—Somehow, in connection with the *intellective ganglia*, self perceives, represents, and thinks. In some unknown way, in connection with the *emotive ganglia*, self feels joy, hope, love. In the above diagram the intellective and emotive ganglia are inserted to give a complete view of the cerebral organism.

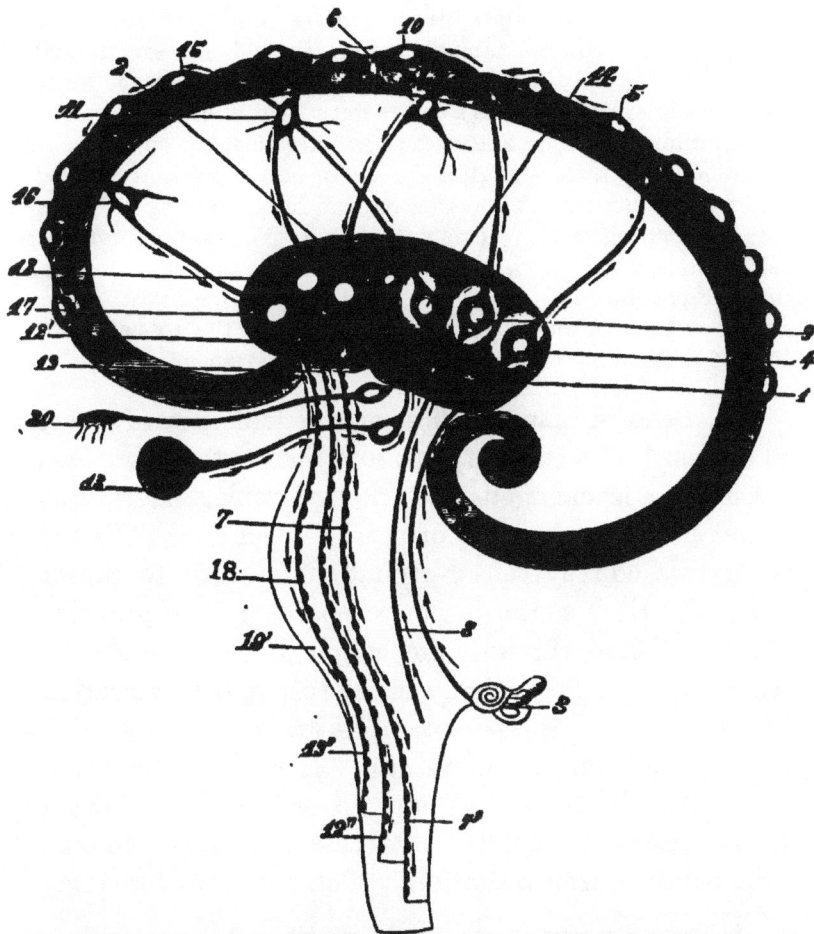

Diagram of the sensori-motor processes of cerebral activity. 1, *optic thala-
mus* with its centers and ganglionic cells. 2, *corpus striatum.* 3,
course of the propagation of acoustic impressions : these arrive in the
corresponding center (4), are radiated toward the *sensorium* (5), and
reflected at 6 and 6' to the large cells of the *corpus striatum*, and thence
at 7 and 7' toward the motor regions of the spinal axis. 8, course of
tactile impressions : these are concentrated (at 9) in the corresponding
center, radiated thence into the plexuses of the *sensorium* (10), reflected
to the large cortical cells (11), and thence propagated to the large cells
of the *corpus striatum*, and finally to the different segments of the spinal axis. 13, course of optic impressions : these are concentrated (at 14)
in their corresponding center, then radiated toward the *sensorium* (at
15); they are reflected toward the large cells of the *corpus striatum*
and afterward propagated to the different segments of the spinal axis.—
(Luys, "The Brain and its Functions," p. 61. Inserted by permission.)

Here we have an Inside View. Observe closely. A bell rings; the sound-waves vibrate through the air, through the ear, through the auditory nerves, in the auditory ganglia. Self feels the vibrations and interprets them as a call to duty. Duty emotions occasion the determination to go to church; the determination causes motor agitation in the motor-ganglia; the motor-nerves transmit the excitation to the muscles; the muscles respond by contracting and relaxing, thus causing motion; I walk to church. You do not know how self makes connection with ganglia. No one does, no one can. You must accept the fact. Place the above cuts on the board. Trace sensor excitation from objects through each of the special sensor lines to self and back through motor lines to movements.

II. **Sensor-Organs.**—These organs look inward as well as outward. In these organs, *somehow*, external molecular motion is changed into internal molecular motion, called nerve-commotion, or sensor-excitation. The sensor-nerves convey sensor-excitations inward to sensor-ganglia. Each sensor-organ responds to its appropriate stimuli. Thus, through the action of light on the eye we see, and we hear when the ear responds to vibrations of sound. The *end-organs* of hearing are situated in the internal ear, or labyrinth. Here acoustic waves transmitted by the tympanum are analyzed and changed from a physical molecular process to a nerve commotion, called sensor-excitation, which occasions hearing.

1. The *end-organs of sense* are the special mechanisms which are adapted to convert the molecular motions called nerve stimuli into molecular motions called neural excitations. It is the office of the great mass of the eye to transmit and refract the rays of light, but when the nervous elements of the retina receive the physical processes transmitted to them, they transmute these physical processes into physiological nerve processes.

2. The sole office of the nerves is the transmission of neural processes. The *sensor-nerves* transmit neural processes from end-organs to sensor-ganglia. Motor-ganglia transmute sensor-neural

processes into motor-neural processes. The *motor nerves* transmit motor-impulses to the muscles, and these respond by contracting or relaxing, thus causing bodily movements.

3. *Cerebral-sensor-ganglia* are terminal organs of sensor-nerves. The sensor-nerves have their roots in the cerebral substance as the tree has its roots in the earth. Here self and the material world touch. Self consciously feels the neural excitations of his sensor-ganglia; these feelings are *sensations*. Through his sensations self perceives material objects; this is sense-perceiving.

III. Sensor-excitation is the affection of the nervous organism by external or internal sensor stimuli. Sound-waves affect the auditory apparatus, producing *sensor-excitation*. Wherever we find nerves we may infer sensor-excitations when these nerves are acted on by the appropriate stimuli. Light-waves excite the optic apparatus; the agitation caused is sensor-excitation. Sensor-excitation is caused by external or internal stimuli, and when transmuted into motor-impulse expresses itself in automatic or reflex bodily movements. Sensor-excitation occasions sensations when the excitation terminates in cerebral-sensor-ganglia. Sensor-excitation is caused by physical agencies and is wholly physical.

IV. Unpurposed Sensor Action.—The motorium is the mechanism for bodily movements. It includes the motor-ganglia, the motor-nerves, and the muscles. In motor-ganglia sensor-excitation is transmuted into motor-excitation called motor-impulse. The motor-nerves transmit motor-excitation from motor-ganglia to muscles. The muscles respond to motor-excitation by contracting and relaxing, thus causing motion. Unpurposed movements are usually termed reflex, but are more definitely known as automatic, reflex, and instinctive.

1. **Automatic Action** is rhythmic movement caused by internal stimuli and tending to definite ends. Winking, respiring, and heart-throbbing are automatic. Instinctive action is largely automatic. Habitual action tends to become automatic, as walking, talking, and singing. Automatic action may be compared to the movements of a pendulum.

2. **Reflex Action** is reaction from *sensor-excitation* caused by external stimuli. A movement caused by a sudden noise, an unexpected touch, or a thrill of pain, is reflex action. A large part of walking, mechanical work, talking, and singing, is reflex action. Indeed, it enters largely into all habitual movements and instinctive acts. Reflex action is response to stimuli; it is the conversion of sensor-excitation into motor-impulse.

Automatic action and reflex action occur in connection with the lower nerve-centers. An animal from which the cerebral hemispheres have been removed responds to appropriate stimuli with all the reflex action of which the perfect animal is capable; but it is not aware of its acts, and is incapable of any mental act. Consciousness in man, and probably in all animals, occurs in connection with the cerebrum. Automatic and reflex movements occur in connection with the lower centers, and are strictly physical.

3. **Instinctive Action.**—Animal life is the vital energy that adjusts environments to individuals; instincts are the native energies that adjust individuals to environments. Endowed with animal life and animal instincts, the animal germ builds up a physical organism. Instincts lead to specific ends; they are the regulating impulses. Instincts act automatically through nerve-excitation, moving and guiding the animal to do the best for itself and for its species. Every instinct is an im-

pulse. Instinctive impulses lie below the realm of consciousness; instincts are organic and not mental energies. To speak of religious instincts, mathematical instincts, and art instincts, is surely incorrect.

Automatic, reflex, and *instinctive* action are organic and non-voluntary. *Automatic* applies to regular movements, as breathing, caused by internal stimuli. *Reflex* applies to reactions from external stimuli, as sneezing. *Instinct* applies to guiding impulses, as the mating instinct.

Make your Nervous System an Ally.—One becomes a mental millionaire by early and always rooting all right and useful actions into habits. Habitual acts tend to become automatic, and self is left free to expend all his energies in making new conquests. Most movements in walking and talking are automatic. A marvelous mechanism is the ready servant of self to do the drudgery of life. Probably more than nine-tenths of all our movements are automatic, reflex, or instinctive. When these are organized into right habits there is no friction. Only when our habits are wrong do we have to waste our energies in inhibiting these tendencies.

Cerebrum and Self.—So blended are mental activity and brain activity that self is sometimes confounded with his physical organism. But a self-conscious physical organism is not even conceivable. With sensor-excitation in the sensor-cerebral-ganglia the series of physical forces terminates. Self initiates a *new series.* Mental acts are occasioned but not caused. Self does these acts; self is the cause. To establish the theory of one substance and one series the votaries of materialism are forced to sacrifice self, God, immortality. They think of mind as mere fleeting phenomena, a succession of nervous shocks, a secretion of the brain. Materialism is a cruel master, annihilating even hope.

Unconscious Cerebration is a vicious expression. implying that a brain thinks; that the cerebrum goes on doing acts of knowing of which self is not aware. This notion is one of a nest of vipers that prey upon the vitals of a true psychology. Self-scrutiny is the antidote. Self, not organism, does all mental acts. Self is ever aware in some degree. A brain is merely a physical organism in connection with which self, in some unknown way, thinks, feels, and wills.

II. Sensation.

Sensor-excitations occur in the cerebral-sensor-ganglia. Self feels and is aware of feeling these excitations. These *feelings* are *sensations*. With sensor-excitations in the cerebral ganglia the *physical series* of cause and effect terminates. Self transforms these sensor-excitations into sensations, and thus initiates a NEW SERIES, called the *mental series*. The term, sensation, is used to designate the capability to feel sensor-excitations as well as the feeling.

I. **Sensor-Excitations.**—Nerve-commotion conditions but does not cause sensations. In the mind series, self causes; mental acts are occasioned, not caused. All connection of self with the outer world comes primarily through the sensor-excitation of the nervous organism. The excitation of the cerebral-sensor-ganglia is the last link in the chain of physical effects. Self consciously *feels* the excitation; here body and mind clasp hands; here there is a uniform psycho-physical connection between the two worlds; here self converts physical sensor-excitations into mental feelings, into sensations. The process, like all ultimate processes, is inscrutable to mortal vision. We only know that self consciously feels cerebral sensor-excitations, and that out of these feelings he makes his sense-ideas.

II. **Sensation.**—This is the capability of self to consciously feel sensor-excitations. Sensation is also used to designate the feeling occasioned by sensor-excitation. A sensation is the conscious feeling of sensor-excitation. The clock strikes: the sound-waves vibrate through the air, through my ears, through my auditory nerves, in my auditory ganglia. I consciously feel the sensor-excitation: this is *sound-sensation* The moon rises. The light-waves vibrate through space, through my eyes, through my optic nerves, in my optic ganglia; I consciously feel the sensor-excitation; this is *light-sensation*.

The Economy of the Senses.—By sensation we mean the result in consciousness of any affection of the sensorium. It is a feeling occasioned by something independent of self. Through sensations we perceive the outer world. Each sense makes special contributions, but each borrows from all the others. Nothing is more admirable than the economy of the senses.*

Cerebral-Sensor-Ganglia.—Sensation occurs in connection with these ganglia. Animals whose cerebral hemispheres are removed are incapable of sensation of any kind; nerve-excitations can only terminate in reflex movements. Sensation and consciousness are wanting. Sensor-excitation terminates in sensor-ganglia, and in the lower centers it expresses itself in automatic and reflex movements. In the cerebral ganglia, self feels the excitations and transforms them into sensations. There are no sensations where self is not aware of the sensor-excitations. The clock strikes, but you do not hear it.†

III. Sensation is Feeling.—I know something, I feel somehow, I make some effort. Self feels as well as

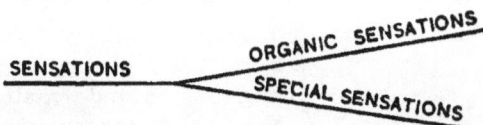

SENSATIONS — ORGANIC SENSATIONS / SPECIAL SENSATIONS

knows and wills. Feelings are agreeable or disagreeable experiences. Sensations are feelings occasioned by sensor-excitations. All sensor-excitations of which self is aware are sensations. Sensations of sound, sensations of light, sensations of bodily movements, sensations

* Hopkins.   † Ladd.

of pain, sensations of hunger, sensations of cold, are some of the myriad sensations that one feels. These feelings are grouped as organic and special sensations.

1. *Organic sensations* are occasioned by internal stimuli. The sympathetic nervous system is a marvelous automatic mechanism unitizing the bodily organism. Visceral sensations, respiratory sensations, sensations of weariness, sensations of comfort or discomfort, sensations of hunger, motor sensations, are some of the countless forms of organic sensation. The cerebro-spinal system has direct connection with the organic sensor organs, thus bringing together self and his entire body. The quickening or retarding of the circulation caused by different emotions, and the gloom and unreasonableness occasioned by dyspepsia are familiar illustrations. A man's religious and philosophic views are strikingly affected by the condition of his body. The hale man is an optimist; the rheumatic dyspeptic is likely to be a pessimist. On the other hand, how astonishing the influences of the mind on the body! Gloom and despair sap vitality, but cheerfulness and hope cure better than medicine.

2. *Special sensations* are occasioned by external stimuli, and are the elements out of which self makes his ideas of material things. The special sensor organs are special adaptations to the influences of external stimuli. The ear is adapted to sound, and the eye to light. The eye receives molecular light-waves, and changes these into *nerve-commotion* called sensor-excitation. The nerve-commotions pass through the optic nerves to the optic ganglia. Self consciously feels the sensor-excitation of his optic ganglia; this feeling is *light-sensation*.

Special Sensor Organs and Special Sensations.
$$\begin{cases} \text{Eyes.......Light-sensations.} \\ \text{Ears......Sound-sensations.} \\ \text{Nose......Odor-sensations.} \\ \text{Mouth.....Flavor-sensations.} \\ \text{Skin ...} \begin{cases} \text{Tactile-sensations.} \\ \text{Temperature-sensations.} \end{cases} \\ \text{Muscles....Pressure-sensations.} \end{cases}$$

Temperature nerves as well as tactile nerves have their end-organs in the skin. Pressure nerves as well as organic sensor nerves have their end-organs in the muscles. (See diagram, p. 19.)

V. **Sensations and Sense-Ideas.**—Sensations are the stuff out of which self makes sense-ideas. I am dependent on sensations for all I know or can know of the material world. But through sensations I may perceive all that the outer world has to present. Out of sensations I make sense-ideas and think these into concepts and judgments and reasons. But, somehow, I must continually go back to sensations and so keep touch with the material world. Sensations are fundamental experiences of self. The infant self, first of all, experiences sensations, and through sensations slowly gains sense-ideas. Material things act on a sensorium, causing sensor-excitations which occasion sensations. Self perceives things, gains sense-ideas.

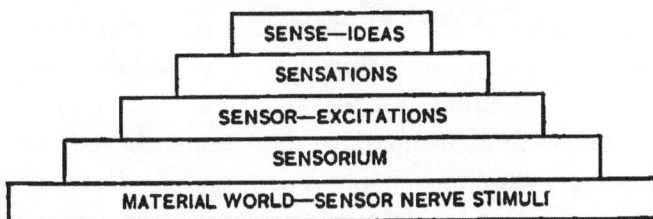

```
            ┌──────────────────────┐
            │     SENSE—IDEAS       │
          ┌─┴──────────────────────┴─┐
          │       SENSATIONS          │
        ┌─┴──────────────────────────┴─┐
        │    SENSOR—EXCITATIONS         │
      ┌─┴──────────────────────────────┴─┐
      │          SENSORIUM                │
  ┌───┴──────────────────────────────────┴───┐
  │  MATERIAL WORLD—SENSOR NERVE STIMULI      │
  └───────────────────────────────────────────┘
```

III. Sense-Perception—Sense-Intuition.

This is the capability of self to gain sense-knowledge. Self lives in and acts through a material organism. We dwell in a material world. The native energy of self to master the sense-world is termed sense-perception or sense-intuition. Sense-perception is self perceiving external objects. It is direct insight into the matter world. It is sense-intuition. Self as sense-perception intuitively gains sense-ideas termed sense-percepts.

I. **Sensation and Sense-Perception.**—I see the apple red, and feel it smooth, and taste it delicious, and smell it fragrant. The sight-sensations and touch-sensations and taste-sensations and smell-sensations are occasioned by the apple-excitations of my sensorium. Out of these sensations, immediate and remembered, I form the idea, this apple. My native power to gain sense-ideas through sensations is sense-perception. I am aware of feeling the excitations of my sensorium, and I learn to call these feelings sensations. Out of my sensations, immediate and revived, I make my notions of material things. Sensation makes sense-perception possible. The native energy of self to intuitively perceive sense-ideas through sensations is sense-intuition, is sense-perception.

II. **Sense-Percepts.**—These are notions of individual material things. My notion of this tree, this book, this house, this pencil, or this hand, is a sense-percept. What I know about a material object is a sense-percept. Sensations, immediate and remembered, are the stuff out of which sense-ideas are made. *Sense-percept* is one of the few terms now generally used in the same sense in mental and educational science and in literature. Every one understands by a sense-percept a notion of a material thing. A sense-percept is a particular sense-idea, a notion of a particular sense-object.

Sense-Percept.—The process of localizing sensations and referring them to definite objects is known as sense-perception. To perceive an orange is to refer orange-sensations to an object called an orange. The complete psychical product is called a sense-percept.*

Sense-perception gives us the idea of externality. We perceive material objects as out of and independent of self. We perceive

* Hopkins.

things as extended and exercising energy. Sense-perception is a property of the mind just as certainly as gravity is a property of matter. It is the native energy of self to perceive material things. We look directly on material objects.*

Sense-percepts do not resemble the material objects; they are signs which represent to us the objects. Sensation and perception are subjective, but the thing perceived is objective; hence sense-percepts are said to be objective; they are notions of things independent of the mind.† *Our notions of things with qualities are sense-percepts.* Some writers make unnecessary complexity by calling an idea gained through a single sense, as *this red*, an individual sense-percept; and the notion of an object gained through all the senses, as *this red apple*, a general sense-percept. These distinctions merely confuse and do not help. An idea is either a percept or a concept. My notion of a particular thing, as this horse, is a *percept;* but my notion of a class of things, as quadruped, is a *concept.* There can be no excuse for the misuse of these terms. *A sense-percept is a notion of a material object.*

III. **Self makes Sense-Percepts.**—A nervous system intervenes between a self and a material world. An object having physical properties affects my sensorium and occasions sensations. I feel this orange rough, I taste it delicious, I smell it fragrant, I see it orange-color, I hear it dull, I weigh it heavy. Out of my orange-sensations, old and new, I form the idea, this orange. I discriminate and assimilate; I interpret sensations as the operator interprets the clickings of the telegraph. I gain distinct ideas of individual objects. These ideas are sense-percepts. My power to gain sense-percepts is sense-perception.

IV. SELF-PERCEPTION.—SELF-INTUITION.

This is the capability to gain self-knowledge. It is the power of direct insight into the mind-world. I

---

* McCosh.　　　　　† Compayre.

perceive myself remembering the diameter of the earth, and I gain the notion, *this memory.* As the remembering is an act of self, and as I perceive myself remembering, I call the idea gained a self-idea, a self-percept, a self-intuition. The native energy of self to gain self-percepts is called self-perception, self-intuition, conscious-perception, and self-consciousness. Self-perception or self-intuition clearly expresses the meaning. *Self-perception is self perceiving himself knowing, feeling, willing.* It is the mind knowing itself in its knowledge, emotions, and volitions. It is the power of introspection.

I. **Awareness and Self-Perception.**—Awareness of knowing, feeling, and willing is consciousness. I am aware of my own acts; I am conscious. I am aware of feeling sad, of seeing the rainbow, of preferring Chicago to New York. *Consciousness is awareness of present mental acts.* Out of his awareness, self makes notions of his own acts. I perceive myself admiring Gladstone, and I gain the notion, *this admiration.* This is self-perception, and the product is a *self-percept.* As self makes his sense-ideas out of his sensations, so he makes his self-ideas out of his awareness.

The brute feels sensations, but, as Darwin says, gains no well-defined sense-ideas. The brute is vaguely aware of its acts, but it gains no self-ideas; is not aware of itself as doing the acts. Only persons gain self-ideas. Only persons are self-conscious. The brute is not self-conscious, is not a person. At most, brute mentality is impersonal. The brute is not a self.

II. **Self-Percepts are Self-Intuitions, or Conscious-Percepts.**—These are self-ideas. I look directly into the

mind-world and gain notions of my individual acts, and
of my capabilities to do these acts. I perceive myself
imagining, hoping, judging. By direct insight I gain
self-knowledge. My notions of my individual mental
acts are self-percepts. I perceive myself recalling my
visit to the Golden Gate. The notion I have of self
remembering this visit is a self-percept. My notion
of each of my acts of knowing, feeling, and willing, is
a self-percept, a self-intuition, a conscious-percept.
Self-percepts are notions of particular mental acts.
Sense-percepts are particular sense-notions, and self-
percepts are particular self-notions.

"Introspection is internal observation—our consciousness of the
activity of the mind itself. The subject who observes is the object
observed Consciousness is knowing of self. This seems to be the
characteristic of mind.

"Outward observation is objective perception or sense-perception.
It perceives things and environments. Things are always relative
to their environment. Things are therefore dependent beings.
They stand in causal relation to other things, and if moved are
moved from without by external forces.

"Introspection or internal observation, on the other hand, perceives the activity of the mind, and this is self-activity and not a
movement caused by external forces. Feelings, thoughts, volitions
are phases of self-activity. A feeling, a thought, or a volition implies subject and object. Each is an activity and an activity of the
self. External perception does not perceive any self. It perceives
only what is extended in time and space and what is consequently
multiple, what is moved by something else and not self-moved. If
it beholds living objects it does not behold the self that animates
the body, but only the body that is organically formed by the self.
But introspection beholds the self." *

III. **A Self is a Conscious Person.**—A self is a spirit
entity, a real being, a self-conscious person. This liv-

* W. T. Harris.

ing tree is an individual thing endowed with vegetable spontaneity; this dog is an individual animal endowed with animal spontaneity; but we never think of trees and dogs as persons. A self is an individual person endowed with mental spontaneity. Each mental act is an event of which self is conscious, and which he cognizes as his own act. The web of a long life is a personal unit. Those *were* my acts, and this *is* my act. For those acts I deserve praise but for this act, blame. Self as consciousness weaves the web of life. I am conscious of building a character, of being intelligent, benevolent, free. Conscious personality elevates me almost infinitely above the brute.

IV. **Physical Basis of Consciousness.**—It is certain that awareness occurs in connection with the cerebral hemispheres. When the cerebrum is removed the animal, though capable of reflex action gives no indication of consciousness. But all attempts to connect consciousness with special ganglia, or to express awareness in terms of nerve-commotion, have proved and must prove dismal failures. I am aware of my own mental acts, and of self doing these acts. I perceive myself doing acts different in kind. Intuitively I gain notions of my individual acts and of my capabilities to do these acts, and I call these notions self-ideas, or self-percepts; I am a self-conscious, self-determining person. This is about all that can be said. Here the no-soul theorist must forever pause. Conscious personality is the grandest of all conceptions, and to the materialist the profoundest of all mysteries. It means an enduring self, forever becoming more and more noble. It means spirituality, immortality, God. It is the key to the mysteries of the universe.

3

V. Necessary-Perception.—Necessary-Intuition.

This is the capability to gain necessary knowledge. It is the power of direct insight into the world of necessary realities. Self is endowed with the capability to perceive necessary realities and gain intuitively necessary ideas. Space *must* be, that things *may* be; space is a necessary reality. I notice the objects in this room; I gain the idea, *this where things are;* I gain the idea, *this space.* Because I can not think of things as local and extended without having the space idea, I call this a necessary idea. Necessary ideas are notions of necessary realities. The capability to gain immediately necessary ideas is termed necessary perception, or necessary intuition. *Necessary perception is self perceiving necessary realities.*

I. **Necessary realities** are the realities that *must* be, that things *may* be. We may roughly group necessary realities as necessary elements, necessary conditions, and necessary relations. In our times the enduring realities that make *phenomena* possible are called *noumena.*

1. *Necessary Elements.*—Matter and mind are the elements of the universe. This magnet is heavy, cohesive, magnetic, hard; the material entity that is heavy, cohesive, magnetic, hard, is material substance. Material substance is the matter element of the universe. That physical phenomena *may* be, material substance *must* be. Matter is the material element of which we affirm physical phenomena.

The conscious self that knows, feels, and wills is an actual being, a spirit entity, a mind. That mental phenomena *may* be, self *must* be. Mind is the spirit element of the universe. A self is the mind element of which we affirm psychical phenomena. Matter and mind are necessary realities—are noumena and not phenomena. Matter and mind *must* be, that physical and mental phenomena *may* be.

Matter and Mind.—These are elements. Matter is that out of which material things are made; mind is the spirit element of the universe. Everything perceived through at least one of the senses is a material object; every self-conscious thinker is a spiritual self. Inertia, extension, and impenetrability characterize matter; spontaneity, sensation, and awareness characterize mind. Bound up in matter are the physical forces—gravity, cohesion, chemism, sound, light, heat, electricity, magnetism; bound up in a mind are the mental energies—intellect, sensibility, will. A material thing is an object; a mind is both object and subject. I perceive myself thinking. Physical effects are *caused;* mental acts are *occasioned*—self is the cause. Material things are moved; a mind is self-moving.

2. *Necessary Conditions.*—Duration, space, cause, are the necessary conditions of phenomena. Every thing must be some when, some where, and some how. That things *may* be, time, space, and cause *must* be. Time, space, and cause are necessary realities; are noumena and not phenomena.

3. *Necessary Relations.*—These are truth-relations, beauty-relations, and duty-relations. These articulate the eternal fitness of things, and make science and art and character possible. Truth is correspondence with reality. That ice is cold is a truth. But I must have the truth idea before I can say "*this is true.*" In the same way we know beauty and duty and infinity and axiomatic relations as necessary realties.

Necessary Correlations are classed as necessary realities. These truths are the axioms we gain by direct insight. They are the ful-

crum that makes it possible for us to move the world. I can not say
$a = c$ when $a = b$ and $b = c$, unless I have the idea that things which
are equal to the same thing are equal to each other.   This is a
necessary truth.   The axioms of logic, science, and life, as well as of
mathematics, are necessary truths, expressing necessary correlations.
Truth, beauty, duty, infinity, are necessary realities; are noumena
and not phenomena.

. II. **Necessary Percepts.**—The notions we gain intuitively of necessary realities are termed necessary percepts, necessary intuitions, necessary ideas.   Like all
percepts, these are concrete ideas.   I perceive this space,
not infinite space.   I perceive this cause, not that every
effect must have a cause.   I perceive this time, and not
infinite duration.   I perceive this material object, and
not that there must be material substance back of all
physical phenomena.   I perceive myself acting, and not
that there must be a self back of all mental phenomena.
I *perceive* the *particular* and *think* the general.   Necessary percepts are particular notions of necessary
realities.   These notions are necessary ideas, which we
generalize into necessary truths.   I must have the beauty-
idea before I can say this is beautiful.   I must have the
duty-idea before I can say I ought.   I must have the
self-idea before I can say self thinks.   Sense-ideas and
self-ideas are phenomenal percepts.   Necessary ideas
are noumenal percepts.

III. **Gaining Necessary Percepts.**—Self is endowed
with the native energy of direct insight into the world
of necessary realities.   I gain particular notions of necessary realities intuitively, as I gain sense-ideas and
self-ideas intuitively.   The space in this room is environed and continued by the space outside. of the room.
The space within the solar system is environed and con-

tinued by the space beyond the solar system. The space within the known universe is environed and continued by the space beyond the known universe. There can be no limit to space; it is infinite. Thus by direct insight I gain the idea, this infinity. Finite duration is environed and continued by duration. The present is bounded by two eternities. Duration is boundless. Intuitively I gain the idea, *this infinity*. I look immediately into the world of necessary realities and intuitively gain notions of these realities. These notions are necessary ideas, necessary intuitions, necessary percepts.

IV. **Characteristics of Necessary Ideas.** 1. *They are self-evident.*—I stand face to face with necessary realities as I do with the sense-world and the self-world. I know space and cause just as I know color and memory, by direct insight. Truth shines by its own light. No proof is needed to satisfy me that these equals divided by these equals give equal quotients; it is self-evident. No proof is needed to satisfy me that something makes the pot boil, or that these things are somewhere. I perceive this cause, this space. This is immediate insight into the nature of things; this is perception, intuition; this is self-evidence.

2. *These Ideas are necessary.*—Noumena *must* be, that phenomena *may* be. We *must* have necessary ideas, that we *may* have phenomenal ideas. I must have the space-idea before I can have the idea of length, breadth, or thickness.

3. *All accept Necessary Ideas.*—They are universal. No sane person ever questions them. Endowed with necessary intuition, every man dwells in the immediate presence of necessary realities; necessary ideas are

the common furniture of human minds. Notions of
necessary realities are self-evident, necessary, and universal, and are the basis of all our knowing.

V. **Necessary Ideas and Necessary Truths.**—Self as
necessary intuition gains immediately necessary ideas.
As thought, self elaborates his necessary ideas into necessary truths. That this straight line is the shortest
distance between these two points is an intuitive idea;
the generalization is a necessary truth. Axioms are
necessary truths derived from necessary ideas. I gain
directly necessary percepts and think these into necessary truths. It must be emphasized that *intuitions* are
particular notions which we think into *general* notions.

VI. Perceptive Knowing.

This is immediate knowing. It is gaining a direct
elementary knowledge of self and his environments.
Since self gains this knowledge first hand, perceptive
knowing is classed as experimental knowing.

I. **Perceptive Powers.**—Self is endowed with capabilities to look directly into the three worlds. *As sense-
perception*, self looks directly into the matter-world and
gains sense-ideas; as *self-perception*, self looks directly

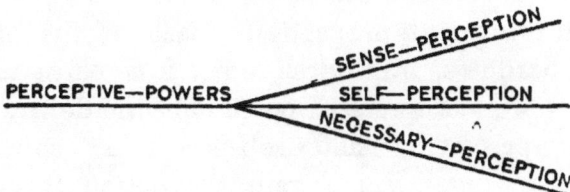

PERCEPTIVE—POWERS
SENSE—PERCEPTION
SELF—PERCEPTION
NECESSARY—PERCEPTION

into the mind-world and gains self-ideas; as *necessary-
perception*, self looks directly into the world of necessary
realities and gains necessary ideas.

II. **Perceptive Acts.**—Self is endowed with distinct energies. Each capability has its specific office. But self acts as a unit and commands the entire key-board of his capabilities. Mental acts are complex, never simple. While I know, I also feel and will. While I perceive, I remember and think and desire and attend. The great fact of the mental economy, "*All the capabilities supplement and re-enforce each*," needs to be kept continually in view. We say a mental act is perceptive when perception characterizes it; is representative when representation predominates; is elaborative when thought is most prominent; is emotive when emotion is its leading feature; is volitional when volition characterizes the act. Acts of immediate knowing are perceptive acts. These acts are grouped as sense-perceiving, self-perceiving, and necessary-perceiving.

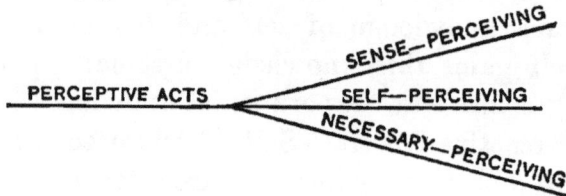

PERCEPTIVE ACTS
SENSE—PERCEIVING
SELF—PERCEIVING
NECESSARY—PERCEIVING

Sense-perceiving is self gaining intuitively sense-notions. I perceive this silver dollar. I know it is a material thing with properties. Back of the phenomena of hardness, brightness, etc., I perceive material substance. I am aware of perceiving the dollar. Thus necessary-perceiving and self-perceiving supplement sense-perceiving. But I gain the notion, this dollar; the act is essentially an act of sense-perceiving.

Self-perceiving is self gaining intuitively self-notions. I perceive myself pitying a suffering child. I know this is my own act. Back of the act I perceive self. Then I see and hear the sufferer. Thus necessary-perceiving and sense-perceiving supplement self-perceiving. But I gain the notion, this pity; the act is essentially an act of self-perception.

Necessary-perceiving is self gaining intuitively necessary notions. I see the apple falling. I know something caused it to fall. I perceive this cause, and know it as a necessary reality. I am conscious of this perceiving. Thus sense-perceiving and self-perceiving supplement necessary-perceiving. But I gain the necessary notion *this cause;* the act is essentially an act of necessary-perception.

III. **Perceptive Products.**—Notions gained by direct insight are percepts or intuitions. These notions are characterized as concrete, individual, particular, because they are notions of particular things.

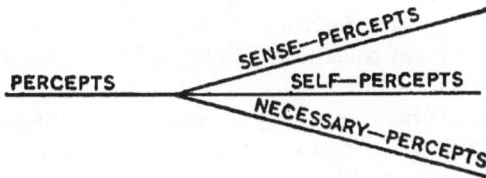

The notions which self as sense-perception gains of material things are *sense-percepts*, sense-intuitions, sense-ideas; the notions which self as self-perception gains of mental acts are *self-percepts*, self-intuitions, self-ideas; the notions which self as necessary-perception gains of necessary-realities are *necessary-percepts*, necessary-intuitions, necessary-ideas.

Assimilation—Apperception.—Self assimilates his new and his old experiences, and views as a whole all his acquisitions. A mind unifies its entire contents. I constantly integrate my present experiences with my past. At every step I discriminate and assimilate, and thus unitize my acquisitions. In doing this I command all my powers. Assimilation is sometimes called apperception. "I have not used the term *apperception*," says James, "because the variations in its usage are absolutely innumerable I consider assimilation the most fruitful term yet used."

SUGGESTIVE STUDY-HINTS.

I. Helpful Books.—A recent physiology comes first, but you need to restudy the nervous organism from the standpoint of self. Ladd's Physiological Psychology is, I think, one of the best presentations of the sensor-organs and sensation. I have found Hopkins's Study of Man, Porter's Human Intellect, McCosh's Cognitive Powers, and Sully's Psychology, suggestive and helpful. Ponderous works are for advanced students and specialists. You must first master elementary works.

II. Letter—Perceptive-Knowing.—I recommend you to write to an appreciative friend a clear, concise statement of your views of perceptive-knowing. This will help you to grasp the subject. The letter is very much better than the essay. Your effort to make this difficult subject clear to your friend will help you more than reading many volumes. You may be called upon to read the letter before the class or reading circle or institute.

III. Sensor-Organism.—Do you clearly grasp the structure of the nervous organism? Draw a nerve-cell—illustrate by a clot of jelly; draw a nerve—illustrate by a small tube filled with liquid or by a pencil; draw and connect several ganglia—illustrate by a galvanic battery. What do you mean by the sensorium? by sensor organs? by end-organs of sense? by sensor-nerves? by sensor-ganglia?

IV. Sensor-Excitation.—Explain nerve-stimuli; external stimuli; internal stimuli. What is nerve-stimulus to the optic apparatus? to the auditory apparatus? to the olfactory apparatus? to the gustatory apparatus? to the tactile apparatus? Where does physical motion become nerve-commotion? How is nerve-commotion transmitted from the end-organs of sense to sensor-ganglia? Do sensor-ganglia transmute nerve-commotions into sensor-excitation? State proofs.

V. Motorium and Motor-Excitation.—What does the motorium include? What do we mean by motor-excitation? Explain auto-

matic action—illustrate by the ticking of the clock. Explain reflex
action. What do you mean by instinct ? Explain instinctive action. How do automatic action and instinctive action differ ?

VI. **Sensation.**—What is sensation ? Prove that sensation occurs always in connection with cerebral-sensor-ganglia. Show the
difference betwen sensor-excitation and sensation—illustrate by the
clickings of the telegraph in absence of the operator. Why do you
object to such expressions as unconscious-cerebration ?

VII. **Sense-Perception.**—Explain sense-perception and sense-intuition. Show the relation between sense-perception and sensation
—illustrate by the operator interpreting the clickings of the telegraph. Show how you gain the notion of this apple, this orange,
this rose. What is a sense-percept ? How do particular notions
differ from general notions ? Give five examples.

VIII. **Self-Perception.**—Are you aware of your own acts ? Do
you perceive yourself perceiving the mountain ? What do you mean
by self-perception ? self-intuition ? self-consciousness ? How does
self-perception differ from awareness ? What is a self-percept ? Give
several examples. Are self-percepts general or particular notions ?
Compare sense-perception and self-perception.

IX. **Necessary Perception.**—What do you mean by realities ? by
necessary realities ? Show that space, time, cause, matter, and mind
are necessary realities. How do you gain ideas of necessary realities ? Show how you gain ideas of the realities named. What is a
necessary-percept ?

X. **All the Capabilities of Self supplement each.**—What capabilities supplement and re-enforce sense-perception ? self-perception ?
necessary-perception ? Give examples. It is hoped that the outline
on page 2 will aid you to better grasp this truth. This presentation
may help you to think of the entire self doing each mental act. A
faculty is merely a capability of self to act in a particular way, as in
sense perceiving, remembering, desiring, choosing.

XI. **Laboratory Work.**—You will find original research in the
mind-world as valuable as in the matter-world. You can do *something,* and the little you do yourself will enable you to appropriate
the experiences of the army of specialists. Sandford says: " As long
as psychologists live upon the crumbs that fall from the tables of
neurology and physiology they will live in dependence. They must
investigate for themselves—no less rigorously and no less broad-
mindedly than others, but from their own standpoint, and must view

what they find in its psychological perspective." But, however fascinating to advanced students, and however valuable in some of its results, the "laboratory methods" are not meant for beginners. Even Aristotle and Hamilton are much easier for young students and more valuable than the "original researches" of Fichte, or Wundt, or Fechner, or Meynert, or Spitzka, or Hartwig, or Herbart. Introspection is the true experimental method. The student looks within, and intuitively gains self-knowledge, just as he looks without and intuitively gains sense-knowledge. This is the natural method, and must ever precede and accompany the laboratory method.

CHAPTER III.

EDUCATION OF SENSE-PERCEPTION.

THE foundation for all forms of mental growth must be laid in sense-activity. Sense-ideas underlie all other ideas; sense-intuition is fundamental in the mental economy. In the acquisition of sense-knowledge the child begins its education.

I. PLACE OF SENSE-PERCEPTION—TERMS DEFINED.

1. *Relations.* Self knows, feels, and wills. All mental energies supplement each other. Self gains a notion of a new material object. In this act revived sensations are assimilated with immediate sensations: there is discrimination as well as assimilation; there is the desire to find out as well as attention. Then the idea gained is remembered, awakens emotion, occasions choice, and leads to action.

2. *Hygiene and sense-perception.* Perfect sensations come of perfect health. The body needs to be kept in the best possible condition. Right hygienic

habits are cardinal. Living is a constant joy to the healthy child, and its sensations are perfect. Its senses require no culture; it is the capability to gain knowledge through the senses that must be cultivated.

3. *Sensation* is the capability to consciously feel sensor-excitations. Sensations are sensor-excitations of which self is aware. The term sensation is used to designate the feeling as well as the capability to feel sensor-excitations.

4. *Sense-perception* is the power of self to gain sense-percepts; sense-perception is also known as sense-intuition and outer-perception and sense-presentation. Sense-perception and sense-intuition are synonyms, and are everywhere used interchangeably.

5. *A sense-percept* relates to a particular material object. Our ideas of individual material objects are our sense-percepts. Sense-percepts are particular sense-notions; sense-percept and sense-intuition are synonymous terms.

6. *Education of sense-perception* is the development of the power to gain sense-knowledge. The education

of the capability to gain sense-ideas makes the difference between the feeble, halting, imperfect perceiving of the child and the vigorous, penetrating, exact observations of the scientist. It is not the senses that we educate, but the capability to interpret sensations.

II. Importance of Sense-Perception Culture.

Mental activity begins with sensations. Light-waves vibrate through my optic apparatus, bringing to me a world of color and form and movement; sound-waves vibrate through my auditory apparatus, bringing to me a world of speech and song; excitations of my tactile and olfactory and gustatory apparatus open to me the worlds of touch and smell and taste. The importance of sense-perception culture can hardly be too strongly stated.

1. *Sense-perception culture gives the mastery of the matter-world.* We learn to so observe as to become acquainted with the things around us; step by step we explore earth and sea and sky.

2. *Sense-perception culture enables us to build on experience.* I experience my sense-knowledge. On this rock I build. I am certain; I know intuitively things having properties; I know for myself. As an educator, I lead the child to build on its own experiences.

3. *Sense-perception culture gives a basis for clear thinking.* It enables me to gain exact sense-percepts. Through these I think up to exact concepts and judgments and reasons. The foundation is laid in sense-knowing; clear perceiving makes clear thinking possible.

4. *Neglect of sense-perception culture.* In our time, this is inexcusable; but, alas! the neglect is still too common. Visit a hundred schools: half are destitute of the best means for sense-perception culture. Neither the teachers nor the pupils seem to realize that the mastery of the glorious world all about them is pre-eminently their work; nevertheless we have a host of wise teachers who lead their pupils in the conquest of the matter-world and thus educate sense-perception.

III. Growth of Sense-Intuition.

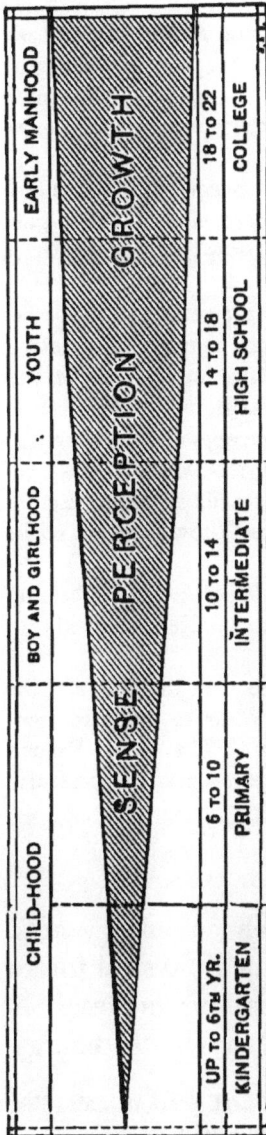

The capability to gain sense-ideas is the first cognitive power to become active. Infant sense-perception is obscure and halting. To observe the slowly-developing sense - activity during the first months of life is highly interesting. Taste, touch, and sight seem to be slightly active when the infant is but a few hours old ; hearing, smell, and some of the organic senses become feebly active within a few days after birth. Very early the sensorium seems to respond to all kinds of sense-excitation. The early sense-impressions of the little ones are not ideas, but something lower, such as brutes gain ; but before the child can talk it evidently acquires many wordless ideas. It is able to understand words before it can say them. Thus the little ones during the first months begin the work of mastering the material world. When the child begins to use words as signs of things, the growth of sense-intuition becomes very marked. By the end of the third year the senses are fully active and the child has gained a considerable stock of sense-ideas.*

1. *From three to six* is now recognized as the *Kindergarten period*. During this period the growth of sense-perception is wonderful. The foundation of future achievement is now laid in sense-experience. Not the culture of the senses, but of the power to gain sense-notions, is the aim.

2. *From six to ten* is the *primary period*. Sense-intuition is now highly active The child is trained to observe closely and to gain and express clear sense-ideas; education is now literally objective work.

3. *From ten to fourteen* is the *intermediate period*, coming between childhood and youth. Sense-intuition is now fully active. Boys and girls gain a deeper insight into things having properties; observation now becomes active and penetrating; clear-cut sense-percepts are now gained and thought into concepts and judgments.

4. *From fourteen to eighteen* is the *high-school period*. Observation now becomes scientific and the youth learns science. Sense-perception, the power to gain accurate sense-knowledge, is at its best. This is the science period.

5. *From eighteen to twenty-two* is the *college period*. Observation is now penetrating, exact, and exhaustive. Nature yields up her secrets to the student.

6. Sense-perception is kept vigorous by use even in old age. The eye may grow dim and the ear dull, but the power to interpret sensations may grow more and more powerful. The great French chemist Chevreul when a century old still prosecuted successfully his experiments.

IV. Laws of Sense-Perception Growth.

A law is a uniform way in which an energy acts. Physical laws are uniform ways in which physical forces act—as, for instance, the laws of falling bodies. A mental law is a uniform way in which a mental energy

* I have found Preyer's Observations of the first years of child-life, vols. vii and ix, International Education Series, very helpful.

acts, as a law of association. An educational law is a uniform way in which a mind must act in order to grow. Some educational laws are common to all our mental powers, and hence are called general laws. Other laws of mental growth are peculiar to certain mental energies, and are termed specific laws.

I. **General Laws.**—The first great educational law is the law of effort—*Effort under guidance educates.* Among the various educational principles lying at the foundation of all true teaching, no one is so universally accepted as this. Education is the development of capability by exercise. But, to make this practical, it is necessary to restate the general law in terms of each mental power:

1. *Law of effort.* Well-directed effort in gaining sense-percepts educates sense-perception. Such effort develops power. Directed exercise strengthens capability. Endeavors to master the world of material things promote the growth of sense-intuition.

2. *Law of means.* Whatever calls sense-perception into vigorous activity is a means for its culture. We gain sense-ideas in the presence of sense-objects. The blind gain no ideas of color, because they have no light-sensations. The deaf gain no ideas of sound, because they have no sound-sensations. Sense-experience is the basis of all mental activity. Acquiring such experience by means of objective work educates sense-perception.

3. *Law of method.* Systematic, persistent, and efficient plans of work, in mastering the matter-world, educate sense-perception. Orderly, continued, and vigorous efforts develop power.

II. **Special Laws.**—The following and similar laws relate to sense-perception growth:

1. *Law of conditions.* A sound sensorium favors sense-perception growth. Perfect sensations come of good health as well as of a sound organism. Physical improvement underlies mental improvement. The wise teacher gives great attention to practical hygiene.

2. *Law of attention.* Interested attention to material things accelerates perception-growth. Distracted attention blurs sense-percepts, and no attention means no percepts. Attention is an indispensable condition of knowledge.

3. *Law of ascent.* The object, the idea, the word; this is the natural order of ascent. The child perceives the object, gains the idea, and embodies the idea in a word.

4. *Other laws.* You will discover other laws. A few laws aptly applied are best. When you realize that all good comes from working in harmony with law, you will search for laws as for diamonds.

V. Means for Educating Sense-Perception.

Sense-perceiving is self gaining sense-ideas by means of sense-objects. A world of material things affords unlimited means for sense-intuition culture. From this boundless store, wisdom seeks the best.

A grindstone is a means of sharpening an axe, and a plow is a means of cultivating the soil. Mathematics is a means of educating judgment and reason. Art is a means of cultivating imagination. In general, whatever tends to call forth normal mental activity may become a means for culture.

I. **Educational Values.**—Studies are valuable for two things: for the *culture* they afford, and for the *use* that can be made of them. By culture here is meant the entire effect of knowledge on the mind, both in acquisition and possession. The word *practical* here signifies value for use.

4

$$\text{Educational values} : \begin{cases} 1. \text{ Culture value.} \\ 2. \text{ Practical value.} \end{cases}$$

Studies calculated to call forth the most vigorous and discriminating efforts in gaining sense-knowledge are of the highest value in educating sense-perception. When such studies are also of the greatest practical value they become doubly valuable as educational means.*

II. **Table of Educational Values.**—Some studies call sense-perception into constant and vigorous activity, and hence are of the highest value in educating this faculty.

SENSE-PERCEPTION CULTURE, VALUE OF	1	2	3	4
Kindergarten work, and general object-lessons..	10	10	....	
Botany, zoölogy, geology, chemistry, geography.	10	10	....	
Manual art-work, penmanship, drawing, molding.	9	8	....	
Reading, spelling, language-lessons, vocal music.	9	8	....|....	
Physiology, physics, astronomy................	8	7	....|....	
Objective arithmetic, objective geometry.......	8	6	....|....	

Explanations.—The aim is to give in this table the comparative values for perception-culture of the leading studies preceding college work. The values in column (1) are the estimates of the author. The values in column (2) are the estimates of Dr. Brooks. Each student will place in column (3) his own estimated values, and then in column (4) the averages of columns 1, 2, and 3. Mathematics, Latin, history, etc., are omitted because of their low value for sense-perception culture. It needs to be emphasized and stated

---

* I am indebted to Dr. Edward Brooks for valuable suggestions on educational values.

again and again that the educational value depends largely on the methods of work. Often and often so-called object-lessons are of little value for sense-perception culture, because the work is subjective and not objective.

Suggestions.—1. Besides the collections made by the pupils, every school-room should have a cabinet of classified minerals, plants, birds, etc. When suitable cases are provided, these things will gradually accumulate, and are likely to be kept in good condition.

2. In every school-room there should be a collection of tools. These tools should belong to the school, and be under the control of the teacher as a part of the school apparatus. Tools are the means by which mankind gain a living, and are not to be despised. They are the indexes on the dial-plate of civilization showing the advances of the race. The essentials are the hammer, the screw-driver, chisels, planes, borers, saws.

3. Every school-room should have a set of weights and measures. The metric weights and measures should be used in connection with the common weights and measures.

VI. Methods of educating Sense-Perception.

A law, a method, a device; these expressions are now specific. An educational law is a fundamental and guiding educational truth. Educational methods are outgrowths of educational laws. Good methods are systematic, persistent, and efficient plans of work. An educational device is a helpful educational expedient. A true educational method is a plan of work in harmony with child-nature and the nature of the subject studied. It is doubtless best to consider methods from the standpoint of the pupil and as adaptations to stages of growth. Kindergarten methods are plans of work adapted to the child from the third to the sixth year. Primary methods are plans of work adapted to children from six to ten. Intermediate methods are plans of work adapted to pupils from ten to fourteen. High-school methods are plans of work adapted to pupils from fourteen to eighteen. College methods are plans of work adapted to college students.

Methods of educating sense-intuition are plans of work that lead pupils to put forth systematic, persistent, and efficient effort in gaining sense-intuitions.

I. **Kindergarten Method of educating Sense-Perception.** —By Kindergarten methods are meant plans of work adapted to children under six years of age. Up to the third year, the mother is the Kindergartner. After the third year, the wise mother, when possible, puts her darling into a good Kindergarten. This is the period for sense-growth and for finding out how to gain sense-knowledge. Kindergarten work is admirably adapted to the promotion of these ends.

1. *Trying things educates sense-perception.* The child becomes acquainted with things through testing them by his senses. The orange is seen and felt and tasted and smelled and weighed. The blind child can not find out color, but it can try the orange by all the other senses.

2. *Doing educates sense-perception.* The child is led to do things purposely. It speaks, sings, draws, molds, handles, measures, makes, exercises, combines, builds. Doing such things brings the child into close

and constant sense-contact with objects. It becomes acquainted with things—gains sense-ideas. This intimate and active contact educates sense-intuition.

3. *Observing educates sense-perception.* As early as the third year the child begins to linger over objects. It now discriminates more sharply. It now notices that wholes have parts. Its notions become fuller and clearer. We say the child begins to observe. Kindergarten work trains the little ones to so observe as to gain correct notions of things.

Kindergarten Work.—Every teacher should study some good Kindergarten manual, such as The Mother's Songs and Games, as well as Froebel's Education of Man. The insight thus gained will help in any line of work. In the near future, our high-schools as well as our normal schools will give young ladies a short course at least in Kindergarten work. Mothers will thus be better prepared to give wise direction to the activities of their little ones, and primary teachers will be better prepared for their work.

II. Primary Methods of educating Sense-Intuition.— These are plans of work adapted to children from six to ten years of age. Sensation is now at its best. At home, in the street, in the Kindergarten, the children have been busy, heretofore, exploring the wonder-world around them. It is astonishing to find what a store of sense-percepts they have acquired. Somehow, even the little ones most unfortunately situated, have attained considerable sense-perception culture. But how striking the difference between these waifs and the children wisely trained from infancy! The Kindergarten graduate enters the primary school with at least two years the start of the less fortunate child. The primary teacher is compelled to do a good deal of Kindergarten work to make up for the loss of wasted years.

1. *Acquiring sense-intuitions educates sense-perception.* At six the child hears and sees and tastes and smells and touches and weighs almost as perfectly as the adult; but the capability to interpret sensations and make exact percepts is still comparatively feeble. This is the golden period for storing the mind with ideas of things in land, sea, and sky. The efforts put forth in gaining these ideas develop sense-perception.

2. *Objective experimental work develops sense-perception.* The child reaches sense-intuitions through material objects. He continually experiments by sense-tests. This apple tastes sour; this rose smells sweet; this board feels rough. He discriminates the properties of objects and assimilates these into notions. Such work educates perception.

3. *Doing educates sense-perception.* Notice those children making mud-pies, mud-dolls, mud-houses. How intently they work! Lead them on to do better things, as molding, drawing, making things; as reading, talking, singing; as *handling, combining, separating, weighing, measuring.* You will thus lead the children to put forth their best efforts in the best ways. They get close to things, and thus gain a mastery over them.

4. *Teaching well primary arithmetic, primary geography, primary reading, and primary language lessons educates sense-perception.* These subjects must necessarily be taught objectively. The child perceives these five apples and these five marbles and these five marks; it thus gains the idea—*five.* It perceives this body of water, and this, and this; it thus gains the idea—*lake.* From things to ideas and to words is the fundamental law. The child is led to

perceive things having properties.   Out of its own experiences, immediate and revived, it makes its number notions, and its geography notions, and its notions used in reading and language lessons.   It builds on the rock.   It learns how to see and hear and taste and smell and touch, so as to gain clear and full notions of things.

III. Intermediate Methods of educating Sense-Perception.—By these we mean methods suited to boys and girls.   Sensations are now readily transformed into sense-ideas.   The easy work of childhood does not satisfy boys and girls.   Now, book instruction supplements oral instruction.   Semi-science takes the place of miscellaneous object-lessons.

.1. *Observing critically educates sense-perception.* The pupil examines things minutely.   He is no longer contented with vague ideas, but wants to know all that can be known about objects.   His penetrating scrutiny enables him to gain clear and exhaustive sense-notions, and greatly strengthens sense-intuition.

2. *Analyzing and synthesizing material things cultivates sense-perception.*   Intermediate pupils take delight in these processes as applied to objects.   By analyzing and synthesizing objects, they gain exact knowledge and deeper insight.   The discrimination and assimilation required give the very best culture.

3. *The study of objective science develops sense-perception.*   The objective side of geography, botany, zoölogy, etc., calls forth the best efforts of the pupils. Technical terms are used sparingly ; exhaustive classification is not attempted ; but a solid foundation is laid in the experience of the learner.   This work gives a higher development to sense-intuition, and prepares the

pupil for science-work in the high-school and the college.

4. *Manual training educates perception.* Besides drawing, molding, etc., boys and girls must be trained to use tools and make things. This is an educational necessity, and must in some way enter into the education of intermediate pupils. I venture the prediction that it will be found best to give this manual training in connection with the school-work. Doing educates perception because it awakens interest, fosters attention, and secures vigorous, sytematic, and persistent exercise of this faculty.

5. *Good methods of teaching reading, language, vocal music, drawing, geography, botany, zoölogy, educate sense-perception.* To the pupil each word in the reading or language lesson becomes a jewel glittering with meaning. All other lessons prepare for these. But details here would hinder and not help. The wise teacher will provide herself with a good manual of methods in each subject. These manuals supplement normal work and are full of helpful suggestions. They are working plans.

6. **Practical Suggestions.**—Geography, liberally defined, includes botany, zoölogy, geology, and meteorology, as it treats of the earth and its products. Sometimes your geography work will be devoted for a few weeks to vegetable life and sometimes to animal life. For the systematic culture of sense-perception, these are the best of all studies. The pupils need no book except the book of Nature, but you need for yourself a working manual for each subject.

IV. **High-School Methods** are plans of work adapted to the high-school. Sense-perception is now fully active and observation becomes scientific. The exact and penetrating observation demanded by science gives the highest culture to sense-perception. Botany, zoölogy, geology, and chemistry are the best studies for this culture. Books are now used, but the student must still build on his own experience. The laboratory method is coming into vogue for high-schools and colleges; the student conducts original investigations.

Culture of sense-perception is incidental in the high-school. Thought-culture now predominates, but to verify conclusions the student needs constantly to go back to sensations; then, to make advances, he must continue to make new and closer observations. Thus the power to gain sense-knowledge is not only kept vigorous, but is steadily improved.

Oral Work and Book-Work.—At first the child learns about things by direct insight; it gains ideas directly from material objects. As the months multiply, it more and more unites revived and immediate experiences in forming its notions of things: later, the pupil appropriates the experiences of others. Teacher-experience supplements child-experience: the teacher stimulates and guides the efforts of the child, but its ideas are gained directly from things. *This is oral work.* When prepared for it

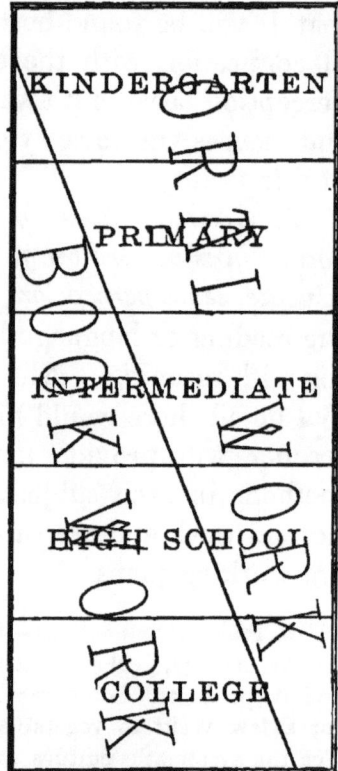

the pupil is led to find out from books. Printed and written words now represent to the pupil ideas of things; the pupil learns from the book. *This is book-work.*

In the Kindergarten the work is necessarily oral; in the primary, most of the work must be oral; in the intermediate, book-work becomes more and more prominent. As most pupils do not advance beyond the intermediate grade, it is of the utmost importance that boys and girls be educated to gain knowledge from books as well as from Nature. In the high-school and the college book-work predominates, but the pupil tests and verifies the statements of the book by his stored experiences and by work in the laboratory.

V. **Mistakes in Education of Sense-Perception.**—Violations of educational laws and improper applications of educational principles are educational mistakes. Errors of this nature are legion. Attention is called to a few of the most hurtful:

I. SOCIETY MISTAKES —1. *Poor facilities.* School buildings improperly constructed, imperfectly heated, poorly ventilated, and scantily furnished are still the rule. In view of the momentous interests involved this is a monstrous mistake. Every citizen is deeply interested in supplying our schools with the best hygienic and educational agencies.

2. *Employment of incompetent teachers.* The chief error is the employment of persons without skill as teachers. They neither understand child-nature nor the nature of the subjects to be taught. Surely the time is coming when none but trained teachers will be employed.

II. HYGIENIC MISTAKES. — The teacher does not know; pupils are not trained to hygienic habits; hygienic laws are disregarded; eyes are injured; bending over the desk becomes a habit; pupils work in vitiated air; invigorating exercises are neglected; the law of frequent change is disregarded; the tendency is to

physical deterioration.   What a revolution is needed!
Physical vigor conditions mental vigor; perfect health
conditions perfect sensations; perfect sensations condition perfect sense-percepts.

III. TEACHING MISTAKES.—Violations of educational
principles, or injudicious or unskillful application of
educational principles, are mistakes of this class.   The
teacher promotes growth when he works in accordance
with law.

1. *Book-work before oral work.*   The inexperienced child is required to study the unmeaning book.   This is the old education.
Unmeaning words, unmeaning definitions, and unmeaning rules en-
cumber memory.   Sense-perception is not exercised and hence is
not developed.   What could be more vicious?   Such education does
not educate.

2. *Words before ideas.*   From things the pupil must gain the
ideas which he embodies in words.   This is the law.   But visit a
school kept by a well-meaning ignoramus.   What do you observe?
No effort is made to lead the pupil to understand; memory is
crowded with words, but the child does not know their meaning.
The multiplication table is memorized but not learned.   Words
without ideas characterize every exercise.   This is the Chinese
method; this is the old education.

3. *Concepts before percepts.*   Percepts are the stuff out of which
concepts are made.   The child perceives this island, and this, and
this.   It perceives likeness and discerns the class notion.   The particular notion, this island. is a percept, but the general notion,
island, is a concept.   Here we obey law; this is the new education.
Under such tuition sense-perception grows.   But visit again the antiquated school.   You find the teacher toiling to make pupils who
have never seen an island define island.   Thus it is all day; but
we forbear even to enumerate the long catalogue of disheartening
errors.

IV. PSYCHOLOGICAL MISTAKES.—These errors result
from a want of knowledge of the nature of sense-perception and of its laws of growth.   A knowledge of

child-nature is now recognized as fundamental in the
art of teaching :

1. *Second-hand work.* It does not develop perception to read
and hear about things. Children must see and hear and feel and
taste and smell for themselves. Perception should be immediately
appealed to through the senses until conception is easy and accurate
without it; it should be developed in breadth, strength, and skill.
Children must gain sense-ideas directly.

2. *Too much hurry.* To the mature mind perception seems almost instantaneous; but the perceptions of the infant are very slow,
probably as slow as the most difficult process of reasoning later in
life; and the teacher does not always realize how long it takes a
child in its first years of school life to gain a clear perception of an
object, a picture, or a figure. There must be time for a permanent
unification, or the perception will not be complete and the activity
begun will degenerate into forgetfulness.

3. *Failure to discriminate and assimilate.* Objects so presented
to the senses as to stimulate a perception of differences are the proper external occasions of perception, and the differences in the objects presented should at first be strongly marked and always clearly
distinguishable; but mental perception is a unification. This is an
act of the mind itself which the teacher can not help the pupil to
perform. The teacher often says, "You see this or that," and the
child says, "Yes," when he sees nothing, or perhaps something entirely different from the thing intended. Such wrong methods
should be carefully avoided. Differences can be presented in an
order that will suggest proper comparison and unification, but some
test of the actual completion of the unification should be sought
besides the questions that can be answered by yes or no. Tests
should be continued until it is known with certainty that the unification of perception is real, true, and clear.*

4. *Appealing to a single sense.* Much of the poverty of school-
work results doubtless from this practice. The most common form of
this error is the exclusive appeal to hearing. Good teaching, whenever
possible, appeals to sight as well as to hearing. Young children
need to test things by several of the senses. In teaching the blind
we must appeal to all the senses except sight; in teaching the deaf

* Palmer.

we must appeal to all the senses except hearing; in teaching children perfectly endowed we must appeal to all senses.

SUGGESTIVE STUDY-HINTS.

At every step the teacher, as well as the student, needs critically to interrogate self. The few hints here given, it is hoped, will prove helpful. Do I fully understand the nature of sense-perception? Am I reasonably familiar with its growth and its activity from youth to age? Am I prepared to promote the growth of this power in my pupils? How can I better qualify myself for this work? Am I thoroughly in earnest?

I. **Helpful Books.**—You will receive most help from educational journals, from attending summer normal schools, from visiting the best schools, and from contact with the best living teachers. The best books are indispensable. As new books are constantly appearing, you need to exercise your book-intuition to discriminate between gold and dross. We live in an age of superior books.

II. **Letter.**—*What I know about the education of sense-perception.* He who tries to help another helps himself. Giving enriches in the mind-world. Nothing besides, in my judgment, will help you so much as writing a thoughtful letter on the education of sense-perception to some earnest teacher who will respond in kind. In the normal school, in the institute, and in teachers' reading-circles, I have found it highly advantageous to have several of these letters read before the class. In writing these letters tell what *you* think.

III. **Position of Sense-Perception.**—In the mental economy where do you place sense-intuition? Why? How is sense-perception related to attention? to memory? to conception? Distinguish between sensation and sense-perception: illustrate. Why do you use sense-perception and sense-intuition as synonyms? What do you mean by the education of sense-perception?

IV. **Importance of Sense-Perception Culture.**—You may state three reasons why you think this culture very important. Illustrate by primary reading and primary. arithmetic. Why do we call the movement initiated by Pestalozzi and others the New Education? What do you mean by the old education? Do you class the methods of Socrates and Plato and Aristotle with the new or the old education? Why?

V. **Growth of Sense-Perception.**—Illustrate. Show that it is the

growth not of sensation but of the power to acquire sense-ideas.
What is the relation between hygiene and sense-perception culture ?
Why ought every teacher to be familiar with the laws of health ?
Trace the activity of sense-perception from youth to age.

VI. **Laws of Perception-Growth.**—What distinction do you make
between general laws and special laws ? What is meant by an educational law ? Illustrate each of the general laws of sense-intuition
growth. State and explain two special laws. What distinction do
you make between an educational law and an educational principle.

VII. **Means of Perception-Culture.**—Illustrate by the grindstone.
Explain the meaning of culture value and practical value. Show
that botany is a better means of sense-perception culture than
algebra. How is it that the culture value of a study depends so
much on the method of teaching it ? Illustrate by primary geography.

VIII. **Methods of educating Sense-Perception.**—Make the distinction between a law, a method, and a device. What do you mean by
Kindergarten methods ? Primary methods ? Intermediate methods ?
High-school methods ? College methods ? What question does the
child ask ? the boy ? the youth ? the man ?

1. *Kindergarten methods.* Who is the natural Kindergartner ?
Why is it better to place children after the third year in a well-con-
ducted Kindergarten ? How does trying things educate perception ?
Explain how doing helps. Illustrate the benefit of observing. What
advantage will be gained by primary teachers who study a good
work on Kindergarten ?

2. *Primary methods.* What do children of six know ? Are their
senses at their best ? Is it a mistake to keep children out of school
too long ? Tell some advantages gained by Kindergarten pupils.
How do primary differ from Kindergarten methods ? Show that
acquiring sense-percepts educates perception. Show how observing
promotes the growth of sense-intuition. Prove that doing educates
perception. Tell how you will so teach the following branches as
to educate sense-intuition: Primary arithmetic, primary reading,
primary language-lessons, primary science-lessons.

3. *Intermediate methods.* How do intermediate differ from primary methods ? Show that objective analysis and synthesis cultivate perception. How will you so teach zoölogy as to educate sense-
intuition ? Will manual training help ? Would you make this a
part of the school-work ?

4. *High-school methods.* Show the difference between intermediate and high-school methods. Why is sense-perception culture made incidental in the high-school? What do you mean by observation now being scientific? Illustrate by botany, by chemistry, by physiology.

IX. **Oral and Book Work.**—Why must the work be mostly oral in the Kindergarten and the primary school? Show the folly of exclusive book-work in the intermediate school. Why should intermediate pupils be carefully trained to gain knowledge from books? Which do you consider the greater educational power in the high-school and college, books or the living teacher?

X. **Mistakes in educating Sense-Perception.**—What are educational mistakes? Mention some society mistakes; some hygienic mistakes; some teaching mistakes; some psychological mistakes.

CHAPTER IV.

EDUCATION OF SELF-PERCEPTION.

By this is meant the development of the capability to gain self-knowledge. I am aware of loving my friend. Out of my love-awareness, immediate and revived, I form the notion *this love.* The notion of this act of love is a self-idea. My native energy to gain self-ideas is self-perception. As sense-perception is the power of direct insight into the matter-world, so self-perception is the power of direct insight into the mind-world. Consciousness is simply awareness of self doing various acts. Self as conscious-intuition coins awareness into ideas.

I. Relations and Definitions.

Awareness, like sensation, is fundamental in the mental economy. Wherever we find mind we find sensation and awareness. A brute is in some degree aware of its sensations; a person is not only aware of his sensations, but also of self feeling these sensations.

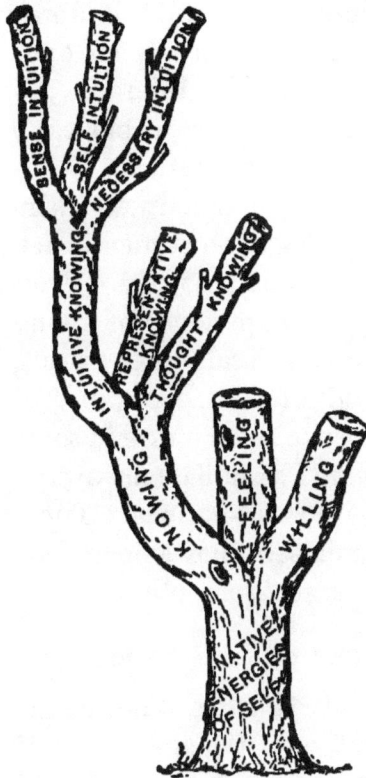

1. *Mental Phenomena.* —I think; I perceive myself thinking. I grieve; I perceive myself grieving. I choose; I perceive myself choosing. I am aware of my own acts; I perceive myself acting. Phenomena are appearances. My mental acts appear to me, and hence are termed mental phenomena. Self is aware of his own acts as his own; awareness can go no further.

2. *Self-perception.* This is the native energy to gain self-ideas. I assimilate my awareness into self-notions just as I assimilate my sensations into sense-notions. Self-perception is known as self-intuition, self-consciousness, inner-perception, introspection, and conscious-perception.

3. *Self-percepts* are notions of particular mental acts. They are the ideas self gains intuitively of his knowing, feeling, and willing. I desire to visit Paris. The notion I gain of self feeling *this desire* is a self-idea, a self-intuition, a self-percept. Notions of individual mental acts and notions of the capabilities

to do these acts, gained by introspection, are self-percepts.

4. *Education of self-perception* is the development of the power to gain self-ideas. The child is dimly aware, but the illuminated mental economy is an open book to the man. Education makes the difference between the feeble, glimmering consciousness of our early years and the clear self-consciousness of maturity.

5. *Relations of self-perception.* Attention, memory, and awareness enter into every distinct mental act, and hence are called our general mental powers. Thus self is able to weave into unity the experience of a long life. I perceive the storm; I attend, recall other storms, feel emotions of sublimity, think of God, am aware of each of these acts. Asleep or awake, I am aware in some degree of my own acts. *Somehow* I assimilate my awareness, immediate and recalled, into self-notions. These are acts of self-perceiving. I gain self-knowledge. The capability to gain self-percepts is self-perception.

II. Importance of the Culture of Self-Perception.

Self-knowledge is the most valuable knowledge. "*Know thyself*" is the imperative of the ages. A self is a *microcosm*, a miniature universe. A knowledge of the microcosm is the key that opens to us the wonders of the macrocosm, the infinite universe. Each self is a type of the race. To one ignorant of self the universe is a maze without a plan. We explore the earth and the heavens, but leave the mind-world unexplored. How little most persons know of themselves! Our schools and colleges send out their graduates rich in sense-knowledge but poor in self-knowledge. Even teachers,

5

otherwise intelligent, do not appreciate the connection of psychology with their work. Not less sense-knowledge but more self-knowledge is the great educational need. A few reasons for the culture of self-perception are presented in brief. You will expand and illustrate these arguments:

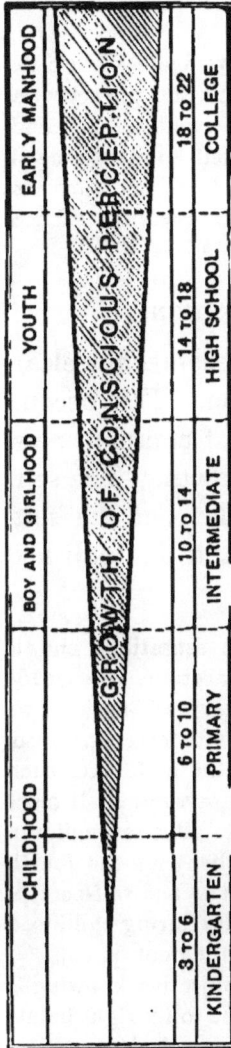

1. *Insight into character.* Self-knowledge is the key to human nature. Knowledge of self makes it possible to understand and appreciate noble characters. I examine myself; I love truth and right and all noble traits, and I grieve when I do wrong. I put myself in the place of my friend. I appreciate his noble traits and sympathize with him when he goes wrong. I read history, and rejoice in all that is great in human character and human achievement.

2. *Self-knowledge opens to us the treasures of history and literature.* Thucydides and Macaulay are without interest and without meaning to one ignorant of self. The Iliad and Paradise Lost have no charms for one unacquainted with self.. How can I understand Homer and Shakespeare and Dickens if I do not understand myself?

3. *Sociology, philosophy, and theology* give up their secrets to one who knows himself. I am a creative first cause; a free, self-determining, responsible person. I can think of God as the infinite creative first cause, the infinite will, the infinite person. I can think of free, self-determining persons, responsible to law, constituting society, immortal.

4. *Cultured self-perception characterizes the great man.* The brute gains no self-ideas. The self-notions of the unreflecting masses

The diagram on the left, from top to bottom, shows columns labeled:

EARLY MANHOOD — 18 TO 22 — COLLEGE

YOUTH — 14 TO 18 — HIGH SCHOOL

BOY AND GIRLHOOD — 10 TO 14 — INTERMEDIATE

— 6 TO 10 — PRIMARY

CHILDHOOD — 3 TO 6 — KINDERGARTEN

GROWTH OF CONSCIOUS PERCEPTION

are few and crude. Here and there we find persons who know the mind-world better than any one knows the matter-world. These are the mighty ones—the Shakespeares, the Aristotles, and the Kants. In proportion as we become acquainted with ourselves, we rise to the digni⁺y of a grand manhood.

5. *Self-perception* is the source of self-knowledge. We are dependent on self-intuition for our ideas of the acts and the activities of self. A being not endowed with self-consciousness has no mind-world. We are as dependent on awareness for self-knowledge as on sensation for sense-knowledge. The culture of self-consciousness opens to us a world infinitely grander than the sense-world. "There is nothing great but mind."

III. Growth of Self-Perception.

The feeble awareness of the child becomes the clear, penetrating self-consciousness of the man. This becoming, this gradual process is the growth of consciousness. Education is the promotion of this growth. The self-notions of the child are few and crude; but the self-notions of the educated man are many and like polished gems.

1. *Childhood.* Very early the infant feels sensations and is dimly aware. How early it assimilates its sensations into crude sense-notions, and its awareness into rudimentary self-notions, we can not know. At first the child is aware of the objects perceived, and nothing more. As early as the third year the child uses such words intelligently as *I, me, my.* Even earlier it says *mine.* It must perceive dimly self knowing, feeling, and willing. But few children give evidence of distinct self-consciousness earlier than the fourth year. From this period the growth is continuous; but self-perception acts feebly for some years. Its feeble activity during childhood indicates that its culture should be incidental (study cut, p. 66).

2. *Boyhood and girlhood.* Awareness of objective knowing is quite active during this period. Now is the time to fix right habits and good manners. We now educate our pupils to attain certainty in their mental experiences.

3. *Youth.* The youth feels irrepressible desires to explore the

inner world. Now self-intuition becomes active and penetrating. Real self-knowledge becomes intensely interesting. This is peculiarly the fitting period for the culture of self-perception. As the child gains an experimental knowledge of the matter-world, so the youth gains an experimental knowledge of the mind-world. This is the golden period for self-perception culture. Educators begin to realize this fact. Within one or two decades geometry, botany, and elementary psychology will be studied, side by side, in all our high schools.

4. *Manhood.* During early manhood self-intuition becomes fully active. It must be that this capability grows more and more powerful as the years advance. The octogenarian gazes with increasing wonder into the profounder depths of the spirit-world.

IV. Laws of Self-Perception Growth.

The uniform ways in which self must act in order to the development of consciousness are the laws of self-perception growth. Because these laws are fundamental and guiding educational truths they are called educational principles.

I. **General Laws.**—These look to the growth of all the mental powers, but need to be stated in terms of each. What are the great laws of self-intuition growth?

1. *Law of effort.* Well-directed effort in acquiring self-knowledge educates self-intuition. As the acquisition of sense-percepts develops sense-perception, so the acquisition of self-percepts develops self-perception.

2. *Law of means.* Subjective work educates self-intuition. I gain self-knowledge only through perceiving myself acting. Studies requiring constant introspection are the best means for educating self-perception.

3. *Law of method.* Plans of work which call self-perception into lawful, systematic, vigorous, and per-

sistent activity, educate this power. Effort under guidance educates.

II. **Special Laws.**—These apply particularly to the development of self-intuition. The wise educator will look well to the special as well as to the general laws.

1. *Law of the brain.* A sound brain conditions perfect awareness as well as perfect sensations. We accept this fact; no one can explain it. Vigorous health and clear self-consciousness are intimately related. Poor health may account for much of the confusion and error in the mind-world. Even insanity is primarily an affection of the physical organism.

2. *Law of origin.* Self-perception becomes active first in connection with sense-perceiving. The child is aware of its sense-experiences. Slowly it becomes aware of its memory-experiences, and its emotional experiences, and its thought-experiences.

3. *Law of growth.* Self-perception develops slowly. From obscure to clear consciousness is the natural order. Indistinct awareness becomes distinct awareness. Glimmering self-percepts become clear self-percepts. Doubts become certainties. From our own experiences we learn to be very patient with our pupils. Here we need to hasten leisurely. Young persons gain self-ideas slowly.

4. *Law of ascent.* The mind ascends through self-percepts to self-concepts. I think memory-experiences into the concept, memory. Through particular self-notions the mind ascends to general self-notions.

5. *Law of conserving mental energy.* Mental energy is conserved by developing awareness into clear-cut self-percepts. The failure to do this is a great source of waste in the mental economy. "The waste of mental energy from failing to develop a perfect consciousness, and from the consequent degradation and dissipation of force, is the most serious loss to which the mind is subject in its struggle to gain power. When we consider the time spent in studying truths which are not incorporated with the mind, we can see something of the fearful waste of energy that comes from making the aim so narrow that effort is dwarfed, and actual achievement loses its value. The loss comes from ceasing to fight before the battle is finished." *

* Palmer.

V. Means of educating Self-Perception.

As the mastering of the matter-world educates sense-perception, so the mastering of the mind-world educates self-perception. Each mental act is an event. Self stands face to face with his own acts, and perceives himself knowing, feeling, and willing. Man looks within as well as without, and gains self-knowledge as well as sense-knowledge. Each mental act may become the *means* of self-perception culture. Any study which quickens self-observation and transforms awareness into self-percepts may be made the means for self-perception culture.

I. **For Children.**—The work during this period is incidental and informal. We do not even mention self, but we lead the child to gain some self-ideas in connection with its daily work.

1. *Certainty in self-perceiving and in remembering.* " Are you sure?" is the best question. Yes or no will not answer this question. The teacher must satisfy himself that the child is really certain.

2. *Truthfulness in telling.* There is no better means than this for the culture of self-intuition.

3. *Forming right habits.* This is an admirable means for educating self-perception. Good manners and morals are the results of the formation of good habits. The child contemplates his own acts and learns to be careful.

II. **For Boys and Girls.**—Awareness is now quite active, so far as the sense-world is concerned. Gaining self-ideas becomes more and more interesting. The means for self-perception culture are various and abundant.

1. *The means for educating child self-perception* may also be used here, but the field is wider and much more can be done.

2. *Self-examination.* Did I intend to do so? Do I understand this? Was that what happened? Why do I desire to go?

3. *Juvenile literature* is a most important means. The pupils now begin to understand the experiences of others.

III. **For Youths.**—All lines of work may now be made the means of educating self-intuition.

1. *Psychology* easily ranks highest. Introspection characterizes this study. Self-percepts become as definite as sense-percepts, and are thought into concepts. The mental powers are defined and grouped. The youth analyzes his own mental acts with more delight than he feels when analyzing flowers. Soon he discovers the laws of the mental economy and the laws of mental growth.

2. *Ethics* has a high value. Character-building develops the power to gain self-knowledge. Self-examination with the view to better living gives a deep insight into the mind-world.

3. *Literature* is of great value. The Bible is incomparably the best book for this purpose. I place Shakespeare next. But the means of self-intuition culture are boundless—life, history, literature, art.

VI. METHODS OF DEVELOPING SELF-PERCEPTION.

Distinctness, certainty, unity; these are cardinal in education. Self is aware of his acts as his, but there must be sunlight clearness. Each act must stand out distinctly, and doubt must give place to certainty. Teacher, have you developed your power of introspection? Then you are prepared to lead others. You will not need many suggestions. Work on in the light of your own experience.

I. **Kindergarten, Primary, and Intermediate Methods.** —Good teaching educates self-perception as well as sense-perception. So blended is self-perceiving with other mental acts that discrimination is not always easy; we think of our acts, but not of self doing these acts. The specific culture of consciousness, however, must be kept ever in view. We can hardly begin these lessons too early, but from the nature of the work all details must be left to the teacher. A few general suggestions are all that is desirable. Work out your own plans in your own way.

1. *Incidental.* At this early stage you give no sepa-rate lessons to educate self-perception, but you do this incidentally in connection with all lessons. You will need to guard against all expressions which the child is not prepared to understand.

2. *Accuracy.* Lead the pupil to observe accurately. Do you really see and hear and smell and taste and touch these things? Are you sure the clock struck four? The ways are endless of training to accuracy, in observ-ing, in recalling, and in thinking.

3. *Distinct memories.* Lead your pupil to recall precisely what occurred. Was that what happened? Was that what I saw? Without thinking of it, the child clearly perceives itself remembering. You lead the child to tell just what it saw, or heard, or did, or read.

4. *Memory and phantasy.* Lead your pupils clearly to distinguish memories and phantasms. Children oft-en fail to do this. Much care is needed here. Self as memory recalls actual experiences; self as phantasy modifies his experiences. The erroneous reports of chil-dren are often the unintentional blending of memories and phantasies rather than intentional falsehoods.

5. *Truthfulness.* The habit of truthfulness compels introspection. From infancy to age it is of the ut-most importance to have the habit of truthfulness in-grained.

6. *Self-examination.* Teach your pupils to question themselves. Inculcate honesty here. What did I mean? What did I intend? Why do I feel guilty? What did I do? These questions become more and more search-ing from year to year. Higher ideals and better living must be the aim.

7. *Stories and Literature.* Lead pupils to put themselves in the place of others. What would you have
done? What would you have said? How would you
have felt? How would you have acted? The wise
teacher will assiduously cultivate this fruitful field so
rich in helpful experiences.

8. *Manners and Morals.* Lead your pupils to form
all right habits. Careful training in right manners and
morals develops self-perception. You do not need further suggestions. You will work out your own methods
in your own ways. You will lead your pupils to gain
self-knowledge as well as sense-knowledge.

II. **Advanced Methods.**—These are plans of work
adapted to the high-school and college periods. Self-
perception is now decidedly active, and seems to reach
full activity about the twentieth year. How may this
power be grandly developed? The answer must always
be, *by mastering the mind-world.*

1. *Gaining self-percepts educates self-perception.*
The youth makes, out of his self-experiences, definite
self-percepts. Awareness, like sensation, is fundamental
in the mental economy. I am dependent on consciousness for all I know or can know of the mind-world.
Making sense-percepts out of sensations educates sense-
perception; making self-percepts out of awareness educates self-perception. We do not educate sensation
and awareness, but the capabilities to gain ideas through
these experiences. Introspection is the capability to
gain self-knowledge. Efforts in gaining self-percepts
develop self-perception.

2. *The study of self educates self-perception.* What
am I? What can I do? With what capabilities am I

endowed ? How may I make the most of myself ? I
know that I am I ; on this rock I take my stand. I
perceive a church and gain the self-percept, *this perceiving*, at the same time that I gain the sense-percept,
this church. I find that I have the capabilities to gain
sense-ideas and self-ideas, and I learn to call my notions
of these capabilities sense-perception and self-perception.
Thus, step by step, I explore the self-world. My power
of introspection becomes more and more vigorous as I
make greater and greater efforts to understand myself.
My self-ideas become as clear and well-defined as my
sense-ideas. The mind-world gives up to me its secrets.

3. *Put yourself in his place.* I consider this one
of the very best ways of cultivating self-perception. To
the teacher this habit is invaluable   Every year I spend
a few days in some school as a pupil. I find that this
experience helps me to put myself more completely in
the place of my students, and thus I am better prepared
to lead them in their investigations. This method of
studying the mind-world may be used constantly. You
observe the words, looks, and acts of the lover : put
yourself in his place and you can understand him. Human nature is the same everywhere. Each man represents all men. Thus you have the key to all human nature. You can interpret history, and literature, and art.
Efforts to understand others educate self-perception,
and the knowledge gained is of the highest practical
value. You can now look at things from the standpoint
of your pupils. You literally take your place beside
them and lead them in their work. You can now view
history from the standpoint of the actors. You can now
contemplate the plays of Shakespeare from the stand-

point of the author. You can now admire the Greek Slave from the standpoint of the artist.

4. *Vicarious experiences help.* One becomes a mental millionaire by appropriating the experiences and achievements of others. This is legitimate. Each person is entitled to the achievements of the race. But the foundation must be laid in self-experience. As I need sense-experience to be able to appropriate the achievements of scientists, so I must have self-knowledge to be able to appropriate the self-experiences of others. I find that I am at all times, whether sleeping or waking, active and in some degree aware of my acts. What is your experience? What is the experience of the race? Hamilton had himself awakened at various times; he tells us that self was always found busy and aware. Self-intuition is cultivated by comparing our own with the conscious experience of others. In literature we study the conscious experience of writers. With these experiences we compare our similar experiences. We are enriched by the experiences of the most gifted. Our hasty inferences are corrected by the common experiences of mankind. Such efforts cultivate self-perception and render the human mind an open book. The insight gained by such efforts is invaluable in practical life. Thus the individual becomes as wise as the race.

5. *Self-examination cultivates self-perception.* From childhood to age the habit of self-examination is of great benefit. As the years go by, self-inspection becomes systematic and penetrating. I count the practice of self-scrutiny invaluable. As at the close of the day the business man posts his books, so the wise character-builder at the close of each day carefully examines his own acts.

We do most for our pupils when we lead them to form the habit of careful and systematic self-examination. I have not found formulated schemes advantageous. Very soon they are dropped. Each one will spontaneously form a plan best suited to his wants. We suggest lines of self-examination, but leave each one to pursue his own method. Self-betterment is the inspiring motive. We strive for perfection. Each·day we try to advance.

6. *Lead the learners to assimilate awareness into self-knowledge.* Pushing awareness into definite, clear, distinct, positive self-knowledge does most to educate self-perception. Failure to do this accounts for the haziness of the self-knowledge of most people Here and everywhere complete success is reached by working on until the victory is won. First, we must attend so closely to our acts that our self-perception will be complete. Secondly, we must compare the results we reach with the results reached by others. Our self-knowledge will thus become broad, exact, clear, positive.

VII. Mistakes in Educating Self-Perception.

A chief mistake is its utter neglect. Even professional teachers are often poor in self-knowledge. Many teachers make no intelligent effort to increase the self-knowledge of their pupils.

1. *Misconceptions.* The capability to make self-ideas out of awareness is as certainly a native energy of self as gravity is a native energy of matter. Some think of each mental act as a *state* of *awareness*. This misconception, as I think, confuses and leads to the neg· lect of self-perception culture. The gain would surely

be immense could the expressions *states of mind* and *states of consciousness* be effaced and *acts of mind* be substituted. To think of memory and reason and hope as *states of consciousness* does not help, but hurts. Nothing is added, nothing is gained. The student simply wonders what can be meant by *states*. Each mental act is complex, but the native energies to do mental acts are simple. It is because all our mental powers supplement each, that mental acts are complex. Much is gained and nothing is lost by thinking of consciousness as our capability to perceive self-remembering, reasoning, hoping.

2. *Haziness.* The self-knowledge of teacher as well as pupil is often shadowy, and self-ideas are vague. A clear-cut self-percept is more valuable than diamonds. What an inexcusable and incalculable waste to stop short of perfect self-ideas! Ask a score of well-informed persons to give you the distinction between *conscience* and *consciousness*, or between a *percept* and a *concept;* you will be astonished to hear their crude and erroneous answers. You must begin with the children. Clear self-knowledge comes of culture.

3. *Second-hand self-knowing.* Nothing develops self-perception but actual self-perceiving. An hour of real introspection is more valuable than weeks of second-hand work. All knowledge of self must begin in self-experience. Many delude themselves into thinking they are studying self, when they are studying what somebody says about self. Direct self-knowledge is fundamental. You must perceive yourself acting, and must coin your awareness into self-ideas.

4. *Children sometimes become too subjective.* "She

never plays," a mother observed about her daughter, "but she reads so much and asks such strange questions." This indicates an abnormal condition. The healthy child lives with nature, likes to play, likes to see things, and is as happy as a bird. The old little child is a sad object. Some one has blundered.

5. *Egotistic awareness is a misfortune.* The big *I* shuts out real self-knowledge and prevents a person thus afflicted from seeing himself as others see him. Inordinate consciousness of self produces timidity as well as egotism. You will study to lead your pupils to think of self-acts and self-ideas, but not of self. True self-knowledge makes one modest and courageous.

6. *A morbid ethical consciousness is a great misfortune.* Why eternally worry over your follies? Do the best you can, and rejoice always. It is wrong and foolish to make yourself miserable brooding over your sins. Ask, and you will be forgiven. Go and sin no more. Make your life useful, and you will be happy.

7. *Failure to develop consciousness into definite, clear, and positive intuitive-ideas* is a fundamental educational error. Mental energy is thus wasted, and the person becomes a dreamer. No mistake in education needs to be more carefully guarded against.

8. *Self-concepts before self-percepts.* This mistake is even more common than that of sense-concepts before sense-percepts. It is the violation of the law of ascent. We must ascend through particular notions to general notions. My notion of this memory is a self-percept, but my notion of my capability to recall my past acquisitions is a self-concept.

9. *Substituting our own awareness for that of the*

learner. We thus read into child-mind what is not there, but in our own minds. Just here we find the source of the failure of the teacher to understand the child. The confusion of his own standpoint with that of the mental fact about which he is making a report, Prof. James considers the great fallacy of the psychologist. In studying comparative psychology we fall into the same error by reading into the brute-mind what is not there, but in our own minds. In studying the Bible many read into it what is not there, but in their own minds.

SUGGESTIVE STUDY-HINTS.

I. **Helpful Books.**—The New Testament is incomparably the best. Each one here sees self reflected back as in a mirror. Most writers have exhausted their energies in discussing sense-perception and its education. However, by substituting self-intuition for sense-intuition, and the mind-world for the matter-world, the best suggestions looking to the culture of outer-perception may be applied in the culture of inner-perception.

II. **Letters—Self-Perception Culture.**—You must look within. How have you managed to gain self-knowledge? How will you lead your pupils to explain the mind-world? Write such thoughts as will prove suggestive to your friend. Be careful to use no word or expression the meaning of which is not clear to you.

III. **Awareness and Sensation.**—Show that self is as dependent on awareness for a knowledge of the mind-world as upon sensation for a knowledge of the matter-world. Illustrate fully and clearly the meaning of these terms.

IV. **Awareness and Self-Perception.**—Show that self makes his self-ideas out of his awareness as he makes his sense-ideas out of his sensations. Analyze five acts of self-perception.

V. **Education of Self-Perception.**—Define and illustrate. Give several reasons why you deem the culture of this power of great importance. Is it as important to develop the power of internal observation as the power of external observation?

VI. **Laws of Self-Perception Growth.**—State the three general edu-

cational laws in terms of consciousness.   Give three special laws
which you think of great practical value.

VII. **Means of educating Self-Perception.**—What means do you esteem valuable in childhood? in boyhood? in youth? Why do you
give psychology the first place? When is the golden period to study
elementary psychology? Why should it have a place in every high
school? Do you consider ethics a valuable means for this culture?

VIII. **Methods of educating Self-Perception.**—State the distinction
you make between a law, a device, and a method. Define Kindergarten, primary, intermediate, and high-school methods in terms of self-
perception. Can you transmute methods of sense-perception culture
into methods of self-perception culture? Try this. Show your plans
of work in educating self-intuition in childhood; in boyhood; in youth.

IX. **Mistakes in educating Self-Perception.**—How do you account
for the astonishing neglect of self-perception culture? Why do
most persons count sense-knowledge more valuable than self-knowledge? Why do you prefer the expression, *acts of self*, to the expressions, *states of mind* and *states of consciousness?* How do you
account for the haziness of the self-knowledge of most persons?
Why is it a mistake to trust to *second-hand* self-knowledge? May
the child become too subjective? State your remedy. May young
people become too self-conscious? What remedy do you suggest?
Is it possible to gain sense-concepts before gaining sense-percepts?
Can you gain self-concepts before acquiring self-percepts? Give
several illustrations.

CHAPTER V.

EDUCATION OF NECESSARY-PERCEPTION.

BY this is meant the development of the power to
gain necessary-knowledge. Education makes the difference between the crude, undefined necessary notions of
the uneducated, and the clear, well-defined necessary notions of the philosopher.*

* Read Chapter VIII, Elementary Psychology ; also, Necessary-intui
tion, p. 34.

I. **Place of Necessary-Perception in the Mental Economy.**—Necessary-intuition is fundamental.   Self as sense-intuition gains sense-knowledge and nothing more. Self as conscious-intuition gains self-knowledge and nothing more. A being not endowed with necessary-perception must remain forever ignorant of the world of necessary-realities. Necessary-intuition is the native energy of self to *experience* necessary realities.   We make our sense-ideas out of our sensations and our self-ideas out of our awareness; but we stand face to face with necessary-realities and gain necessary-ideas by direct insight.

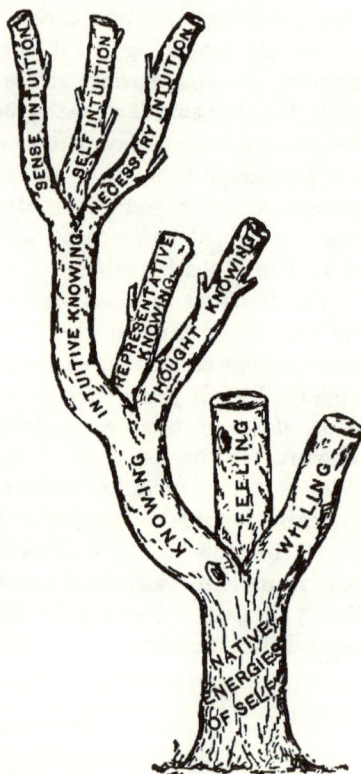

II.   **Definitions.** — We need to tread softly here. The mightiest thinkers still falter on this battleground of thought.   We must each strive to grasp these profound truths as best we can.

1. *Necessary-realities* are the actualities that make possible the physical and the spiritual universes.   These realities are termed *noumena;* they underlie phenomena and make things possible.   Space, time, cause, matter, mind, truth, beauty, duty, are *noumena*.   Each is a *necessary* reality; each *must* be, that *things* may be.

6

2. *Necessary-percepts* are concrete notions of necessary-realities. Because we gain these notions by direct insight they are called necessary-percepts or necessary-intuitions. Like all percepts, our necessary-notions are concrete notions.

3. *Necessary-truths* are necessary-percepts generalized. Socrates died from drinking the poison. That *this effect had this cause* is an intuitive-percept; but *that every effect is caused* is an intuitive truth. We gain *necessary-percepts* intuitively, but we infer necessary-truths. Axioms are necessary-truths.

4. *Necessary-perception* is the capability of self to gain necessary-ideas. We are endowed with the power of direct insight into the world of necessary-realities. We *perceive* necessary-realities; we intuitively gain necessary-ideas. Necessary-perception is self perceiving necessary-realities.

5. *The Education of necessary-perception*, is the development of the power to gain well-defined necessary-notions. All men experience necessary-realities, but the vague, unworded necessary-ideas of children and uneducated persons are vastly different from the necessary-notions of the educated. Necessary-truths are the pillars of science and philosophy.

III. **Importance of educating Necessary-Perception.**— Necessary-intuition is a native energy of self, susceptible of distinct and unlimited culture. Necessary-knowledge is the granite of the thought-world. The mathematician builds on necessary-truths. The scientist builds securely when he builds on this granite. The philosopher is grander than other men because more than others he deals with these sublime truths.

IV. **Growth of Necessary-Perception.**—Every one has the' time-idea and the space-idea and the cause-idea. How early the child dimly perceives necessary-realities we can not know, but it is certain that child-notions of necessary-realities are dim and vague. The power to gain necessary-ideas acts feebly in childhood, becomes more active in boyhood and girlhood, and becomes vigorous in youth. It is the latest of all the faculties to reach full activity. While all persons perceive necessary-realities, only the few gain clear and well-defined necessary-ideas and the power to use them. Most of us are so interested in phenomena that we fail to investigate *noumena.*

V. **Laws of Necessary-Perception Growth.**—(1.) Well-directed effort in gaining necessary-ideas educates necessary-perception. (2.) The mind must ascend through necessary-percepts to necessary-concepts and necessary-truths.

VI. **Means of educating Necessary-Perception.**—Necessary-realities environ us and furnish the means of educating necessary-perception. This space, this time, this cause, this truth, this beauty, this duty, are perceived as readily as sense-objects. Gaining distinct ideas of these realities develops necessary-intuition. Studies involving the acquisition and constant use of necessary truths are excellent for the cultivation of this faculty. Geometry, ethics, logic, and philosophy are the best. The wise teacher will find something in each lesson to familiarize the learner with necessary-realities. Phenomena touch *noumena* at every point.

VII. **Methods of educating Necessary-Intuition.**—Mastering the world of necessary-realities educates ne-

cessary-intuition. All have vague notions of these realities; but, to make these notions clear and definite, and
to state and use them skillfully, are only possible to educated persons. Because most persons stop short of this,
they are incapable of effective thinking. People wander
after every delusion because they fail to master the
world of necessary-realities. They build on the sand.

1. *Lead the learner to perceive things having properties.* Save him from that most hurtful delusion that
he can know only phenomena. We know matter as extended. We know material substance as certainly as we
know material phenomena. We know directly things
in their relations to space and time and cause.

2. *Lead the learner to perceive self doing things.*
Save him from the no-soul delusion. We know the
thinker as certainly as we know the thinking. Self
loves, self reasons, self chooses. Back of these acts we
perceive the self that does the acts.

3. *Lead the learner to build on axioms.* Necessary-
ideas are fundamental. The learner thinks these ideas
into necessary-truths. In geometry, at every step, he
necessarily builds on axioms. Lead him so to build in
all his studies. This is the climax of educational methods. This is building on the rock.

CHAPTER VI.

CULTURE OF THE PERCEPTIVE POWERS.

THESE are our native energies of direct insight. Self is endowed with capabilities to look immediately into the world of matter, the world of mind, and the world of necessary-realities. Exploring and mastering these worlds cultivate our perceptive powers.

Terms used.—Familiar and expressive terms are the best ; but precision is necessary. In some cases we must use technical terms for the sake of clearness. As a rule, it is best to use easy terms. We can then better understand ourselves and each other.

1. *Perceptive—intuitive—acquisitive—presentative* are the common terms applied to our capabilities to know immediately. Each of these terms is used to express the same meaning. They are the general terms used to designate the powers of self to gain particular notions by direct insight. Each term includes sense-perceiving and self-perceiving and necessary-perceiving.

2. *Percept* or *intuition* is a specific name for a particular notion. Percepts or intuitions are concrete notions of material objects, of mental energies and acts, and of necessary-realities. These notions may be sense-percepts, self-percepts, or necessary-percepts. When I think of *percepts* or of *intuitions*, I think of sense-ideas, self-ideas, and necessary-ideas. When I wish to be specific, however, I designate my concrete notions as sense-intuitions, as self-intuitions, and as necessary-intuitions.

II. **Perceptive-Knowing is Immediate-Knowing.**—The practical realization of this fundamental fact has revolutionized our methods of teaching. From the Kindergarten to the university, we lead the learner to acquire directly sense-knowledge, self-knowledge, and necessary-knowledge. From childhood to manhood we lead the learner to build on his own experiences.

1. *The learner must actually do the perceiving.* The pupil and not the teacher must gain the percepts. This is vital. The art of teaching begins with skillfully leading the learner to look directly into the three elementary worlds and thus gain immediate and clear-cut notions of *noumena* as well as phenomena.

2. *The knowing must not be second-hand.* The temptation to substitute book and teacher experience for pupil-experience is greater than some teachers can withstand. It is much less trouble and requires much less time, but it does not educate. They will build on the sand. At any cost of toil and time you must lead the learner to gain his percepts for himself. The knowing must be first-hand. The experience must be the pupil's.

3. *Imagination must not take the place of experience.* The learner must really perceive. Imagination supplements experience, but can not take its place. The learner must taste the sugar sweet, and be aware of self rejoicing and perceive this space. Be not deceived. Real experience is fundamental.

III. **Habits of Exact Observation.**—These habits should be formed in early life. Discriminations and assimilations should be as exact as possible, and this exactness should be rooted into habit.

1. *Sense-observation.* Great attention should be given to educating learners to gain exact sense-ideas through each sense. The power and accuracy of mem-

ory, imagination, and thought depend largely upon the extent and exactness of our sense-knowledge. In practical life such culture is invaluable. Merchants must be able to test the quality of their goods by their senses. Mechanics, cooks, artists, poets, need to have the power of exact sense-observation well developed. Habits of exact observation should be cultivated early in life, and maintained persistently. Gazing around at every thing, and listening to every sound, are not meant by this, but a careful attention to details, plans, and purposes.*

2. *Self-observation.* Man is naturally inclined to look out of himself before he looks within. There is a propriety in this. The mind must have materials of thought before it thinks. But it is of importance that we learn to observe our own activities and thus become acquainted with ourselves.† Great care should be given to the acquisition of exact self-ideas. The habit of exact self-observation is of inestimable value. What do I perceive? What do I remember? What do I think? What were my motives? What is my intention? As we interrogate the outer world and find out its secrets, so we interrogate self and thus become acquainted with the inner world.

3. *Noumenal-observation.* The habit of exact observation of *noumena* as well as phenomena is highly important. All perceive concrete *being. It is.* This is all that can be said. All perceive concrete good. Good is fundamental. *It is right,* is final. We must learn to perceive concrete necessary-realities distinctly and exactly. We perceive that these parts equal this whole, and think these and similar observations into

* Palmer. † McCosh.

axioms. Necessary-ideas, self-ideas, and sense-ideas are
alike reliable.

IV. **Assimilation.**—This is the most fruitful term yet
used to express the union of our present with our previous acquisitions.   Nothing is more congenial, from
babyhood to the end of life, than assimilating the new
to the old. The victorious assimilation of the new is
the type of all intellectual pleasure. The lust for it is
curiosity. The emotion occasioned by discerning the
relations of the new to the old is wonder. What we
partly know inspires us with a desire to know more.

1. *Identification of the new and the old.* New acquisitions have to be interpreted in the light of former
experiences. I see a man near, and I say, "Here comes
my brother." He has changed during our years of sep-
aration, but I readily recognize him. The identification
of the new and the old is uninterrupted, prompt, immediate. The same speed and accuracy of identification
occurs in reading. To assimilate wholly new impressions is difficult. The mind searches its previous knowledge, comparing the new with the old, and in the end
finds a place for the new with the old, and thus enriches
itself.*

2. *Making our acquisitions an organic whole.*
When this is not done, the thinking and acting are
fragmentary and disconnected. Things unorganized can
grow only by accretion, the simple addition of particles
from without, but an organized body grows and develops by an inherent power within. Work of such kind
and in such quantity should be given to pupils as can
be thoroughly assimilated and combined with previous

* Rooper's Apperception.

knowledge, for only in this way and by this means does the mind gain mastery. Many persons who have a vast fund of information seem to be lacking in mental power, and the cause of this is that what they know exists in the mind as isolated facts. They do not comprehend and appreciate the relation of one thing to another and of each to the whole. Their knowledge is like useless rubbish, impeding instead of assisting the growth and development of mind. The viewing of each new acquirement in its relation to previous ones and in its relation to the whole, the assimilation of the new with the old, and its combination with the whole is what makes knowledge of value. The combination of all our acquisitions into an organized symmetric unit is the culmination of method in education.*

3. *Apperceiving is the most important idea in education.* " Prof. James, in his Psychology (vol. ii, page 107), says that the word apperception has carried very different meanings in the history of philosophy—a true remark, though not true of apperception only, but of almost all words used by philosophers and other people. The truth is that apperception has only two meanings that are worth mentioning, and these are : first, the meaning of perception pure and simple—its meaning in French and the meaning in old English of *aperceive;* and, second, that given it by Herbart, which means the assimilation of an idea by associating it with old ideas and thus interpreting it by bringing to bear on it all one's previous experience. Now, this is the most important idea in education, and deserves a new technical term all to itself, if any educational idea deserves

* Elliott.

such an honor. In the Kantian and Leibnitzian sense the word has nearly, if not quite, the meaning given it by Herbart. Leibnitz uses it to mean perception together with memory, and this is in effect Herbart's use of the word. Kant uses it to express the combination of what is received through the senses with the categories of the mind (quantity, quality, relation, and mode), and this is evidently the interpretation and recognition of the new perception by the aid of ideas already in the mind. Prof. James thinks that there are a number of words that will serve to render the meaning of Herbart—he names *psychic reaction, interpretation, conception, assimilation, elaboration, thought.* It is not one of these words, but all of them taken together, that are required to express the word apperception whenever that word is used by an Herbartian, for the word calls up not only *assimilation,* but a special kind of assimilation, namely, an *interpretation* of the new by the old ideas, and it implies also *explanation,* which assimilation does not, for the literal meaning of the latter is digestion, or simply the making-like. The idea of apperception is very complex, containing the following elements never synthesized before Leibnitz and Herbart so as to be denoted by one word : (1) A train of ideas already in the mind as a result of experience. (2) A new idea which is brought into relation to this train so as to be recognized through it, and (3) interpreted and explained by it; (4) this process resulting in a twofold result, namely, a knowledge of the real existence of examples or individual instances of the idea in question ; and (5) the subsumption of those particular instances under a general concept and the recognition that the individual perceived is only a special phase and not the whole reality of the general idea."

V. **Observing Nature.**—The children must be drawn toward, and not away from, the woods and fields and waters, and must be led to see more clearly that Nature lives and feels and acts, and links itself to human inter- . est and sympathy in the strongest and the subtlest ways; that a man cut off from fellowship with the creatures of the open air is like a tree deprived of all its lateral roots and trimmed to a single branch. He may grow down and up, but he can not grow out. It is not creditable that their education should leave our well-bred men and women so blind to the significance and beauty of the world of life. The greater part of the emotional or æsthetic value of zoölogy is lost, if the door of the class-room is shut. A personal knowledge of the habits and activities of animals, and a habit of sympathetic observation of them, are very valuable elements in the result of the skillful teaching of a well-arranged course.*

The best training of the observing powers lies outside the range of school exercises. A habit of close observation of Nature is best acquired in friendly association with, and under the guidance of, an observant parent or tutor, in hours of leisure. A daily walk with a good observer will do more to develop the faculty than the most elaborate school exercises. The training of the observing powers is indeed that part of intellectual education that most requires the aid of other educators than the schoolmaster. The young need to mingle with Nature, and should be trained to observe hill and dale, stream and wave; trained to observe the forms and

* Forbes.

movements of plants and animals, which are the best exercise of the observing faculty; and trained for those simpler and more attractive kinds of scientific observation—e. g., collecting birds' eggs, fossils, etc.—which grow naturally out of children's play-activity.*

* Sully.

PART II.

EDUCATION OF THE REPRESENTATIVE POWERS.

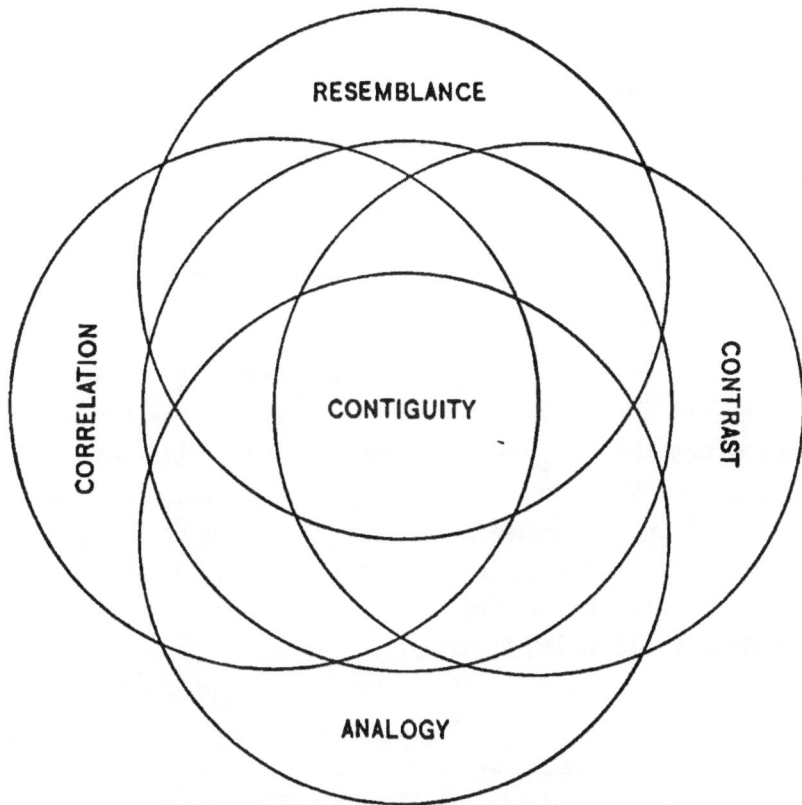

RESEMBLANCE

CORRELATION

CONTIGUITY

CONTRAST

ANALOGY

Laws of association and suggestion. Present ideas suggest other ideas with which they have been associated. The five laws of association named in the above cut are the five ways in which self associates his acquisitions, and the five ways in which associated ideas suggest each other. "These," says Mark Hopkins, "seem to me to be original and irreducible; at least no reduction of them can be made that will be of practical value. They will remain the separate working methods of suggestion and must be studied as such." By five circles we may fitly represent experiences as linked together in five distinct ways: by having each circle cut all the other circles, it is intended to indicate the truth that the suggestion may occur in at least five ways. The possibilities of recalling are thus multiplied many fold.

PART SECOND.

EDUCATION OF THE REPRESENTATIVE POWERS.

CHAPTER VII.

THE REPRESENTATIVE POWERS AND REPRESENTATIVE KNOWING.

SELF as representation makes present again, in old and new forms, his past experiences. *Present* means to make things present originally, but *re-present* (*re*, again + *præsentare*, to make present) means to make present again. Presentative knowing is making things present to ourselves for the first time, but *re*-presentative knowing is making our experiences present to ourselves again; it is re-knowing.

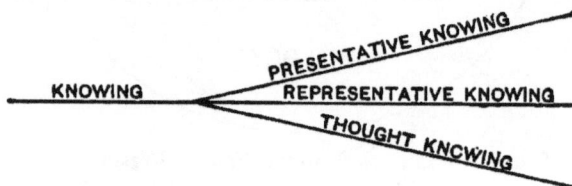

Our representative powers are our capabilities to make our acquisitions present again in old and new forms. They are our native energies to modify as well as to revive our experiences.

Self as memory recalls his acquisitions in the old forms of experience. I remember the home of Emerson just as I saw it. Self as *phantasy* weaves his experiences into new forms called fancies. We thus *re-*

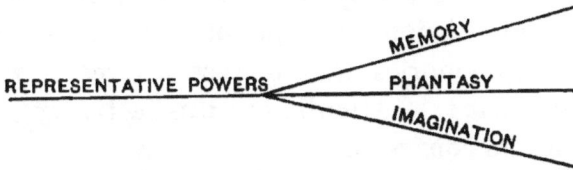

REPRESENTATIVE POWERS
MEMORY
PHANTASY
IMAGINATION

present our experiences in reverie and dreaming. Self as *imagination re-*presents his experiences in new forms called ideals. We so change and rearrange realities as to form ideals. Some psychologists designate these processes as reproductive imagination, passive imagination, and creative imagination. It is better to retain the old names.

I. MEMORY.

This is the native energy of self to reproduce his acquisitions. That memory is a native energy of self is an unquestioned fact. The expressions "I remember" and "I do not recollect" mean almost as much to the child as to the philosopher. We are endowed with the capability to recall our past experiences. Memory is simply the self remembering. Self as memory does *all* his recalling. Memory, like awareness and attention, enters into all our knowing, feeling, and willing.

I. **Memory Products.**—Revived experiences are *memories, remembrances, recollections.* We speak of sweet memories of other days, and cherish the fond recollections of childhood. Our memories are of our emotional and active experiences as well as of our cognitive. We do not recall our emotions, but we recall ideas occasioned by our emotions. The recollection may occasion a new emotion, but the dead emotion is merely a memory. Self embalms his emotions and purposes in ideas; when recalled, these ideas may occasion new emotions. We recall our impressions and notions of all our experiences. Our memories are our lives revived. *Memory makes no changes.* Attention to this fact may prevent much needless confusion.

II. **Memory Processes.**—My memory is my capability to recall my past experiences. For the thousands this is all that need be said. But you seek deeper insight. The actual processes of remembering are inscrutable; but we study to know facts about the processes.

1. *Retaining* is so associating and unitizing our experiences that present experiences will suggest past experiences. This must be the meaning of retention, for it is certain we do not keep our experiences in mind. Suggestion is the key to the storehouse of memory. We may be said to retain our acquisitions when we possess the key to unlock our stored treasures. Our memories become retentive when we thoroughly assimilate and carefully *associate* our acquisitions.

2. *Representing* is restoring the thing remembered with its associations. In acquisition we assimilate into unity our old and new experiences; we form associated experience groups; we make picture-groups. When we *r*emember we *r*ecollect the group. We *r*epresent to ourselves the thing remembered with its environments. We restore the unity. But all mental acts are marvelously complex. Imagination and thought and emotion enter largely into our representations, filling up the outlines of memory.

3. *Reproducing* is bringing back to mind our former experiences. This is pre-eminently the meaning of memory. We express this wonderful act by such words as *r*emember, *r*ecollect, and *r*epresent. You reproduce the problem just as the teacher stated it.

4. *Recognizing* is identifying experiences and memories. You recognize this lady as your friend of former years. You recognize this poem as one you memorized while attending school. I am aware that my memories were my experiences. This is what is meant by recognition. Professor James gives this definition : " Memory is the

knowledge of an *event* or *fact* of which meantime we have not been thinking, with the additional consciousness that we *have experienced it before.*" While this is true of a complete act of memory, we are aware that recognition is wanting in a large proportion of our acts of memory. As a rule, we do not recognize the memories we build into our phantasms, ideals, and thoughts as former experiences.

III. **Memory Laws; Laws of Suggestion.** — Present experiences suggest past experiences. This is a fundamental fact in the mental economy. The child for the first time sees a pineapple; its optic apparatus is energized so that it gains an idea of the object. It asks the name, and is told that it is a pineapple; its auditory apparatus is now energized so that it gains the word. It associates the name and the object, so that thereafter the name suggests the object and the object suggests the name. Here we certainly have a physiological basis for association and suggestion, but the actual revival is surely mental.

We assimilate into unity our experiences. We associate our acts as parts of related wholes. A present idea suggests other ideas associated with it, and thus self restores the unity of his experience. Memory depends on association, but interested attention, systematic arrangement, and determined effort widen and deepen association.

1. *Association by resemblance and contrast* (see cut, page 91). Similar or contrasted ideas associated together suggest each other. The term *ideas* is here used to include all our experiences. The learner observes and assimilates into groups similar things. The similars associated constitute an experience unit. When we think of one of the similars it suggests the other members of the group. I think of birds, and the idea suggests the whole group of vertebrates. Dissimilar related things suggest each other; joy suggests sorrow, and hope suggests fear.

2. *Association by contiguity.* Experiences occurring together or in succession suggest each other. This law is far-reaching and explains most of our remembering. A thousand illustrations will occur to you.

3. *Association by correlation.* Ideas associated as correlatives suggest each other. The word suggests the idea as the idea suggests the word. The sign (+) suggests addition. The effect suggests the cause; the end, the means; the consequent, the antecedent; the conclusion, the premises. Ruler suggests subjects; father, son; uncle, nephew. This may be counted the master law of suggestion, including all forms of thought association.

Other memory laws will be considered in connection with memory culture. When we seek to recall something, we must make search for it just as we rummage a house for a lost object. Success crowns wise and determined effort.

IV. **Memory Cerebration.**—In some unknown way mental processes go on in connection with brain-processes. The mystery of remembering is no greater than the mystery of perceiving. " Conscious memory," says Ladd, " is a spiritual phenomenon, the explanation of which, as arising out of nervous processes and conditions, is not simply undiscoverd in fact, but utterly incapable of approach by the imagination. When, then, we speak of a physical basis of memory, recognition must be made of the complete inability of science to suggest any physical process which can be conceived of as correlated with that peculiar and mysterious *actus* of the mind, connecting its present and its past, which constitutes the essence of memory."

II. Phantasy.*

This is the native energy of self to weave his experiences into new forms called fancies. It is self, spontaneously and without purpose, throwing his experiences into the incoherent and grotesque forms of day and night dreams. Memory furnishes most of the materials. Suggestion comes chiefly through association by resemblance and contiguity. Sensations, chiefly organic, strangely affect our dreams. When all is well, our dreams are pleasant; but, when the body or the mind is disturbed, our dreams are troubled.

Some psychologists treat of phantasy as the passive imagination, as they treat of memory as the reproductive imagination. This nomenclature seems to me objectionable. (1.) We can not think of a passive energy, but we are familiar with unpurposed and undirected activity. (2.) These are not the expressions used in literature or by the people. (3.) These expressions multiply the difficulties of the learner and the teacher. A more fundamental objection is stated elsewhere. It is surely every way better to retain the easy and familiar names of these powers—*Memory, Phantasy, Imagination.* The Greeks meant by *phantasia*, image-making. Fancy, phantasy, and fantasy are merely the three forms of the word. Phantasy is here used because freer from misleading associations than the other forms.

I. **Phantasy Products.**—Self, out of his experiences, immediate and revived, constructs fancies. The panoramas we paint for our own amusement, in reverie and dreaming, are called fancies. We can put into our dreams only our experiences. The blind put no color

* See Elementary Psychology, Chapter XI, also James Mark Baldwin's Handbook of Psychology, Chapter XII. This faculty, called by him Passive Imagination, is admirably treated. As a wonderful exhibition of the play of phantasy, study Shakespeare's Midsummer-Night's Dream.

into their fancies. Adults who have lost their hearing before the fifth year put no sound into their dream images. Self as phantasy deals with the concrete. Our fancies are made up of sense-percepts, self-percepts, and necessary-percepts. Concepts are not used in our dreams. Each one can give many apt illustrations from his own experiences.

II. **Phantasy and Awareness.**—We are aware of our dreams and of self viewing the panorama; but, at the same time, our dreams seem to us to be objective realities. We do not recognize the memories that are woven into our dreams as former experiences, nor are we aware that these fancies are products of our own minds. I am merely aware of self viewing the scenes he makes, and of the varying emotions occasioned by those pictures. In soundest sleep and even in delirium I am aware. The sense-world may fade away, but self never ceases to be conscious of his own acts.

III. **Phantasy and Memory.**—Memory acting through suggestion recalls our experiences for the use of phantasy. Self as phantasy disassociates his experiences and then recombines them into new forms. As thus changed, we do not recognize these as past experiences, but look upon them at the time as new experiences. Our fancies are not usually remembered, as there is slight attention, and as dream-life is apart from waking life. Memory *re*presents our acquisitions in the old forms of experience; phantasy represents our experience in new forms.

IV. **Phantasy and Mesmerism.**—Operators try to induce the mesmeric state and keep their patients in this condition. Phantasy is now peculiarly sensitive to suggestions made by the operator. Phantasms seem to be realities, and the patient *acts* his dreams. In the same way may be explained many things connected with somnambulism, delirium tremens, and insanity. The play of phantasy is the key to many mysteries.

V. Phantasy and Cerebration.—During repose, when phantasy is most active, the blood-supply to the cerebrum is greatly reduced. Perception, and thought, and will are slightly active, and the exhausted brain recuperates. Self drifts. Gentle sensor excitations and present ideas suggest other experiences. Self, without purpose and without plan, goes on linking fancy to fancy. This is scribbling, not writing ; this is the child daubing, not the artist painting. This is the whirlwind piling up the timbers, not the architect constructing the mansion. Phantasy is self representing his experiences in the grotesque forms called phantasms.

VI. Phantasy and Imagination.—A clear distinction between these powers helps the psychologist much, but the educator more. Imagination is purposed and directed effort, but phantasy goes on without purpose and without direction. The one is work, the other play. We educate the one and leave the other to roam fancy free. Phantasy is to the imagination what the kaleidoscope is to the designer ; it gives suggestions which the imagination may work up in higher forms. It is thus a helpful factor in creation. Phantasy is active in childhood. while imagination is feeble and halting.

III. IMAGINATION.

This is the capability of self to transform the real into the ideal. Beecher, it is said, never made a quotation. As the bee transforms sweet into honey, so Beecher transformed everything he touched into Beecherisms. The materials are realities, but the creations of imagination are ideals. Out of your experiences you create an ideal cottage which you hope to make a reality. We *construct* our ideals; this is prose. We *form* our ideals; this is poetry. We *create* our ideals; this is both prose and poetry. Create, as here used, means to make out of our experiences new wholes.

I. **Imagination Products.**—These are called ideals. A reality is something that really exists independent of the mind. This school-house, and this, and this, are real school-houses. Out of my experiences I make a plan for a school-house widely different from anything I have ever seen. This ideal school-house is my own creation and exists only in my mind. Imagination modifies experiences, rearranges them, analyzes them, and makes new syntheses. Imagination makes models, constructs hypotheses, forms systems, creates poems. Realities, touched by the magic wand of imagination, become ideals. Yonder mountain becomes a mountain of gold crowned with crystal palaces inhabited by angels. Ideal is opposed to real, and is used to designate the products of imagination. *Ideas* are notions of realities; *ideals* are creations of the mind. Memory represents our acquisitions in the old forms of experience; imagination represents experiences in the new forms of ideals.

II. **Limits of Imagination.**—We *gain* ideas and *construct* ideals.

1. *We are dependent on sense-perception* for all we know of the material world. Self as imagination is limited to his sense-experiences. The deaf put no sounds into their creations; nor do the blind put color.

2. *We are dependent on self-perception* for all we know of the mind-world. We can endow our ideal man or angel with our own

capabilities and nothing more. True, we are able to vary the degree of knowing, feeling, and willing almost infinitely.

3. *We are dependent on necessary-perception* for all we know of necessary realities. We *must* make our ideals *somehow*, some*where*, and some *when*. We *must* make our ideals out of *matter* and *spirit*. We must construct our ideals in harmony with our axiomatic intuitions. Even in imagination we can not make the whole greater than the sum of all its parts.

III. **Imagination and Memory.**—Self as imagination represents his experiences in new forms called ideals. But memory furnishes the materials from the storehouse of experience out of which imagination makes his creations, as the hod-carrier supplies the mason with bricks and mortar out of which to build the wall. We associate and recall our ideals, as we associate and recall our ideas. On the other hand, no one knows how much imagination helps memory, filling out to completeness the skeletons of the experiences we recall.

IV. **Imagination and our other Powers.**—As the master-builder, self, in creating his ideals, commands all his capabilities; memory contributes materials, will contributes purpose, emotion contributes inspiration, thought contributes wisdom to guide and restrain. Thus we create the enduring works of art and literature and life.

V. **An Ideal is a Working Model.**—It is the harmonious blending into one mental product the idea and the object. My ideal blackboard is grateful to the eye, free from dust and a perfect writing surface. Here the object is the blackboard, and the ideas are those named. I realize my ideal when I make it a reality. All invention, all progress, all education, come from efforts to realize ideals. To the educator, as to the inventor, the ideal is the working model. We labor here and everywhere to realize our ideals. Our ideals, in this sense, are the finished products of our imaginations. Much of the work of imagination consists in modifying and rearranging our acquisitions; still, it is best to call even these imperfect forms ideals as opposed to reals.

CHAPTER VIII.

EDUCATION OF MEMORY.

BY this is meant the development of the power to reproduce past experiences. Last year I visited, with friends, Minnehaha Falls and enjoyed its beauties. The friends are scattered, and I am far away from that delightful scene. But I now recall it with its associations, and I recognize this memory as a past experience. Memory is my capability to reproduce my past acquisitions. When I am able to do this readily and accurately, my memory is said to be educated; you say I have a good memory.

I. RELATIONS AND DEFINITIONS.

Memory stands for recalling. When we think of memory, it is always our power to reproduce our past experiences. We think of retention and association and suggestion and recognition as incidents of memory; memory includes these processes. We simply think of *recalling* when we think of memory. Memory stands for all recalling.

1. *Memory* is the capability of self to recall his past experiences. Acquisition makes knowledge present *for*

the first time ; memory makes knowledge present again. Acquisition presents ; memory *re*-presents. *Present* means to *make present* to ourselves; *re*-present means to make present again ; to recollect ; to remember ; to reproduce ; to recall.

2. *Memories* are recollections of past experiences. Memories, remembrances, and recollections are the prod-

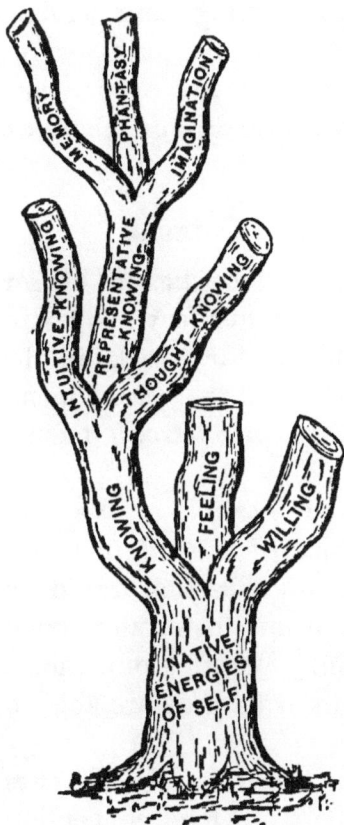

ucts of memory, as percepts are the products of perception. We acquire ideas ; these when remembered are termed *revived* ideas. Remembered percepts are simply *revived* percepts. This is true of all our remembered experiences ; they are simply *revived* experiences. The experience is merely recalled and recognized. Memory makes no changes. Our remembrances coincide with our experiences.

3. *Education of memory* is the development of the native energy of self to recall his past experiences. It makes the difference between the feeble memory of the child and the powerful memory of the man. The ready, accurate, exhaustive memory comes of culture.

4. *Relations of memory.* In the mental economy

memory stands midway between perception and thought. We acquire, we remember, we think. Self as memory records and reproduces his experiences. You know, memory is there ; you feel, memory is there ; you will, memory is there. Memory supplies imagination and thought with materials. Memory holds up to choice alternatives. Attention and awareness and memory are bosom friends who never separate. This trio accompanies all other acts of knowing, feeling, and willing. While we *perceive*, we attend, remember, are aware ; while we *think*, we attend, remember, are aware ; and while we *feel* and *determine*, we attend, remember, are aware.

II. IMPORTANCE OF MEMORY-CULTURE.

A good memory is a friend which sticketh closer than a brother. One with a poor memory gropes in the dark, while one with a good memory works in the light of all he knows. Millions bewail their *weak* memories, while thousands rejoice in their *strong* memories.

1. *Memory makes learning possible.* We can hardly appreciate the importance of a good memory. Without it, skill or progress in any direction would be impossible. The teacher bases all his instruction upon the possibilities of reproduction. We test our pupils and estimate men and women by what they are able to reproduce.

2. *Memory makes thinking possible.* It supplies material for thought. It holds up before conception various objects to be compared and classified. It holds up before judgment two notions, that the agreement

or disagreement may be discerned. It holds up before reason the premises, that the conclusion may be inferred.

3. *Memory multiplies our joys.* It makes a thing of beauty a joy forever. "Pleasures of memory" is classic. True, we do not recall the old joys, but our recollections of our past joys occasion new joys. A good memory brings to us over and over again the sweets of life, while forgetfulness drops out of our lives all bitter things.

4. *A good memory increases efficiency.* The student with a good memory accomplishes many times as much as the student with a poor memory. A teacher with a good memory furnishes his pupils a perpetual feast. A good memory is of incalculable value to the minister, to the lawyer, to all workers.

5. *Neglect of memory-culture.* May all have good memories? Some are more gifted than others, but all, by culture, may develop vigorous memories. Why is this culture so neglected? Why is it that persons with excellent memories are so rare? How may we remedy this evil? Better methods of study and of teaching will work wonders.

III. Growth of Memory.

Macaulay, when a child, remembered the names of his toys; but, when a man, he remembered the facts of human history. *Growth* made the difference between the feeble memory of the infant and the mighty memory of the man. Teaching is the art of promoting this growth.

1. *Infant memory.* Next to sense-perception, memory earliest becomes active. When but a few weeks old, the child remembers the face of its parents and various objects. When but a few months old the child remembers the names of objects as well as the objects. When the child is three years old it uses correctly a considerable number of words to express its acquisitions. But infant memory is feeble, and early impressions are fleeting. The three years of infancy are a blank to the adult. An adult puts no color into his memories when sight has been lost before the fifth year.

2. *Childhood memories.* From the third to the tenth year objective memory is active. The child associates the word with the object. Words occurring in succession are associated. Stories and pictures are remembered. Memory is now fresh and active, but comparatively weak.

3. *Memory in boyhood and girlhood.* During this period objective memory reaches full activity and abstract memory becomes active. Language is easily learned and readily remembered. Semi-science is the delight of boys and girls.

4. *Memory in youth.* During this period memory becomes fully active. The vigorous memory of youth is proverbial. All forms of knowledge are now easily remembered. Impressions are lasting.

5. *Memory in manhood.* Up to the meridian of life, memory certainly becomes more and more commanding. The memories of Webster and Gladstone were vastly more vigorous at fifty than at twenty.

6. *Memory in old age.* At ninety Humboldt's memory was as vigorous as in youth. Bismarck and Gladstone at seventy-five

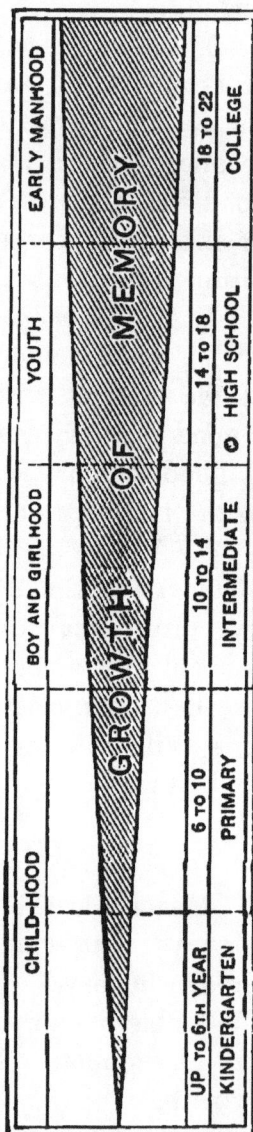

gave no signs of memory failure. But, when the old cease to make new conquests, memory begins to lose its grasp.

IV. LAWS OF MEMORY-GROWTH.

The uniform ways in which we must work in order to promote the growth of memory are termed the laws of memory-growth.

I. **General Laws.**—These are here stated in terms of memory. It is well to keep in mind that memory includes association, suggestion, reproduction, and recognition. It is the native energy of self to recall his past experiences.

1. *Law of effort.* Well-directed effort in associating and recalling our ideas educates memory. We assimilate and associate our new and old experiences. We organize our acquisitions into unity, so that a present notion suggests the entire group of associated ideas.

2. *Law of means.* Studies which call memory into constant and vigorous activity have a high memory-culture value. The study of history is an excellent means for improving memory. The study of algebra is not a good means for memory-culture.

3. *Law of method.* Plans of work which call memory into lawful, systematic, vigorous, and persistent activity develop this power. The methods of study and teaching very largely determine the value of a study.

II. **Special Laws.**—Many valuable laws relating to the culture of memory have been presented by educational writers. A few of the more important are given.

1. *Law of the brain.* A healthy and vigorous brain conditions a good memory. It is certain that self works in and through his physical organism. It is also certain that, the better the condition of his physical organism, the better he can work. This law empha-

sizes the importance of school hygiene. Pupils who take little exercise, and study in a crowded room, poorly ventilated and poorly heated, will likely be noted for poor memories. Boys who smoke cigarettes and girls who chew gum nearly always complain of weak memories. Violation of law brings all our woes.

2. *Law of association.* Vigor of *mind*, interested *attention*, rational *order*, and *repetition* strengthen association. This law gives us the key to good memory. Complete association makes reproduction easy and exhaustive. No one who observes this law will complain of a poor memory.

3. *Law of interest.* Delight in study marvelously strengthens association and suggestion. We rarely forget things which delight us. Pupils who are deeply interested remember well.

4. *Law of determination.* Determined and systematic effort to retain and reproduce our acquisitions develops memory. When we make up our minds to remember, we can usually do so. I *will* remember is almost invincible. We need to learn and remember many things which do not interest us. Determined effort enables us to do this.

5. *Law of retentive memory.* Self must remember *in order to know*, as well as to reproduce *what he knows*. In general we treasure what we understand. But at almost every step memory must keep before self *words and statements not understood*, that he may investigate and master them. Still, to crowd memory with unmeaning words, as the Chinese do, is a fundamental educational error.

6. *Law of time.* Keeping a topic before the mind for a considerable time and recalling it frequently strengthens memory. The matter is examined from various standpoints, and associated in many ways. It is *assimilated*. In acquisition we must hasten leisurely. Hurried work is waste labor in education. Knowledge recalled at intervals *not too great* becomes firmly fixed in the mind. But knowledge not recalled soon fades into forgetfulness.

7. *Memory specifics.* The multitude of these is absolutely bewildering. The art of never forgetting will be taught in ten lessons! While we are grateful for all helpful hints, the sooner we realize that there is no royal road to memory, the better for us and for our pupils.

V. Means for Memory-Culture.

Knowledge is the means for memory-culture. Storing and reproducing knowledge educates memory. Any study may become the means of memory-culture when properly pursued; but studies which call memory into constant and vigorous activity are of the greatest memory-culture value.

MEMORY-CULTURE, VALUE OF	1	2	8	4
Kindergarten work and general object-lessons..	10	10	....	....
Primary language-lessons and juvenile literature	10	9	....	....
Geography, botany, zoölogy....................	10	10	....	....
History, literature, Latin.....................	9	10	....	....
Physiology, physics, chemistry................	8	8	....	....
Reading, drawing, music......................	8	8	....	....
Mathematics, psychology, ethics..............	6	6	....	....

Explanation. Estimates in the first column are the author's; those in the second column are Dr. Brooks's. You may place your estimate in column three, then place the averages in column four. A few hours of earnest work along this line will give you deeper insight into the nature of memory and the relations of knowledge to memory. You will see that almost everything as to the culture value of a study depends on the teacher.

Educational values depend upon study and teaching methods; but, when methods are equal, some studies give better educational results than others. We may thus make an approximate estimate of the comparative educational value of various studies. Aristotle and Plato called attention to this matter. Bacon tells us that there is no defect that can not be remedied by " fit studies." He prescribes mathematics for *thought, history* for *wisdom, poetry* for *wit,* and *science* for *depth.* In our times the contention between the advocates of the classics and the advocates of the sciences has given great prominence to this subject. Whewell and Spencer and Bain and Harris and others have ably discussed "*What knowledge is of most worth?*" Dr. Payne, in his Contributions to the Science of Education, gives a valuable chapter on "Educational Values." Frequent references will be made to his *estimates*, because he, like Dr. Brooks, has ventured to make his estimates specific. For memory-culture Dr. Payne esteems of *high value*, botany, geography, history, literature; of *medium value*, arithmetic, physiology, grammar; of *low value*, physics.

VI. Methods of educating Memory.

These are efficient plans of work in getting, retaining, and reproducing knowledge. As teachers we can command the most favorable conditions. We can manage to arouse and hold the interested attention of each pupil. We can use such illustrations and expedients as will enlist all the activities of the learner. We can lead the learner to thoroughly associate his acquisitions by assimilating into unity his old and new experiences. We can train the learner to the habit of recalling and using his knowledge. In these ways we promote the growth of memory.

I. **Kindergarten Methods.**—The ideas gained by the child during its first three years fade away, but the impressions and habits endure. During these years the mother is the loving kindergartner. Happy the child that is wisely led during these precious years!

The Kindergartner suggests and manages, but still leaves the little ones almost as free as the birds. The child is led to explore the world around. It sees and

8

hears and tastes and smells and touches and uses all it
comes in contact with. Its sense-experiences become
sense-ideas. These it embodies in words, which become
signs of the ideas. New experiences and old are assimilated and associated. The narrow child-world is a unit.
The child remembers because a present experience suggests its associates. It is trained to recall often and
accurately its few experiences. As its world becomes
larger, its memory grows stronger.

II. **Primary Methods.**—Memory of words as the
signs of objects is at its best during the primary period.
During these four years the child becomes widely acquainted with things and their properties. This is the
golden period for objective language-lessons. Now the
child easily learns to speak and read and write. Stories,
hymns, precepts, and memory gems which touch child
experience, educate child memory. Leading children
to find out and tell about the earth and the animals
and the plants develops memory. This is a fitting
time to ingrain good habits. Acquiring good manners
and morals cultivates memory. Here and everywhere
primary lessons must be objective and concrete. The
effort of the child to remember and *act* good manners
and morals strengthens memory.

The excellent manuals of primary methods, now
within easy reach of every teacher, render details here
unnecessary. Good primary teaching educates memory.

III. **Intermediate Methods.**—During this period objective and verbal memory are highly active, and memory of the abstract begins to be active. Girls and boys
are anxious to do more work and more difficult work.
Feats of memory delight them.

1. *Lead your pupils to study science.* In geography and botany and zoölogy manage to have your pupils observe closely, classify roughly, and find out some terms of science. No studies can elicit deeper interest or command closer attention. The experience gained is assimilated, associated, and constantly recalled. There is no better way to improve memory. A solid foundation is now laid for the study of science in the high-school and college.

2. *Lead your pupils to study history and litera-ture.* We are rich in the choicest books for this purpose. Now is the time to cultivate a taste for good reading, and to train the pupils how to read. Everything must in some way connect with the pupil's experience. The wise teacher leads his pupils to *un-derstand, assimilate, associate,* and *recall.* The inter-est is intense and the attention complete ; memory grows strong.

3. *Reading, language-lessons, music, manners, and morals* must be so taught as to educate memory as well as the other capabilities. Every advance step must be based on the experience of the pupil. The learner will remember because he knows.

4. *Doing educates memory.* What the pupil does is seldom forgotten. You show the pupil the map of South America and talk to him about it, but he soon forgets. Have him mold South America and draw a map ; now he remembers. In our modern methods the pupil literally *works* out his own salvation.

IV. **High-School Methods.**—During the high-school period memory, in all its forms, is highly active, and seems to reach full activity about the eighteenth year.

The student now thinks his knowledge into system, and logically associates his experiences.

1. *Lead the student to master botany and zoölogy.* For memory-culture these studies are among the best. The student now multiplies his own experiences by appropriating the experiences of others. You lead him to rediscover the classifications of science, and to construct anew his botany and his zoölogy. Memory is called into constant and vigorous use.

2. *Lead the student to master the Latin language and Greek and Latin literature.* No other work will develop a more vigorous memory. The modern methods of teaching the classics are admirable for memory-culture.

3. *Lead the student to study properly history and literature.* Facts are grouped and associated by their cause relations. The main events are thought into unity while minor matters are treated as scaffolding. The student toils to make his historic world a history of the race. Such studies grandly educate memory.

4. *Lead the student to cultivate a discriminating memory.* To forget is as important as to retain. The important things must be seized and held, and the rubbish must be rejected and dropped. All our memory energies are thus expended in retaining and recalling our most valuable experiences. For the younger pupils the teacher manages the discriminating, but the learner is gradually trained to select the best things for retention. To remember everything would be to bury self in a sea of details. Selection is the basis of good memory, and forgetfulness is its partner.

5. *Train the student to organize his knowledge.*

Self is not an *organism* but an *organizer*. Through organization we gain mastery. Organization means numerous associations; and the more numerous the associations the greater the power of recalling. This is why we lead children to test objects as far as possible by each sense. This is why we must lead the learner frequently to recall his old knowledge and assimilate it and associate it in many ways with his new acquisitions. We forget proper names because we do not thoroughly organize them into knowledge unity. Usually the student's memory is best in the studies in which he takes the deepest *interest*, for in these he organizes his knowledge most completely.

V. General Directions for Memory-Culture.— Many find a few terse rules helpful. These should be so stated as to stir the student like bugle-blasts.

1. *Fuller's rules.* These quaint but unique rules have assisted thousands :

(1) Soundly infix what thou wouldst remember.

(2) Marshal thy notions into method.

(3) Overburden not the memory with details.

2. *Colburn's rules.* These rules shine like stars. They have incited countless numbers to study better and teach better :

(1) Learn one thing at a time.

(2) Learn it thoroughly.

(3) Learn its connections with other things.

3. *Rules for study.* Each of the following rules is a golden link in memory's chain :

(1) Take a deep *interest* in what you study.

(2) Give your entire *attention* to what you study.

(3) Thoroughly assimilate and associate the old and the new.

(4) Push effort to complete mastery.

VI. **Control over Memories.**—Each person can in a great measure remember or forget what he will. What we wish to remember we study thoroughly, associate in many ways, and recall often. Knowledge thus organized sticks like burrs. We give slight attention to what we wish to forget, and refuse to assimilate it, and when such thoughts occur we refuse to entertain them. Things thus treated, like unwelcomed visitors, soon cease to trouble us. The teacher may, to a marvelous extent, control the recollections, and thus determine the characters of his pupils.

1. *The teacher determines the lessons.* He controls presentation directly and representation indirectly. This far-reaching principle makes it possible to mold races of men, as witness the Jews and the Chinese.

2. *The teacher controls methods of acquisition.* Thus by keeping the things he wishes remembered before the pupil he makes the memory certain. Do you realize how completely your pupils are in your hands?

3. *The teacher controls illustrations.* Objects, board work, moulding, charts, maps, experiments, etc., are so used as to impress deeply the thoughts he wishes remembered. Modern methods intensely interest, deeply impress, and secure system. These are the conditions of good memory.

4. *The teacher controls the physical conditions.* The habits of the pupils, the temperature and the ventilation of the school-room, etc., are very much under

the direction of the teacher. These conditions wonderfully influence recollection.

5. *Teachers' responsibilities.* Clearly, you largely control the ideas of your pupils. But ideas pass over into emotions, and emotions into acts. You thus determine the lives of your pupils. Shrink not, appalled by the responsibility, but courageously press on, leading those in your charge up to a higher and better life.

VII. **Mistakes in educating Memory.** — In our earnestness to have our pupils learn the most possible, we sometimes make grievous mistakes. As educators we must try to be law-abiding, and thus avoid hurtful blunders.

1. *Stated examinations and reviews at long intervals.* Much waste labor in education is thus caused. During each lesson, true teaching calls up the past in connection with the present. The habit of commanding our knowledge grows. I have not found stated examinations and formal reviews helpful.

2. *The Chinese method—words without ideas.* This certainly stultifies the mind. No wonder China has made little progress for two thousand years. Do you know any teachers who use the Chinese method? If so, hasten to teach them more perfect ways of education.

3. *Memory before experience.* The arch-enemy could hardly have invented a method more hurtful. Thus are committed unmeaning definitions, rules, tables, classifications, facts. It is infinitely better for the learner to *make* these out of his experiences. He thus associates and remembers things understood and so grows stronger and wiser.

4. *Books in place of Nature.* The sources of knowl-

edge are all around the child. It has but to look to know. What can be more stupid than to have it memorize the book? This does not even cultivate memory. When you lead the child to gain knowledge directly from nature it will know and remember. Later it will be able to appropriate the experiences of others as contained in books.

5 *Indiscriminate remembering.* This crowds the mind with rubbish, and tends to weaken memory. Not *how much* but *how little* is the safe rule. Selection lies at the base of learning. Lead the learner to treasure only the *best*, only the *essentials*. Memory thus becomes *strong* and useful.

SUGGESTIVE STUDY-HINTS.

Memory becomes retentive, ready, and exact, when experiences are carefully selected and thoroughly organized into unity. Interested attention, intelligent and determined effort, and vivid imagination re-enforce memory and make it commanding.

I. **Helpful Books.**—Next to sense-perception memory-culture has elicited most discussion. Among many excellent works may be mentioned, Memory, by David Kay, International Education Series; Sully's Psychology; Bain, Education as a Science; Palmer, Science of Education; White, Elements of Pedagogy; Garvey, Manual of Human Culture. The subject is treated at great length in works on Physiological Psychology, by Spencer, Ladd, James, Wundt, etc. You will find it safe to ignore all systems of artificial mnemonics.

11. **Definitions.**—Give your definition of memory; of remembrances; of education of memory. Give your views of the relations of memory to perception; to phantasy; to imagination; to thought; to emotion; to will.

III. **Importance of Memory-Culture.**—State and illustrate three original reasons why *you* consider the education of memory highly important.

IV. **Growth of Memory.**—Trace the growth of memory from infancy to the meridian of life. When do you think objective memory becomes fully active? abstract memory? Explain the loss of memory by old people. How may memory be kept vigorous even in old age?

V. **Laws of Memory-Growth.**—What do you mean by educational laws? State the law of effort in terms of memory; law of means; law of method. Mention two special laws that you have discovered. Which of the special laws given do you consider most helpful?

VI. **Means of Memory-Culture.**—Tell what you mean by this. What branches do you esteem of highest value in memory-culture? You may make and explain a table of the memory-culture value of the leading school studies.

VII. **Methods of educating Memory.**—What do you mean by this? Tell how you would manage kindergarten work so as to develop memory; primary work; intermediate work; high-school work. Explain the assimilation of ideas; the association of ideas; the organization of your knowledge.

VIII. **Mistakes in educating Memory.**—Why do you think stated examinations a mistake? formal reviews? What are your objections to the Chinese method? to memory before experience? to books in place of Nature? to indiscriminate remembering? You may suggest two additional mistakes which teachers make in their treatment of memory.

IX. **Control over Memories.**—How do you remember? How do you forget? Tell how the teacher controls the memories of his pupils. To what extent is the teacher responsible for what his pupils become?

X. **Letter on Memory-Culture.**—Put into your letter to your friend the *best* things you know about the education of memory. Write what you think.

CHAPTER IX.

EDUCATIONAL TREATMENT OF PHANTASY.

PHANTASY is the native energy of self to *re*present his experiences as fancies. Phantasy is commonly written fancy or fantasy. In psychology it is often called the undirected imagination. When we rest, it is revery; when we sleep, it is dreaming. In childhood it makes the stick a horse and the fairy tale a reality. Later, it makes the novel a history and the drama real life. It fills the drunkard's boots with snakes, changes the demented woman into Queen Victoria, and leads the somnambulist to act his dreams. Surely the educator can not afford to ignore an activity that enters so widely into our lives.

I. **Characteristics of Phantasy.**—These are marked. You can test them for yourself:

1. *Fancies seem to be realities.* Your dreams seem to be new experiences. At the time you are not aware that you are merely representing old experiences in new forms.

2. *Phantasy activity is undirected.* Without plan and without purpose self spontaneously links fancy unto fancy. This is the play faculty of the soul.

3. *Phantasy disassociates and recombines.* Self as phantasy breaks up his experiences into *elements* and weaves these into new forms. It never occurs to us, however, that our fancies are made out of our experiences. At the time, our fancies seem to be new experiences.

II. **Relations of Phantasy.**—While our other powers

are least active phantasy is most active. Memory supplies materials. The laws of suggestion, chiefly those
of contiguity and resemblance, are in force in dreamland.

Immediate sensations, mostly organic, are woven
into the fabric. When thought is slightly active, our
dreams become arguments. When imagination is some-
what active, our reveries and dreams become inventions,
plans, romances. When our affections are slightly active, our dreams become love-scenes. When will is sufficiently active, we act our dreams. When memory is
slightly active, we remember our dreams. Dreamland
is indeed a wonder-land.

III. **Control over Phantasy.**—Wishing our dear ones
pleasant dreams means much. It means refreshing
sleep. Very largely this depends on ourselves. Good
digestion, physical comfort, an hour or two of physical
and mental rest, and a conscience void of offense, are
the conditions of sweet sleep and refreshing dreams.
A sour stomach, overwork, and a troubled conscience,
bring unrefreshing sleep and troubled dreams.

*Our waking experiences largely determine our
dreams.* Let our reading, our associations, and our
emotions be habitually pure and elevating, and our
dreams will be pure and peaceful. Let our reading,
associations, and emotions be low and degrading, and
our dreams will be unwholesome.

Rarely tell your dreams. On waking, fancies
should dissolve like mists before the sun. No one desires to retain his dreams; but, if you tell your dreams,
you will remember them more and more. As you
awake, you will seize on your dream and associate it
with your waking life, that you may tell it.

IV. **Phantasy** in **Childhood.**—The baby weaves its little joys and griefs into its dreams: now it laughs, now it weeps. The child seems to suffer new punishments and engage in new plays. But the healthy child rarely remembers its dreams.

1. *Play is a thing of sense and phantasy.* Play is spontaneous activity; work is directed activity. Watch the little ones at play; without plan and without purpose they weave and act their fancies. See how they weave into their plays past and present experiences.

2. *Fairy-land is reality to the child.* Fairy stories give unbounded pleasure. St. Nick, too, is a reality. Child literature is largely based on the activity of phantasy. The illusions fade out as years advance, but in childhood they must be wholesome. Anything is better than stupid materialism.

V. **Phantasy and Illusions.**—Self as phantasy forms out of his experiences images which seem to be realities. Macbeth saw the dagger, but, when he tested the appearance by another sense, he knew that it was his own creation, a thing of phantasy. You could not be mistaken? True, but what you saw was a phantasm and not a reality. A few grains of common sense will usually dissipate these illusions.

VI. **Phantasy and Imagination.**—We do not educate phantasy; we study it, and so treat it as to make its activity wholesome. Classing fancies as products of phantasy greatly simplifies the study of imagination. Phantasy is very active in childhood, but imagination acts feebly. Phantasy makes our fancies; imagination creates our ideals.

CHAPTER X.

EDUCATION OF IMAGINATION.

IMAGINATION rules the world. So Napoleon believed. Because the soul is progressive, it never quite repeats itself, but in every act attempts the production of a *new* and *fairer* world. So taught Emerson. All progress comes from efforts to realize ideals. So the masters tell us. Ideals are our approaches to the perfect. So poets and sages proclaim. Education of imagination is the development of our ideal-making power.

I. PLACE OF IMAGINATION—
   TERMS DEFINED.

1. *Relations.* Imagination is a master power, commanding all our other capabilities. Memory, from our stores of experiences, supplies imagination with materials, and also associates and recalls the products of imagination. Will contributes purpose and concentrated and sustained effort. Emotion gives wings to imagination. Thought contributes discretion and law. Imagination is the

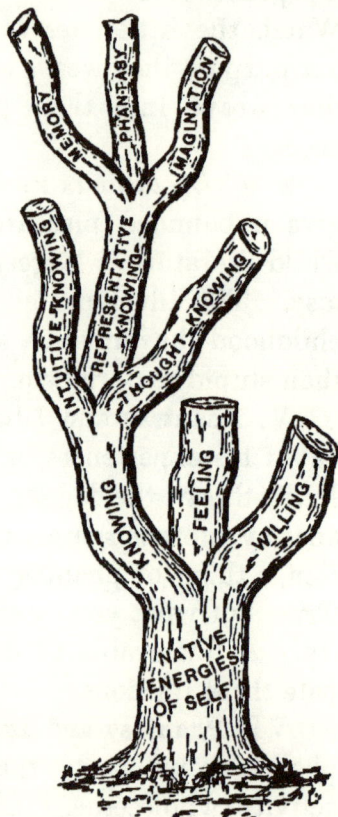

master-builder, and our other powers are the co-operating workmen.

2. *Imagination is the native energy of self to create ideals.* The phonograph was first an ideal in the mind of Edison. Imagination is self imagining. Purposely we put our experiences into *new forms.* We disassociate our experiences and recombine them in new ways. We modify and rearrange our acquisitions. At the magic touch of imagination the hillock becomes a mountain, the rock becomes bread, and the figures, 1, 2, 3, 4, 5, 6, arrange themselves in seven hundred and twenty different ways.

3. *Ideals are products of imagination.* Realities are independent existences; ideals are mental creations. We become acquainted with realities and their relations and so gain ideas; out of our experiences we make our ideals. Ideas are notions of things and their relations; ideals are ideas and objects blended. This and this and this are *real* school-houses; my *ideal* school-house blends the ideas of beauty, comfort, and adaptability with a building embodying these ideas. Realities have their excellences; ideals surpass realities as they embody the *best* of many realities. The *ideal* landscape of the artist combines the beauties of a thousand *real* landscapes. The ideal *manhood* of the teacher combines the best characteristics of the grandest men.

4. *Self as imagination creates ideals.* Create here means to so combine experiences as to make new wholes. Edison *created* the phonograph. No one thinks of his creating the materials; he simply made such new combinations as to give us a talking-machine. His ideal phonograph was a creation of the imagination. Homer *created* the Iliad. His experiences were *real;* but the poet wrought these experiences into heroic forms. Many think of imagination as

of moonshine—something vague and intangible, and, at most, as the power to make mechanical combinations or weave vagaries. How mistaken, how false, how inadequate is such thinking! A deeper insight reveals self really creating his ideals.

5. *Education of imagination.* We educate imagination when we develop the power to create high ideals. It makes the difference between Aristotle, the child, making new combinations of his playthings, and Aristotle, the man, creating the science of logic.

II. Importance of educating Imagination.

In practical life, in art, in literature, and in education, imagination stands for originality and progress. The leaders, in all ages, have been persons gifted with powerful imaginations. Some are naturally more gifted than others, but in all cases a vigorous and disciplined imagination is a result of education.

1. *Imagination represents experiences as ideals.* I am aware of making my ideals just as I am aware of thinking. As imagination, I create my ideals out of my experiences, but the experiences are so changed that I do not recognize them as experiences. I am aware that I purposely make my ideals and that they are my own creations. As memory, I associate, recall, and recognize ideals, just as I associate, recall, and recognize ideas. In the *act of creation* I represent or make present again to myself my experiences in *new forms* called ideals.

2. *Culture of imagination leads the way in high achievement.* Ideals of a perfect government led Washington and his compeers in creating our marvelous Constitution. Your idea of a superior manhood leads you

in your character-building. Lofty ideals, in every field of achievement, lead to high results.

3. *Culture of imagination stimulates mental energy.* It enables one to do more and better work. New devices, new combinations, new illustrations, and new applications make learning a delight and memory easy. The student with a good imagination easily leads the class.

4. *Imagination inspires effort.* We can not tell how much we owe to imagination. The despairing Bruce was inspired to achieve the independence of Scotland by the efforts of the spider. One with a cultured imagination never commits suicide; hope springs eternal in such a mind. Every day, every hour, imagination fires our souls and inspires us for achievement.

5. *Cultured imagination adds immeasurably to our joys.* Even in common life, the ideal gives more pleasure than the real. Cultured life is made a perpetual joy by the rich products of genius. A cultured imagination enables us to appreciate and enjoy and create the best things.

6. *A cultured imagination is the fountain of perpetual youth.* It keeps the world fresh and growing. It keeps us ever young and buoyant. It fills the world with movement and poetry and song.

7. *Dangers of imagination.* The express train has its dangers; still, most travelers prefer it to the ox-cart. Stupidity may be safe, but is a stupid life worth living? Imagination like reason may be misused and so lead to disaster. The educator fortifies against these dangers. Neglect is most dangerous. Education is a positive process. If we neglect to so educate the imagination that it becomes the greatest possible good, it may become wayward and produce evil.

III. Growth of Imagination.

"There is," says Herbert Spencer, "a certain sequence in which the faculties spontaneously develop, and a certain kind of knowledge which each power requires during its several stages of growth. It is for us to ascertain this sequence and supply this knowledge." That the time for culture is during the period of growth, is one of the settled educational principles. But when does imagination become active? What are its stages of growth? What studies are best during each of these periods?

1. *In childhood imagination is moderately active.* Much of what seems to be imagination is in reality phantasy. Without purpose the child weaves its few experiences into fancies. But the play of imagination also enters largely into child-life. The child-imagination is feeble, and its ideals crude. Compositions written by children best show this. Few poets are proud of poems written in childhood. How early the child imagines we can not know. Currie claims that even infants are strongly imaginative, but he evidently uses imagination in the sense of phantasy. Madame de Saussure declares that at the beginning of life imagination is *all-powerful*, but she clearly means phantasy. Similar statements abound in educational works, and apply to phantasy, the play faculty of the mind. As I see it, the truth is that imagination is undoubtedly active in childhood, but that it acts feebly and gives crude and weak products. Paul might have said, "When I was a child I imagined as a child."

2. *In girlhood and boyhood imagination is quite*

9

active. Compare a composition written by a boy of twelve with one written by him a few years earlier. You will note a marvelous growth of imagination. Invention delights boys and girls. They never weary of suitable imaginative literature.

3. *In youth imagination is marvelously active.* The man works out the plans his boyish fancy wrought. About the fourteenth year imagination bursts into wonderful activity and becomes more and more vigorous as the years go by. Compare the composition of the youth with the composition of the boy. Literature that delights the boy has no charms for the youth.

4. *In manhood imagination is fully active and powerful.* About the twentieth year this faculty may be said to reach full activity. Compare the essay of the college student with the composition of the youth. You note a marvelous growth of the imagination. This faculty seems to grow more and more powerful to the meridian of life, and may be kept vigorous even in old age. Homer's Odyssey, Tennyson's Locksley Hall Fifty Years After, and Humboldt's Cosmos, show towering imaginations in old age.

IV. Laws of Imagination-Growth.

Even imagination is subject to law. Here and everywhere growth comes from lawful effort. The great educational laws are in full force in educating imagination.

I. **General Laws.**—These, stated in terms of imagination, are as follows: 1. *Law of effort.* Well-directed effort in creating ideals educates imagination. All the new forms into which we purposely mold our experiences are termed ideals. Dreaming does not educate. This law requires determined effort under guidance. 2. *Law of means.* Studies which demand constant and vigorous imaginative effort have a high value as a means of educating imagination. Literature and art rank highest. 3. *Law of method.* Plans of work which call imagination into lawful, vigorous, and persistent activity educate this power. Roaming fancy free does not educate.

II. **Special Laws.**—These look directly to the improvement of imagination. 1. *Imagination is educated by illustrating the abstract.* This law is an abstract statement. What is meant by putting the abstract into a concrete form? Imagination answers, by giving an illustrative example. Thus a *concept* is a *general* notion; as the notion *oak* is *general* to all acorn-bearing trees it is called a *concept.* Imagination seeks a particular instance; it furnishes examples. Good writers thus make clear their abstract statements, and so enable the reader to grasp their meaning. Where this is not done, the student asks, " Why did he not give an example?" 2. *Efforts to realize ideals educate imagination.* This is true of character-building, of the art of teaching, and of all art work. The sculptor toils to embody his ideal. The teacher toils to educate his pupils up to his ideal. The inventor toils to realize his ideal in the new engine. As we advance we make our ideals higher and higher, and make greater and greater efforts to realize them.

V. Means of educating Imagination.

An instrumentality used to accomplish an end is a means—e. g., a plow is a means of cultivating the soil. Whatever calls forth normal activity is a means of mental culture—as geometry is a means of cultivating reason. Lines of work calculated to call forth the vigorous and persistent effort of a faculty are counted superior means for its development—as botany is an excellent means for cultivating conception. What lines of work are intrinsically best for the development of imagination? The educational value is largely dependent on methods of teaching and well-guided study. Good teaching and well-guided study are understood in the following estimates:

Table of Educational Values.—Some studies call imagination into vigorous and constant activity; these have a *high value* in the culture of imagination. Some studies give considerable exercise to the imagination, but not so constant or vigorous; these have a *medium value* in the culture of this power. Other studies require comparatively little imaginative effort; these have a *low value* as a means for educating imagination. In the education of imagination, Dr. Payne counts of high value, geography and history; of medium value, literature; of low value, arithmetic, botany, physics, physiology, and grammar. The estimates in column 1 are the author's; in column 2, those of Dr. Brooks. In column 3 you will write your estimates; in column 4 you will write the averages.

ESTIMATED IMAGINATION-CULTURE. VALUE OF	1	2	3	4
Language, composition, literature..............	10	10	....	....
Drawing, molding, music, elocution, reading ...	9	9	....	....
Geography, history........	9	8	....	....
Botany, zoölogy, physiology, physics.	7	7	...	....
Arithmetic, algebra, geometry	6	5	....	....

1. *Language, composition, and literature.* It seems to me that these studies easily rank highest. Imaginative literature, from childhood to age, does most to awaken and educate imagination.

2. *Art*, as I think, comes next to literature. Drawing, molding, music, and elocution take high rank. Painters, sculptors, and architects are classed with poets in the realms of imagination.

3. *Geography and history* are entitled to come next. Of all our common-school studies, composition excepted, we rely most on these branches in the culture of imagination.

4. *Mathematics.* By having the pupils *make* many of the problems, considerable culture can be given to imagination even in arith-

metic and algebra. Imagination is only second to reason in the right study of geometry.

5. *Teaching is an excellent means.* Hence, from childhood up each learner is trained to teach. This is a striking feature of the best teaching. The teacher puts herself in the place of the learner and creates illustrations and invents applications. She leads the pupil to make questions and conduct classes.

VI. METHODS OF EDUCATING IMAGINATION.

Plans of work that secure well-directed effort in constructing ideals are methods of educating imagination. At this point a radical reform in our educational work is imperative.

I. **Kindergarten Methods.**—Here we find embodied the philosophy of education. Imagination acts feebly but it is cultivated by easy objective work. The child is led to make new combinations of blocks and sticks and lines; to make new forms in paper and wood and clay, to make new arrangements in stories and plays and pictures. Every wise mother is a natural kindergartner and will lead her little ones to do things in their own childish ways. These crude efforts are the beginnings in the development of imagination.

II. **Primary Methods.**—Here too often we find organized stupidity. The child is treated as a repeating machine. All originality is considered pertness and is stifled. The tendency is to make the child a mere drudge. All honor to the noble exceptions now rapidly multiplying! The wise teacher will gather inspiration from the best teachers and the best literature; and will so use art in its varied forms as to permit imagination growth.

1. *Lead the child to make new combinations.* You

can hardly do better at first than to adapt kindergarten
methods to the wants of your pupils. Your drawing,
molding, object-lessons, and language-lessons will afford
ample opportunities. Only so manage that the child
originates the combinations and forms his own crude
ideals.

2. *Lead the child to image what it reads.* The
primary readers of our times are printed object-lessons
suited for child-culture. Good teaching works wonders.
Take, to illustrate, a single sentence—

"See the pretty snow-flakes falling from the sky."
Draw a picture of a snow-flake. Cut out of white
paper a figure of a snow-flake. "Who can make a
snow-storm?" "I can." Mary gathers a handful of
the paper flakes and hurls them through the air. Each
child now images the above and reads it perfectly.

3. *Lead the child to construct.* Botany and zoölogy in their
simplest objective features are now made a part of the geography
work in our best primary schools. The plan of work in geography with slight modifications applies to the branches named.
Divisions of land and water; of animals, plants, and minerals;
races, states, and nations are splendid object-lessons. The pupils are
led to construct geographical playgrounds, making rivers and seas,
making mountains and valleys, making the various divisions of land
and water. The pupils are then led to construct in imagination
rivers, lakes, and seas; islands, mountains, countries, and continents.
Putting forth these efforts wondrously increases the vigor of imagination. Hasten leisurely. Remember that the wings of child-
imagination are not strong. The flights must not be high or long.

4. *Lead the child to drink in the beautiful.* Beauty
marvelously stirs the imagination. The beautiful world!
We are charmed with the beauty of form and color and
motion; with beauty of speech and music and songs of

birds; with beauty of truthfulness and good manners. Make the surroundings as beautiful as you can. Always have pictures and flowers in your school-room. Lead the children to draw beautiful objects, and in various ways produce beautiful objects.

5. *Lead the child to drink in child literature.* Our readers and supplementary readers now furnish the best. You can supplement these by stories and suitable papers and books. Biographical stories and suitable histories strengthen the imagination. This is a most fruitful field, but discretion on the part of the parents and teachers is highly necessary. " Every first-class bit of food for the imagination has become classic. Classical literature focused for the imagination always has room for any choice gem. An untrained teacher or parent is safe when he turns to the classics for material with which to entertain children. Santa Claus has furnished little people of all climes with healthful inspiration for the imagination; has hallowed the pioneer day of winter; has brightened and heightened gift-receiving, by delightfully dissociating gifts and giving from the personality of the donors. Mother Goose Melodies, although nonsense as compared with classic literature, have been an acceptable prelude for infantile imagination. The fables season it with wholesome character truths. Fairy-tales, mythologies, and tales of chivalry, when winnowed, inspire chivalric sentiments. Who that was brought up on Hawthorne's Tanglewood Tales can estimate the service they rendered him?" *

III. **Intermediate Methods.**—Boys and girls have

* Winship.

vivid imaginations. Their ideals are not lofty, but
they are well defined. You are often surprised at the
materialistic and personal nature of the ideals of this
period. But the experience, so far, has been largely
material. The pupil can put nothing in his ideals but
his personal experiences. You must not expect too
much. Pupils of this age are incapable of sustained
flights; this fact indicates the teaching and the literature now demanded.

1. *Lead the pupils to write original compositions.*
Whenever the pupil tells what he knows in his own
way, it is original. The ideas are old, but the combination is new. You must not expect too much; imagination is still feeble and its products crude. Only manage to have pupils to construct daily, as best they can,
brief compositions. No other work gives such vigor
and discipline to imagination. For detailed methods
you are referred to the excellent language-lesson manuals.

2. *Lead the pupil to construct his geography world.*
In the primary school a foundation was laid in actual
experience. This experience must now be greatly extended. Charts, globes, maps, molding-boards, etc., must
be provided. Now the real work begins. The pupil
has never seen a mountain. He has seen hills of various
heights; out of his hill experiences he must construct a
mountain. This is an achievement for the boy as great
as that of the creation of Paradise Lost for the man.
You lead your pupils to victory after victory. Their
geography world grows larger and larger. They begin
to be able to appropriate the experiences of others.
Give them time. For detailed plans of work you are referred to the valuable manuals of methods in geography.

3. *Interest your pupils in juvenile literature.* You will do most for them in this way. Teaching *what* to read and *how* to read is the most valuable school work. Without dictating, manage to have your pupils read only the *best.* Take a few minutes daily and read with your pupils some choice book. Robinson Crusoe is one of the very best for this purpose, and will intensely interest your pupils for many weeks. McDonald's Sir Gibbie is a treasure, and will engage you during several months.

4. *Lead the pupil to create his history world.* Gradually you lead your pupils to substitute history for fiction. Read with them two or three of the best juvenile histories, such as Dickens's Child History of England and Eggleston's United States. Lead them to construct in imagination the geography, the people, the scenes. It will become almost as real to them as if they were actors. In connection with the studies in literature and history you may impress every noble trait.

5. *Lead your pupils to teach.* Nothing is better to awaken interest and strengthen imagination. Have your pupils *make* most of the problems in arithmetic. This doubles the value of the study. Lead your pupils to make their own definitions and rules and invent their own illustrations. You must never fail to encourage originality. You lead each pupil to make his own arithmetic. Each pupil is ready to take the class and teach the topic in his own way. I recommend you to pursue a similar course in each study.

6. *Lead the child to idealize character.* "The character element in the processes and habits of the imagination should be early and largely considered. Some of the characters in Shakespeare's plays

and Dickens's novels have such a vivifying effect that they are more real than the historical personages of Hume or Macaulay. Indeed, historic characters are real only through the imagination. Everything that appeals to the imagination ought at a reasonably early age to move on a plane above mere sentiment. It should be attractive, from its purpose, its earnestness."

IV. **Advanced Methods.**—In youth imagination is very active, and its systematic culture is not less important than that of reason.

1. *Lead the student to construct science.* The fatal error is studying definitions, descriptions, and classifications in books and nothing more. No wonder that stupidity rather than power is the result. What is the *educational* method? Clearly the student must begin with realities, and work up to ideals. Books and teachers suggest, direct, give information. The student experiences everything and images everything. The learner sees, feels, touches, tastes, and smells the plant. He analyzes and synthetizes it. He compares it with other plants. In imagination he constructs the typical plant and associates with it a name. So at every step knowledge is both actualized and realized.

2. *Lead the learner to construct history.* For the time the student is a Greek. He visits in imagination the cities and valleys and mountains of Greece. He worships at the shrines of the Grecian gods. Now he takes part in the siege of Troy, fights by the side of Ajax or Achilles. He helps build the wooden horse. Now he fights, bleeds, and dies at Thermopylæ. Thus imagination enables him to put himself in their place and thus understand the Greeks. Greece, Greeks, Grecian history, Grecian literature, become a part of

himself. In the same way we study Roman, German, English, and American history.

3. *Lead the student at every step to make concrete the abstract.* Few can understand thoroughly abstract truths without first considering the concrete basis. It is well to say, "Honesty is the best policy"; but it needs to be illustrated. Mr. Jones from boyhood has been known for integrity. Every one respects and trusts him. He has gradually accumulated a competence and is happy. In his case honesty proved to be the best policy. The habit of illustrating everything is invaluable. Only in this way can we build on the rock and firmly grasp general truths.

4. *Lead the student to study art from the standpoint of the artist.* The artist created these ideals; creating them over again educates imagination. How much more does it develop imagination to create original ideals and strive to realize them!

5. *Lead the student to form and try to realize an ideal character.* From the lives of the grand and great of all ages we construct an ideal life, our highest conception of a grand manhood. Now we think and feel and will to realize in ourselves the ideal.

VII. General Directions for the Culture of Imagination.

Concise rules for imagination-culture may prove helpful

1. Be original :
   - *a.* Create your world of geography.
   - *b.* Create your world of history.
   - *c.* Create your world of geometry.
   - *d.* Create your social world.

2. Form high ideals and work up to them.

3. Associate with the pure and good.

4. Avoid bad literature : $\begin{cases} a. \text{ Low literature.} \\ b. \text{ Weak literature.} \end{cases}$

5. *Read wisely the best literature.* Poetry and fiction come first. The real novelist is a genius, a man whose stock in trade is a knowledge of men. His story is the portrayal in print of actual characters, idealized and so combined and interwoven as to reveal the motives which actuate mankind. The reading of such an author leaves us richer in the knowledge of men, and enables us to judge, speak, and act more wisely.

VIII. Errors in Educating Imagination.

We have here errors of omission as well as of commission. No feature of our educational work is now in greater need of reform.

1. *Repeating instead of memorizing.* By dint of repetition, forms and statement are acquired. But the labor is immense and the tendency is to weaken inventiveness and make plodders rather than originators. Imagining, illustrating, actualizing, enable the learner to realize things. He now feels delight and remembers with little effort.

2. *Drudgery instead of mastery.* This is the dominant educational sin of our times. The student is weighted down with facts. Thus, instead of the powerful and fleet Arabian steed we get the stupid dray-horse.

3. *Too much explaining.* The school of to-day has perhaps no phase more vicious than the habit of explaining everything so fully that the mind has little stimulus to wrestle with problems; has almost nothing left with which the imagination can play. From the first hour of school life to the last, the teacher's opportunities for directing and training the imagination are limitless. There is scarcely a fact so patent, a problem so simple, or discipline so trying, that the teacher may not, if she will, enliven the hour and intensify

the thought and ennoble the character by an appeal more or less definite to the imagination.

4. *Saying instead of doing.* Describing a tree helps, but drawing a tree is better. Saying the tables is well, but actual weighing and measuring are better, as the learner is thus enabled to *construct* tables. Let drawing, molding, and constructing take the place of mere saying.

5. *Leaving imagination to roam fancy free.* The student needs to learn to draw sharp distinctions between reals and ideals. Then he needs constantly to subject his ideals to unsparing criticism. Thus may be prevented a dreamy, sickly, sentimental life.

6. *Cherishing or even tolerating low ideals.* " Like gods like people," expresses our tendency to become like our ideals. " Let me write the songs for the people and you may make the laws." Boys and girls saturated with low literature form low ideals, and will likely live low lives.

7. *Neglect of imagination-culture.* The culture of imagination seems to be more uniformly neglected than that of any other faculty. The ability to represent correctly to one's self a thing, a scene, a person, a story, from a verbal description is very rare. Few pupils in studying history, geography, or astronomy, form any distinct and true pictures of what is described. Fewer still are able to create ideal personages and scenes. Training of the imagination should result not only in capacity to receive, but in power to create.

SUGGESTIVE STUDY-HINTS.

I. **Helpful Books.**—Much has been written about imagination, but not much that will help the teacher. "The notion," says Sully, "that the educator has a special work to do in educating and guiding the imagination of the young is a comparatively new one." Porter, McCosh, James, and others give us good suggestions in their psychologies. But, for the most part, you will need to glean. Shakespeare, Shelley, Browning, Ruskin, etc., abound in good things calculated to develop imagination. Emerson's essays are gems.

II. **Letter.**—Give your friend your views on the education of imagination. In this you will need to think as well as to imagine. The effort will repay you. Your views will grow clearer and your grasp of the subject larger as you attempt to make it plain to another.

III. **Memory, Phantasy, Imagination.**—Define each and illustrate the distinctions you make between these powers. Do you prefer these names, or reproductive, passive, and constructive imagination? Why? Do we educate phantasy?

IV. **Importance of educating Imagination.**—Name three reasons why you consider the culture of this power important. How do you account for the neglect of this culture?

V. **Growth of Imagination.**—Show the growth of imagination as indicated by the compositions of the child; of the boy; of the youth; of the man. How early does the child create crude ideals? Do writers always distinguish between child phantasy and child imagination? When does imagination become fully active? Prove that this power may be kept vigorous even in old age.

VI. **Laws of Imagination-Growth.**—State the three general laws in terms of imagination. State and illustrate two special laws. Give a special law that you have discovered. Why do you call it a law?

VII. **Means for promoting the Growth of Imagination.**—What studies do you consider of the highest value for this purpose? Why? Give Dr. Payne's estimates.

VIII. **Methods of educating Imagination.**—Outline your notion of kindergarten methods; of primary methods; of intermediate methods; of high-school methods; of college methods. Give your plan for teaching geography, history, language lessons.

IX. **Mistakes in educating Imagination.**—What mistake in educating imagination do you esteem most hurtful? Why? May the teacher do too much explaining? Name some errors that you have observed. How do you propose to lead your pupils to form pure and lofty ideals?

CHAPTER XI.

CULTURE OF THE REPRESENTATIVE POWERS.

HERE representation means memory and imagination. The earnest teacher asks, How can I so teach as to best develop these powers? What valuable suggestions do educators give to aid me in my efforts to cultivate memory and imagination? This chapter, it is hoped, will help you in your efforts to find answers to these questions. We mean by the culture of our representative powers the development of our capabilities to represent our experiences in *old* and *new* forms. The old forms are *memories;* the new forms are *ideals.*

Phantasy is not considered, as it is not susceptible of cultivation. Self in dreams and revery, without purpose or plan, spontaneously weaves his experiences into fancies. This is phantasy. Self is aware of beholding these panoramas, but not of making them; they seem at the time to be new experiences. Phantasy is active in childhood and in the weak-minded, and is often mistaken for imagination, or called the *passive* imagination. The teacher and the physician as well as the psychologist must needs study phantasy and its office in the mental economy. Its activity affects our lives more than we are willing to admit. As the artist gains innumerable suggestions from the kaleidoscope, so we gain innumerable suggestions from our fancies. Phantasy, though most active during repose, is certainly in some degree active at all times. Many persons *dream* away their lives; they do not think and do not imagine; they drift. The dreamy child or adult must be awakened. We can not educate phantasy, but we can *manage* it. We accept its hints for what they are worth.

We refuse to dream when awake; we work. We occupy ourselves with good thoughts and high ideals and useful deeds, and thus leave no place for revery. Phantasy is marvelously affected by the conditions of our bodies; these we can largely control. We refuse to let the vagaries of phantasy mislead us. Early and always we fill our lives so full of realities and ideals and thoughts and deeds that there is no room for vagaries.

I. **Memory and Imagination.**—Deeper insight into the mental economy awakens ever-increasing wonder. Each native energy of self is unique, is elemental. As gravity and cohesion and electricity and the rest are elementary forces in the physical world, so perception and memory and our other powers are elementary energies in the mind-world. As in the matter-world the various physical forces work in harmony to produce physical results, so in the mind-world all the native energies of self co-operate, supplementing and re-enforcing each other in producing mental results. Thus it is that our simplest acts are wonderfully complex. We must learn to think of self as doing each act of knowing, feeling, and willing, and of our capabilities as merely native energies of self. For convenience we personify each faculty, as when we say, "Memory *recalls* and imagination *creates.*" But these are figures of speech. Memory is self remembering and imagination is self imagining. Psychological insight clears away the mists, and we behold self doing each mental act.

1. *Self as memory does all his recalling.* Imagination does not recall any more than does reason. Self as imagination constructs, but memory supplies imagination with materials, and also stores and recalls its products. In the same way memory furnishes reason with materials and also stores and recalls its products. Our experiences die as soon as completed. As soon as we cease to be aware of our

acquisitions they cease to exist. Storing knowledge, retaining ideas, impressing on memory, and similar figurative expressions, mean simply associating ideas. We assimilate our old and new experiences into organic unity. We so systematize and associate our ideas that present experiences suggest past experiences. This is recalling, this is memory. We recognize our remembrances as former experiences. Eradicate memory and we become incapable of thought or imagination. Memory is the only capability of self to recall, and we embody in this term all processes connected with recalling. Memory includes association, suggestion, reproduction, representation, and recognition.

2. *Self as imagination creates all his ideals.* All products of imagination are *ideals* as opposed to *realities*. Imagination is simply the native energy of self to construct ideals. Because imagination makes present to us again our experiences in new and picturesque forms, we say it is a *representative* power; but it must be emphasized again and again that memory *recalls* the experiences out of which imagination makes the ideals. Culture of memory is the development of our *recalling* power; culture of imagination is the development of our *creative* power.

II. **Ideals.**—Ideals are products of imagination, and are our nearest mental approach to perfection. " The ideal," says Fleming, " is to be attained by selecting and assimilating into one whole the perfections of many individuals, excluding everything defective." The teacher and the student gain deeper insight into the nature of the producer by studying the products. Thus the psychologist gains many of his best lessons from language and literature and art. Through the study of ideals we become familiar with our creative power and its culture.

10

I. *Ideals are ideas and objects blended into harmony.* Some years since the notion occurred to me that I might regulate my school by bells that would ring *automatically*. The programme clock helped me. I now invented an attachment to so connect battery and bells with the clock that it would strike my programme. The idea and the object were thus blended in harmony. This was my *ideal* electric programme clock. I then proceeded to place bells in the various rooms and make the connections as planned. At last I set my clock so as to ring my programme. It worked well. I had realized my ideal. I used this crude invention to regulate my school for nearly twenty years.

2. *Ideal of intellectual greatness.* At certain times we observe ourselves at our best. Now we acquire with surprising ease; now imagination towers; now our thoughts are penetrating. We observe ourselves at these supremest moments and learn what high intellectual activity means. Through reading, hearing, and observing, we appropriate the experiences of the mightiest men at their best.

"Then from ourselves as known to ourselves we eliminate all dullness, vacillation, forgetfulness, confusion, and all other sources of intellectual weakness; while we retain and combine into permanent form all the exhibitions of superior intellectual power that have been revealed to us, and this combination constitutes our ideal of intellectual greatness. This ideal, though composed of what was ultimately experienced in ourselves, is so much superior to ourselves that it perpetually acts as a stimulus to higher intellectual activity." * Our efforts to realize this ideal tend to make intellectual greatness.

3. *Ideal of moral greatness.* We observe ourselves

* Larkin Dunton.

at our best moments. Now our whole being thrills
with philanthropic impulses; now we resist fearful
temptations; now we discharge trying duties. We
observe ourselves at our supreme moments and learn
what high moral activity means. Through observing
and hearing and recalling we appropriate the experiences of great moral heroes. Then from our accumulated experiences we create our ideals of moral greatness. These ideals become a perpetual stimulus to
higher moral activity.

4. *Ideal of teaching greatness.* I observe myself at
such moments as I excel in teaching. Now I hold the
entire attention; now I lead the pupils to put forth
their best efforts; now I inspire my pupils to act nobly.
By observing myself at these supreme moments I learn
what high teaching power means. Through observing
and hearing and reading I now appropriate the best
experiences of the great teachers. Their experiences
become mine. Out of my accumulated experiences I
select the best and construct my ideal of teaching
greatness. This ideal becomes a constant and powerful
stimulus to higher teaching activity. Well-directed
efforts to realize this ideal tend to make me a greater
teacher.

5. *The ideal is a preparation for the actual.* Our
rational acts are planned. Our plans are our ideals.
The general plans to-morrow's battle and thus organizes
victory. The teacher plans her school before it opens
and thus organizes success. The bride who went
through the marriage ceremony without embarrassment
said that she had been married in imagination a thousand times. Demosthenes had made his great oration ·

many hundred times in imagination before he electrified the Athenians.

6. *Ideals lead to actions.* When ideals are pure and ennobling they lead to pure and ennobling acts; but when ideals are base and degrading they lead to base and degrading acts. No one goes to the bad whose imagination is not first corrupted. How superlatively important it is that the associations and readings of the young should be pure and elevating!

7. *Ideals grow.* The artist's ideal is the highest he can now create; but the widened experiences of other years will enable him to make vastly higher ideals. Child ideals are low and crude; boy ideals are higher; youth ideals are vastly higher. My ideal of teaching greatness now is much higher than that of twenty years ago. We make our ideals as high as we can to-day, but to-morrow's experience will enable us to construct higher ideals. Slowly and little by little the child writes its crude composition; the man plans his essay in advance, and writes with a master-hand. What are the ideals of your pupils? How will you lead them to form higher ideals? You look well to the ideas of those under your care. Is it not even more important that you should look well to their ideals?

III. **Time to memorize.**—Memorizing in its best sense is the assimilation and association of our new acquisitions.

Mr. Bain says that memorizing is an exercise which makes the greatest demands upon the nervous energies; that the use of ideas in the making of new combinations —in new constructions—demands a less degree of brain-vigor, and that writing, drawing, and searching reference-books for information, and noting what is found, make the least demands upon the nervous power.

"There are periods of the day that can be most economically employed for memorizing and other severe intellectual labor, and others for performing the lighter and easier work. The three periods of greatest mental vigor are: (1) in the morning for three or four hours after breakfast; (2) for two or three hours following a period of rest after dinner; and (3) one or two hours following a period of rest after supper. The adult mind will use time most economically if he shall employ its periods of greatest vigor in making new acquisitions, reserving its constructive work for periods of less mental energy, and setting apart all merely mechanical and routine labor for those portions of the day when the mind is least vigorous. With the child, memorizing is easier than construction, since the constructive powers have not yet reached their full development." *

The elementary school "will always have the character of memory-work stamped upon it, no matter how much the educational reformer may improve its methods. It is not easy to overvalue the impulse of such men as Pestalozzi and Froebel. But the child's mind can not seize great syntheses. He bites off, as it were, only small fragments of truth at best. He gets isolated data, and sees only feebly the vast network of interrelation in the world. This fragmentary, isolated character belongs essentially to primary education. But just as surely does secondary education deal with relations and functions and processes. It is the stage of crude generalization. But college education strives to induce on the mind the habit of seeing the unity of things." †

IV. **Conditions of Effective Association.**‡—There are some well-defined conditions under which ideas may be acquired and grouped

* George P. Brown.   † W. T. Harris.
‡ Larkin Dunton.

in the mind, which increase the probability that the presence of an idea will be followed by the idea of a similar thing, and that, on the representation of one of a group of ideas, the whole group will be represented.

1. The longer ideas are kept before the mind, or the less the lapse of time since ideas were in the mind, the greater is the probability that these ideas will be represented. It is not what we merely see, or hear, or read, that is most likely to be revived; but what we reflect upon and discuss. It is not what we heard ten years ago that we discuss to-day, but what we have recently heard.

Aged people often recall the scenes of childhood with more fullness than those of recent years. This appears to be an exception to the rule; but the exception is only apparent, for there are other influences at work. But the exception does not hold in regard to recent events. The events of to-day are more easily recalled by the aged than those of a week ago.

2. The more frequently ideas are present in the mind and grouped together, the greater the probability that they will be represented, and in the order in which they have been arranged before. The parts of our homes which we have known together day after day have left such an impression upon our minds that an idea of one part is at once followed by the ideas of all the parts. It is the presence of ideas, not that of words, which creates the tendency to representation.

3. The more intense the attention while a group of ideas is before the mind, the greater is the probability that one of the group will be represented on occasion of the presence of a similar idea, and that then the whole group will be represented. An hour of intense application is of more value than a day spent in turning from one thing to another. To secure this, require the pupil's eye to be on what is represented, or on the teacher, and often call for an expression of what ought to be known.

4. The greater the interest in the things known during the process of learning, the more probable is it that the ideas will be represented.

V. Good Memory is Discriminating Memory.—A good memory has its obvious advantages; but a *good* memory is something more than merely a retentive memory.

It is quite as important to shut one's memory against
that which should be forgotten, and against that which
is not worth remembering, as to open one's memory to
that which is worthy of being borne in mind. A memory that receives and holds important facts and truths,
while it rejects those which are unimportant, is far pref-
erable to a memory that is always overloaded with
things good, bad, and indifferent. Deciding what to
remember, and remembering that, is better than remembering everything.

VI. **Blackie's Self-Culture of Memory.**—It is of no use gathering
treasures if we can not store them ; it is equally useless to learn what
we can not retain in the memory. Happily, of all mental faculties
memory is that one which is most certainly improved by exercise ;
besides, there are helps to a weak memory such as do not exist for a
weak imagination or a weak reasoning power. The most important
points to be attended to in securing the retention of facts are : (1)
The distinctness, vividness, and intensity of the original impression.
Let no man hope to remember what he only vaguely and indistinctly
apprehends. It is better for the memory to have a distinct idea of
one fact of a great subject, than to have confused ideas of the whole.
(2) Nothing helps the memory so much as order and classification.
Classes are always few, individuals many ; to know the class well is
to know what is most essential in the character of the individual,
and what least burdens the memory to retain. (3) The next important matter is repetition : if the nail will not go in at one stroke, let
it have another and another. In this domain nothing is denied to a
dogged pertinacity. (4) Again, if memory be weak, causality is perhaps strong ; and this point of strength, if wisely used, may readily
be made to turn an apparent loss into a real gain. (5) Lastly, whatever facilities of memory you may possess, despise not the sure aids
so amply supplied by written record. To retain stores of readily
available matter, in the shape of written or printed record, enables
a man to command a vast amount of accumulated materials, at
whatever moment he may require them.

PART III.

EDUCATION OF THE THOUGHT-POWERS.

THE INTELLECT.

```
                    REASON, REASONING, REASONS.
        THOUGHT
        KNOWING.    JUDGMENT, JUDGING, JUDGMENTS.

                 CONCEPTION, CONCEIVING, CONCEPTS.

              IMAGINATION, IMAGINING, IMAGINATIONS.
     REPRESENTATIVE
       KNOWING.    PHANTASY,  FANCYING,  FANCIES.

                MEMORY, REMEMBERING, MEMORIES.

            NECESSARY         NECESSARY           NECESSARY
            PERCEPTION.       PERCEIVING.         PERCEPTS.
   PERCEPTIVE
    KNOWING.    SELF-PERCEPTION,  SELF-PERCEIVING,  SELF-PERCEPTS.

          SENSE-PERCEPTION,  SENSE-PERCEIVING,  SENSE-PERCEPTS.
```

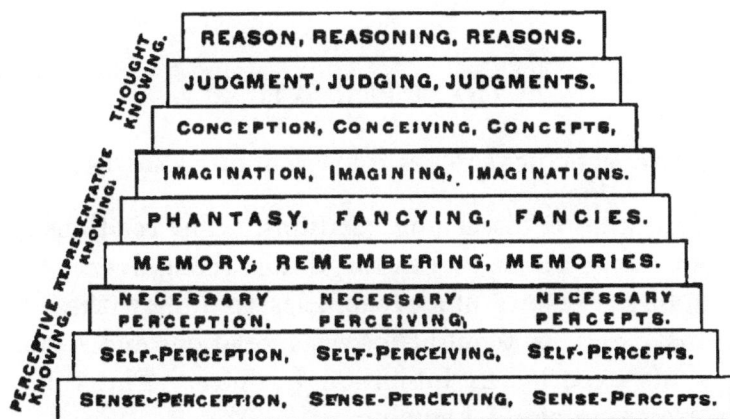

As gravity is the fundamental physical force, so perception is the fundamental psychical energy. Sense-perception is the base of the cognitive pyramid and reason the crown. As we ascend we find that each capability rests on and is chronologically and psychologically dependent on all the capabilities below it; as, for example, imagination could not act but for perception and memory. This psychological insight is confirmed by practical experience, as the practice of all educators proves. Teachers now uniformly present the intellectual powers in the above order. The claim that these powers are not elemental, but merely eddies in the stream of thought, forms of consciousness, modes of analysis and synthesis, is based, as I think, on the failure to discern clearly the co-operative nature of the mental economy. When we once gain the insight that each capability of self supplements and re-enforces all his other powers, it is not difficult to gain the deeper insight that the stream of thought and assimilation and analysis and synthesis and apperception are in reality *resultant* co-operative processes. Each capability is a native energy of self, and is elemental in the mental economy.

PART THIRD.

EDUCATION OF THE THOUGHT-POWERS.

CHAPTER XII.

THE THOUGHT-POWERS AND THOUGHT-KNOWING.

THINKING is discerning relations. The relations between things are as real as the things themselves. Our thought-powers are our capabilities to discern these relations. Self as thought discerns relations and assimilates his experiences into thought-unity. Thinking is the crowning act of knowing.

I. **The Thought-Powers.** — We discover that some things are related to other things by common properties; we discern these group relations and think individuals into classes; our capability to do this is termed *conception*. We discover that our notions agree or disagree; that they are related as true or false; we discern truth relations and think our notions into truths; our capability to do this is termed *judgment*. Finally, we discover that the universe is a cause-unit; we discover cause relations and think truths into reasons and systems; our power to do this is termed *reason*.

THE THOUGHT POWERS ARE
- CONCEPTION
- JUDGMENT
- REASON

II. **Thought-Processes.**—We discern *class* relations and think things into groups. Thus we think our notions of individual birds into the concept bird; this is *conceiving*. We discern *truth* relations and think our ideas into truths. Thus we think our notions, high and mountains, into the truth, *mountains are high;*

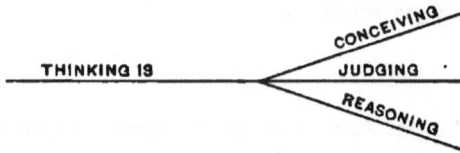

THINKING IS

CONCEIVING

JUDGING

REASONING

this is *judging*. We discern *cause* relations and think truths into reasons. Thus we think our judgments, men have rights and slaves are men, into the conclusion, *slaves have rights;* this is *reasoning*. Discerning sameness is the " keel and backbone of thinking."

III. **Thought-Products.**—Conceiving is thinking our notions of individuals into notions of classes; group notions are termed general notions, or conceptions, or *concepts*. Judging is thinking our notions into truths; sentences express truths or *judgments*. Reasoning is thinking judgments into reasons. Interlocked judgments express *reasons*.

THOUGHT PRODUCTS ARE

CONCEPTS

JUDGMENTS

REASONS

IV. **Thought-Knowing is Mediate Knowing.**—Through the *medium* of particular notions we reach *general no-*

tions. Through the *medium* of particular and general notions we reach *truths.* Through the *medium* of related judgments we reach *conclusions.* Perceptive knowing is *immediate* knowing, but thought-knowing is *mediate* knowing.

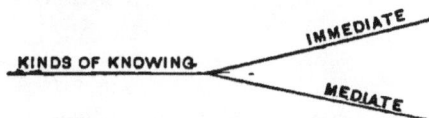

KINDS OF KNOWING {
    IMMEDIATE
    MEDIATE

V. The Thought-Powers are our Comparative Powers.—"Even as the objects perceived to be related are real, so also are the relations discerned. Man's knowledge begins with things. We discern the relations of things known; we discern the relations because we know the things. I am sure that we discern eight kinds of relations: 1. *Identity.* We see a tree in blossom; we recognize the tree as the *same* we saw yesterday, though the blossoms are further advanced. 2. *Whole and parts.* We consider separately the *blossoms,* but as blossoms of the tree. 3. *Resemblance.* We notice that the tree *resembles* other trees standing near it. 4. *Space.* We observe the *shape* and *size* of the tree. 5. *Time.* We calculate how long the blossoms will continue. 6. *Quantity.* We try to estimate the *number* of blossoms. 7. *Active property.* We find that they *emit* a pleasant odor. 8. *Cause and effect.* We observe that some are blown away by the wind. Thinking is discerning relations; but we discern the relations of things. In order to discover relations we must compare; hence our powers to think are our comparative powers. These are our faculties to discern relations."*

VI. Logic and Psychology.—Psychology gives insight into the nature of the thought-processes; logic gives insight into the laws and forms of thought. Psychology asks, "What does self do when he thinks?" Logic asks, "How may we so think as to reach truth?" Formal logic shows us the laws of the judgment and the syllogism. E. J. Hamiltons says, "*Logic is the science of the operations and products of the rational faculty in the pursuit and use of truth.*" You are referred to works on logic for the extended treat-

* McCosh

ment of this subject. The brief discussion here is directed to the psychological view, and may help by way of review and suggestion.

VII. **Thinking is healthful.** — "It is not intellectual work that injures the brain," the London Hospital says, "but emotional excitement. Most men can stand the severest thought and study of which their brains are capable, and be none the worse for it, for neither thought nor study interferes with the recuperative influence of sleep. It is ambition, anxiety, disappointment, the hopes and fears, the loves and hates of our lives that wear out our nervous system and endanger the balance of the brain." "Peaceful mathematics," "peaceful philosophy," "peaceful literature" express the nature of thought. Our great thinkers ought to be healthy, happy, and long-lived.

I. Conception and Conceptive Knowing.

Self as conception gains general notions. Conception is self conceiving. This is the native energy of self to think particular notions into general notions. I gain the particular notions, this and this tree, this and this shrub, this and this plant; I think these *particular notions* into the general notion *vegetables*. As the reaper grasps and binds the grain into bundles, so self as conception grasps and binds his percepts into concepts.

I. **Conceiving, Conception, Concepts.** — We intuitively gain notions of individual things, and we call these notions intuitions, percepts, particular notions. You see this new three-bladed, pearl-handled knife; your notion of this knife is a *particular notion*, a *percept*. As you make this notion out of sensations, you call it a sense-percept. You gain percepts of many different knives, and think these particular notions into the general notion *knife*. This notion applies to all knives; it is general. You think all knives as one group of things.

You call this a class-notion. As you grasp or bind all your particular knife-notions into one notion *knife*, you call this a *general notion*, a *concept*. Conception is the capability to gain concepts. The brute is lost in a wilderness of particulars. The savage makes crude classifications like those of children. The scientist thinks the wilderness of individuals into a few classes, and thus begins to make science. *Conceiving* is discerning class relations; *conception* is the power to gain class notions; *concepts* are general notions.

II. **Percepts and Concepts.**—As we make our sense-percepts out of our *sensations*, so we make our *sense-concepts* out of our *sense-percepts*. As we make our *self-percepts* out of our *awareness*, so we make our *self-concepts* out of our *self-percepts*. Thus, too, we make our *necessary-concepts* out of our *necessary-percepts*. Percepts are the stuff out of which we make our concepts. An idea is either a particular notion or a general notion. Our particular notions are our *percepts* and our general notions are our *conceptions* or *concepts*. When we think of *percepts* we think of *particular notions*, and when we think of *concepts* we think of general notions. Only when we wish to be specific do we speak of sense-percepts, self-percepts, and necessary-percepts; or of sense-concepts, self-concepts, and necessary-concepts.

"**A Conception is not a Mental Picture.**—Perceptions relate to individual objects; conceptions relate to general classes or to abstractions—such is the current doctrine of psychology—and the mental acts of perceiving and conceiving form the most important topics of psychology. What constitutes a general notion or conception? It is not a mental image, but a definition The general notion *tree* should include all trees of whatever description, and it is expressed by a definition. But no sooner do I attempt to conceive the notion *tree* than I form a mental image, but the image is not general enough to suit the notion. No particular image of any object in any class can be general enough to satisfy the definition. Every image must be of an individual, and the definition is broad enough to include all individuals. The definition serves as a rule by which we form an image which will illustrate it. The difference between the conception and the specimen is known to the child and the savage, though it is not consciously reflected upon. Take a different class of conceptions. Take the abstractions of color, taste, smell, sound, or touch—for example, redness, sourness, fragrance, loudness, and hardness. Our conception includes infinite degrees of possible intensity, while our image or recalled experience is of some definite degree, and does not correspond to the general notion.

"Let us take more general notions, such as force, matter, quality, being. If some image or example of these can be called up, it is felt to be a special example that covers only a very small part of the whole field. An image, strictly considered, can not be made of force at all, nor of any special example of force. We can image some object that is acted upon by a force. We can image it before it is acted upon and after it is acted upon—that is, we can image the results of the force, but not the force itself.

"If we conceive existence, and image some existent things; if we conceive quantity in general and image a series of things that can be numbered, or an extension or degree that may be measured; if we conceive relation in general and try to illustrate it by imaging particular objects between which there is relation—in all these and similar cases we can hardly help being conscious of the vast difference between the image and the conception. In realizing the conception of relation, as in that of force or energy, we do not image even an example or specimen of a relation or force, but we image only the conditions or termini of a specimen relation: but the relation itself must be thought, just as any force must be thought, but can not be imagined. We can think relations but not image them." *

III. **Conceptive Processes.**—Conception stands for classification as memory stands for remembering. The

* Dr. W. T. Harris.

steps by which we reach general notions must be counted as merely processes in conceiving ; these are *experience, comparison, abstraction, generalization, classification,* and *naming.*

1. *Comparison.* That we may discover common properties and discern class relations we must compare things.   Comparison here includes experience ; thought deals with ideas, not with things.   When we conceive we compare our ideas of things and not the things themselves ; but we gain our ideas through experiences. We find that these figures are three-sided and those four-sided ; we find that these apples are red and those white.   This is *observing* and *comparing.*

2. *Abstraction.* This is leaving out of consideration the *many properties* that we may consider things with reference to a *single property.*   We disregard everything else, and consider these figures with reference to the number of sides and these apples with reference to color.   This is *abstracting.*

3. *Generalization.*   This is finding a common property and extending it to many individuals.   This figure and this and this are three-sided ; three-sidedness is general to them ; we generalize by extending this property so as to include all three-sided figures.   This is *generalization.*

4. *Classification.*   This is grouping things into classes.   We have abstracted *number of sides* as the basis for classifying these figures.   These figures all have the *general* property of three-sidedness, and we think them into the three-sided figure group ; but those have the general property of four-sidedness, and we think them into the four-sided figure group.   As a basis

11

for classifying these apples we *abstracted* color.   These
apples have the *general* property red, and we think
them into the red-apple group; those have the general
property white, and we think them into the white-apple
group.   We discern sameness as to form, and thus
think all figures into a few classes.   This is *classifying*.

5. *Naming*.   This is giving names to our general
notions.   We call our three-angled figure group *triangles* and our four-angled group *quadrangles*.   We
have reached these general notions and named them;
conception can go no further.   When we think of conception we do not think of these processes, but simply
of self thinking his particular notions into general notions.   Conceiving is discerning class relations, and is
the first step in thinking.

II. Judgment, Judging, and Judgments.

The native energy of self to think his notions into
truths is called judgment.   We judge when we discern
truth-relations.   *Kant was a philosopher*.   We discern
the agreement of the notions, philosopher and Kant,
and think them together into the truth.

Self as judgment discerns and asserts the agreement of notions, as, pleasures are fleeting.   Self as
judgment discerns and asserts the disagreement as well
as the agreement of notions, as, teachers are not infal-
-lible.   Judgment is the truth-discerning power of the
soul, and is considered one of the most important and
fruitful of all our faculties.

1. *A judgment is the assertion of a truth*.   Truth
is correspondence with reality, as *sugar is sweet*.   Un-
truth is the assertion of agreement which does not ac-

cord with reality, as *the earth is square*. Self as judgment discerns the untruthfulness of this proposition
and changes it into a truth by inserting *not*. We
express our judgments in propositions which we call
sentences; hence, judgment is sometimes termed our
sentence-making faculty.

2. *Synthetic and analytic judgments.* We embody
and treasure our knowledge in sentences, and thus we
connect all our progress in the acquisition of knowledge with sentence-making. *Synthetic judgments* extend our knowledge by making ·new predications, as
cows are ruminating animals. To his previous knowledge of cows the learner now adds a new characteristic.
Analytic judgments make our knowledge fuller and
clearer by predicating component parts or properties,
as *birds have wings*, or *gold is yellow*.

3. *Processes in discerning truth.* The steps in
forming judgments are judging processes. Take the
two notions *sponge* and *animal*. We compare these
notions. A *doubt* arrests us. "Is the sponge animal
or vegetable?" We *investigate* and find that sponges
are really animals. We discern the *agreement* of the
notions, and *think* of the sponge as animal. Finally,
we express the judgment in the sentence, sponges are
animals. But no one thinks of these processes when
judging, any more than the orator thinks of the elementary sounds when addressing his audience. From
early childhood we constantly judge, so that an act of
judging comes to seem to us to be a single simple step.

4. *Percepts, concepts, and judgments.* Percepts
and concepts are the materials out of which self makes
his judgments. *Solomon was wise; all men are falli-*

ble. In the first, the subject is a percept; but in the
second, the subject is a concept. In these cases, and in
fact in all judgments, the predicates are concepts. Self
as judgment elaborates his ideas into judgments. Judging is discerning truth relations, and is the second step
in thinking.

Kant defines judgment as the faculty that discerns examples of
universals. It is regarded as the faculty that adapts means to ends
and discriminates applications. One with a good judgment is called
a wise man. From the educational standpoint, however, it is deemed
best to treat judgment as the power to discern and assert truth.

III. Reason, Reasoning, and Reasons.

Reason is the native energy of self to discern
grounds and reach conclusions. Whenever we say intelligently *because, hence, therefore,* we reason. Reasoning is grasping the relation of two judgments into a
conclusion. Thus:

> All mammals are vertebrates;
> The horse is a mammal;
> .˙. The horse is a vertebrate.

Self as reason infers conclusions from premises.
Through two related truths we discern a new truth.
Reason is the capability to originate a judgment expressing the relations of two given judgments. The
constitution of things is such that, certain related truths
being known, we can infer other truths. You know
that $x = y$ and that $y = z$; and you infer that $x = z$.
Reason is the power of inference.

Reason in the Mental Economy.—Infinite reason planned the universe. All things from atoms to systems of worlds are unitized by
cause-relations. Cause and effect, means and ends, antecedent and
consequent, link all into unity. Endowed with reason, we think

the thoughts of God after him. Reason, through interlocked judgment, discerns cause-relations. Self, as reason, lays under contribution all his other intellectual capabilities, and supplements and reenforces each. We think our percepts into concepts—reason is there; we remember and imagine—reason is there; we form judgments—reason is there; we feel emotions of truth and beauty and duty—reason is there; we choose and act—behold, reason is there.

I. **Reasoning Forms.**—Reason stands for the power of inference. Self reasons when he infers a third truth from two related truths. Reasoning as to form is either full or abbreviated

1. *Informal and formal reasoning.* Ordinarily in conversation, in books, in science, and in discourse we reason informally. We say, *men are happy because they are law-abiding.* This is *informal* reasoning, as the major premise is not expressed. When the argument is stated in full it is formal reasoning, as—

Beings who are law-abiding are happy;

Men are law-abiding;

∴ Men are happy.

Rarely do we thus state our arguments in full; but, in all cases, the omissions are implied, and our *informal reasons* may be expanded into *formal reasons.*

2. *Induction and deduction.* These are merely different forms of reasoning. Through particular truths we reach general truths. This magnet and this and this attract iron; since Nature is uniform, we infer that all magnets attract iron. This is *inductive* reasoning. It is inferring a general truth from particular truths. Thus we think up to principles and laws. We deduce particular truths through general truths. Since all minerals gravitate, we infer that diamonds gravitate. This is *deductive* reasoning. It is inferring a particular

truth from general truths. Reason is simply our capability to discern new truths through related truths. Whatever form it takes it is ever the power of inference.

II. **Reasoning Processes.**—These are steps which self takes in reaching conclusions. When we reason we do not think of these processes; we simply discern through the medium of known truths new truths.

1. *Regulative truths.* Our notions of *necessary realities* and the *eternal fitness of things,* gained by direct insight, are termed necessary-ideas. Our axioms are our *generalized* necessary-intuitions and are called *necessary-truths, first truths,* and *regulative truths.*

"**Without the idea of causality** there could be no experience. Experience can not begin until the idea of causality awakens in the mind. Space and time are primary logical conditions which make an objective world possible. Causality is equally fundamental for the existence of experience. Without the idea of causality the mind can not recognize itself as the producer of its deeds, nor can it recognize anything objectively existing as the producer of its sense-impressions. All sense-impressions are mere feelings and are subjective. We can not derive the idea of cause from experience, for we have to use it to begin experience. The perception of the objective is possible only by the act of passing beyond our subjective sensations and referring them to external objects as causes of them. Whether I refer the cause of my sensations to objects and thereby perceive, or whether I trace the impressions to my own organism and detect an illusion of my senses in place of a real perception—in both cases I use the idea of causality. The object is the cause, or I am the sole cause. . . . A real cause is an originator of changes or new forms of existence. It is not something which demands another cause behind it, for it is self-active. The chain of relativity ends in a true cause and can not be conceived without it. The true cause is an absolute, inasmuch as it is independent. That which receives its form from another is dependent and relative. That which is self-active is a true cause, gives form to itself or others, and is independent of others. Our idea of cause, therefore, is the basis of our ideas of freedom, of moral responsibility, of selfhood, of immortality, and, finally, of God." *

Reason makes necessary-truths the ground and the guide of thought. *Things which are equal to the same thing are equal to each other.* This truth, in some of its modifications, doubtless gives form to all our mathematical reasoning. The mathematical syllogism does not, like the real syllogism, subsume. The following example illustrates both :

$y < x$; or x includes y;

$z < y$; y includes z;

$\therefore z < x$. $\therefore x$ includes z.

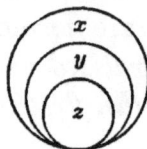

2. *Judgments* are the stuff out of which arguments are made. Self as judgment discerns *truth-relations* and thinks his percepts and concepts into judgments. These we embody in sentences and call them *propositions.* Self as reason discerns *grounds* and thinks judgments into reasons.

3. *Terms and propositions.* In every *reason* three *terms* and three *propositions* are expressed or implied. For example :

All men are mortal ;

Poets are men ;

$\therefore$ Poets are mortal.

As *mortal* is the larger term, it is called the *major* term ; as *poets* includes least, it is called the *minor* term ; as *man* comes between the major and minor terms and is the term with which the others are com-

* Dr. W. T. Harris.

pared, it is called the *middle term*. As the first proposition includes most, and is the one on which the others
are based, it is termed the *major premise*. In the
major premise *all men are mortal*, the middle and major
terms are compared. As the second proposition includes less, and is based on the major premise, it is
called the *minor premise*. *Poets are men;* here the
minor and middle terms are compared. As the third
proposition is the necessary inference from the premises, it is called the *conclusion*. *Poets are mortal;*
here the major and minor terms are compared.

4. *Reasoning* is discerning grounds and reaching
conclusions through the medium of premises. Since
$a = b$ and $c = a$, we discern the conclusion that $c = b$.
We compare the major and minor premises and *infer* the
conclusion. We so interlock related propositions as to
reach conclusions. We so grasp related judgments as
to *press* them to a conclusion. We discern the cause-
relations between judgments and thus reach new truths
which we term conclusions. As *all men desire happiness*, and as the *Arabs are men*, we reason that the
Arabs desire happiness.

5. *Verifying our conclusions*. This means investigation. Reason presides, but in this search for truth
all our powers contribute. We analyze; we reduce the
argument to propositions, and the propositions to concepts, and the concepts to percepts. We synthesize;
we convert percepts into concepts, and concepts into
judgments, and judgments into arguments. We find
that the major premise is true; we find that the minor
premise is true and related to the major premise; we
find that the conclusion is true and that it follows from

the premises. Going back to our intuitions, we investigate every point connected with the argument. We thus verify our conclusions.

III. **Inductive and Deductive Reasoning.**—"*Induction* and *deduction*, like analysis and synthesis, of which they are special forms, accompany each other in all the higher processes of thought. The two blend together so intimately that it is often difficult to sever them, or to find or. trace the line where the one begins and the other terminates. They run together so readily and are so intimately united that it is often hard to decide whether the process is *inductive* or *deductive*, because it is difficult to decide with which the mind begins, the particular or the general, or whether both these relations are not considered together." * We find that in this case and this two parts of hydrogen combined with one part of oxygen give us water; we infer that this will be true in all cases. We demonstrate that a square described on the hypotenuse of this right-angled triangle equals the squares described on the other two sides, and we infer that this is true of all right-angled triangles. This is *inductive reasoning*. Because all men are fallible, we infer that teachers are fallible. Since all flesh-eating animals are carnivorous, we infer that panthers are carnivorous. This is *deductive reasoning*. Induction ascends through particular truths to general truths; deduction descends through general truths to particular truths. When we ascertain the representative facts we *induce* the general ; thus we infer that heat expands all minerals. We *deduce* through general truths particular truths ; thus we infer that heat expands

* Porter.

diamonds, since it expands all minerals. Though we reason through particulars to generals and through generals to particulars, the act of reasoning is ever the same. Reason is the power of inference.

The Reason and Necessary-Intuition.—These are the terms used to designate the native energy of self to gain intuitively *necessary-ideas*. In logic and literature and practical life, *reason* stands for the power of *inference*. It must prove an immense gain to use *reason* uniformly in its popular sense. *Necessary-intuition* is the capability of self to gain by direct insight *necessary-ideas*. This is specific; necessary-intuition expresses *all* that writers mean by *the reason*. Necessary-intuition is the power of direct insight into the constitution of things, and is the regulating principle of mind. Bascom tells us that the *regulative* ideas are existence, number, resemblance, space, time, cause, spontaneity, consciousness, truth, beauty, right, and infinity. Self as thought generalizes *necessary-ideas* into *necessary-judgments;* these are the axioms of mathematics and logic and life, and are called *necessary-truths*. It seems every way fitting to call our power to gain directly necessary-ideas *necessary-intuition*, just as we call our power to gain sense-ideas *sense-intuition*, and our power to gain self-ideas *self-intuition*. Reason, then, may be used uniformly as the power of inference.

Reason and Faith.—We investigate, we reason, we reach conclusions. We *believe* in our conclusions, for we *trust* them and *act* on them; this is *faith*. Rational beings are so constituted that they accept as true conclusions based on sufficient reason. Faith introduces us to the larger life of the race. The historian, through historic premises, infers historic conclusions which he *trusts*. Our history-world is a thing of faith. The scientist experiences one truth and accepts a thousand on faith, and thus builds into science the experiences of the race. Blind credulity is not rational, is not faith. Self, as reason, investigates, and, when the reasons are sufficient, comes to a *conclusion*. Self, as faith, *assents* to the *conclusion*, confides in it, and acts on it. The engineer concludes that the bridge is safe; the conductor accepts this conclusion, trusts it, risks his life and that of the passengers on it; he *believes* that the bridge is safe. This is faith. The Christian reasons that the Bible is completely adapted to man, and hence must be the work of the Author of our being; he *believes* this conclusion, trusts in it, risks his eternal all on it. This is faith.

CHAPTER XIII.

EDUCATION OF CONCEPTION.

By this is meant the development of the power to think individuals into classes. Uneducated persons lack power and grasp of mind because they do not discern things in their relations; do not think many resembling things as one class. The uncultured, like children, think in particular rather than in general terms. Culture of conception increases thought-power almost infinitely. It enables one to think billions of individuals as a single class. You think *animal*, and this is equivalent to millions of living creatures. You think crude knowledge into science.

I. RELATIONS OF CONCEPTION AND DEFINITIONS OF TERMS.

The position of conception in the mental econ-

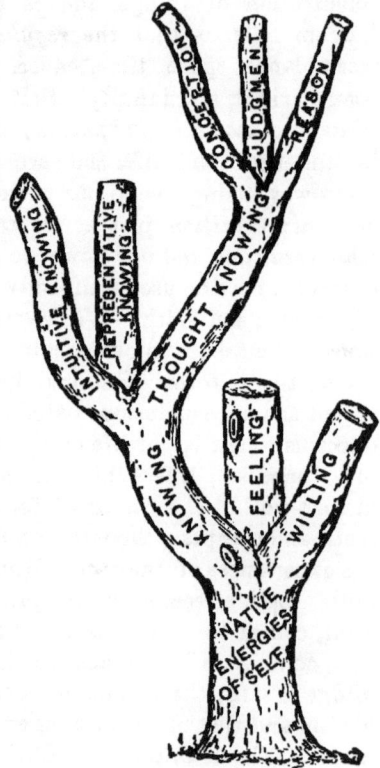

omy may be indicated as in the margin. Its place as one of the thought-powers is unquestioned.

1. *Relation to intuition.* Conception is dependent on intuition for the materials out of which concepts are made. Sense-intuition gives us ideas of material things having properties. Self-intuition gives us ideas of the activities, and acts of self. Necessary-intuition gives us ideas of necessary-realities. But these ideas are individual concrete notions. Self, as conception, compares individuals, discerns class relations, and thinks particular notions into general notions.

2. *Relations to memory and imagination.* Self as memory recalls his particular notions and keeps them before the mind for comparison and assimilation. We certainly can not picture our concepts, and yet imagination helps us amazingly in our classifying labors. Often we need to create experiences. You have seen but one elephant, but from your knowledge of other animals you can imagine elephants, large, small, young, old, white, black, and gray. Then you think your real and imaginary experiences into the concept elephant. In some degree, at least for a time, the learner dimly pictures concepts with particulars blurred or left out of view, as when we think triangle, or soldier, or tree. In thinking tree, some familiar tree flits before the mind and helps us to think the general notion.

3. *Relations to judgment and reason.* In forming concepts we judge. In fact, a concept is a plexus of judgments. Often, too, the learner needs to stop and reason, as when he comes to classifying the sponge. On the other hand, conception furnishes general notions to be appropriated by judgment and reason.

Definitions.—Teachers, even more than students, need to define their terms sharply, and especially the terms that they constantly use. Conception may be termed the capability to make definitions.

1. *Conception* is the native energy of self to think particular notions into general notions. Self, as conception, thinks the particular notions *John, James,* and *Henry* into the general notion *boy.*

2. *Conceiving* is the act of discerning class-relations and assimilating individuals into classes. I discover that some of these apples are sweet and some are sour, and I assimilate all into two classes, and call these sour apples and those sweet apples.

3. *A concept* is a general notion: Boston and Chicago and Nashville are particular notions, but *city* is a general notion. Class-notions are concepts. Our ideas are either *percepts* or *concepts.* Our particular notions are *percepts,* but our general notions are *concepts.* Percepts are *concrete,* concepts are *abstract;* percepts are *individual* notions, concepts are *group* notions; percepts are *particular* notions, concepts are *general* notions. The notions this dog, this horse, and this elephant are percepts; the notions quadruped, vertebrate, and mammal are *concepts.*

4. *Culture of conception* is the development and training of the power to acquire and use concepts. Culture makes the difference between the weak and crude conceptive powers of the child and the savage, and the vigorous conceptive powers of the scientist.

II. Importance of the Education of Conception.

Thinking is discerning relations. Conceptive thinking is discerning class-relations. As soon as the child begins to observe similar objects it begins to group them. This is the feeble beginning of thought. It is important to so develop the classifying power as to make the student a master.

1. *Culture of conception greatly increases mental vigor.* Uneducated persons deal with percepts, and their thinking is narrow and child-like. Educated persons deal with concepts, and their thinking is broad and vigorous.

2. *Culture of conception conserves mental energy.*
Percepts not crystallized into concepts are squandered.
The complete assimilation of discriminations into a
unity is the culminating principle of education. We
compare, discriminate, and then assimilate; we think
as one class things having one or more common characteristics; we think our notions into larger and still
larger mental units; we crystallize our particular notions into general notions. Concepts are more precious
than fine gold.

3. *Culture of conception makes science possible.*
Savages make no science. Persons whose classifying
power is undeveloped neither make nor understand
science. Science is classified knowledge. Development of conception prepares one to make science and
comprehend the products of human thought.

III. Growth of Conception.

The cut illustrates the gradual growth of conception. The child begins its mental life by gaining sense-
percepts. Out of these sense-percepts it soon begins to
form sense-concepts. The degree of activity indicates
kind of culture required.

1. *Kindergarten period.* Before the end of the first year the infant seems to begin to group things. When two or three years old
the child makes many amusing classifications. By the end of the
sixth year the intelligent child has roughly classified the objective
world around it. Wise mothers lead children to use proper terms
to express their concepts. The Kindergartner leads her pupils to
crystallize their sense-percepts into sense-concepts.

2. *Primary period.* From six to ten, verbal memory is decidedly
active and objective conception is moderately active. Now is the
time for objective language-lessons and classifications of geometri-

cal forms and colors, as well as for the foundation work in geography, zoölogy, and botany. Easy but correct names of concepts are acquired.

3. *Intermediate period.* Boys and girls take delight in objective analysis and synthesis and in discovering group notions. Their classifications are bold and striking; obscure and minute groupings are made later. Pupils are led to work up to concepts and make their own definitions. The work of this period is of the utmost importance.

4. *High-school period.* During this period conception reaches a still higher activity. This is the science period, and youths delight in discovering over again the classifications of science.

5. *College period and afterward.* Conception is moderately active in childhood, and is highly active from the tenth to the eighteenth year. This is pre-eminently the period for its vigorous use and systematic culture. After the eighteenth year classification becomes philosophic and exhaustive. Conception seems to increase in power throughout active life. In manhood our classifications become more accurate and far-reaching. By constantly pushing our researches into new realms we may keep the classifying power vigorous even in old age.

IV. Laws of Conception-Growth.

Education is that development and training which fits a man for the highest usefulness and highest happiness of which he is capable.

I. **General Educational Laws.**— It is necessary to restate these laws in terms of conception; thus stated they guide the teacher:

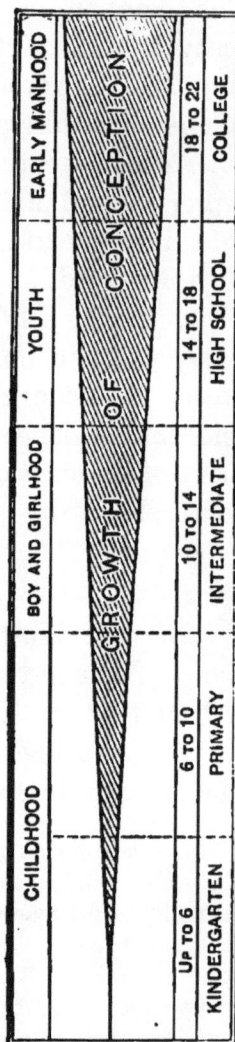

1. *Law of effort.* Well-directed effort in conceiving and using general notions educates conception. This law requires the learner to do his own classifying. Relations must be discerned. Individuals must be thought into groups, and concepts must be incorporated into the mental life.

2. *Law of means.* Studies which call conception into the most vigorous and most constant activity are of greatest value for conception-culture. Zoölogy and botany rank highest.

3. *Law of method.* Plans of work which lead the pupils to put forth, in the best ways, their best efforts in acquiring and using concepts educate conception. It is understood that this work must be systematic and persistent.

II. Special Laws of Conception-Growth.—The tendency to classify is exceedingly human. Children and men feel the impulse to master things by grouping them. The uniform ways in which all must work in order to strengthen the grouping faculty are termed the laws of conception-growth. Attention is directed to two or three special laws: 1. *Ascending through percepts to concepts educates conception.* This law requires that the learner should make the ascent. 2. *Organizing particular notions into general notions educates conception.* Object-lessons which stop with percepts are waste labor in education. In order to save its particular notions the child must be led to assimilate them into general notions. Observe critically the classifying efforts of your pupils. How *must* they make these efforts in order to growth? You will discover other special laws of great practical value.

Above all, you will teach your pupils to work in accordance with law.

V. Means of educating Conception.

Food is necessary to growth. The plant feeds on inorganic substances, but the animal on organic. Knowledge is our intellectual food. Self as perception organizes sensations and awareness into percepts. Self as conception feeds on organic knowledge, assimilates percepts into concepts. Studies are best for conception-culture that give the widest exercise in gaining general notions. The classified sciences—botany, zoölogy, mineralogy, and chemistry—stand pre-eminent. Objective arithmetic, including the construction of tables of weights and measures, language-lessons in connection with objects, constructing outlines and working out definitions, must rank very high. Studies of a low value in educating conception, such as advanced arithmetic and algebra, are omitted from the table.

Table of Educational Values.—Studies which call the classifying power into most vigorous and most constant activity are of the highest value as a means of cultivating conception. You will make your own estimates and insert in column 3. You can then find the averages.

CONCEPTION-CULTURE, VALUE OF	1	2	8	4
Zoölogy, botany	10	10	....	....
Objective language-lessons and objective arithmetic	9	8	....	....
Mineralogy, chemistry, geography	9	8	....	....
Grammar, history, literature	7	7	....	....
Geometry, physiology, physics	5	6	....	....

The educator relies largely on language-lessons, zoölogy, and botany as the means for educating the conceptive power. These

12

studies extend from the Kindergarten to the university. The animals and the plants in city and country are all around us. No other studies interest children and youths more than the classification of plants and animals. Geography may easily be defined so as to include zoölogy and botany, and these studies may be made a part of the work in geography. In our elementary schools, one quarter each year may be devoted to zoölogy and one quarter to botany, leaving half the school year for the usual geography work.

VI. Methods of developing Conception.

"Education can be in nothing more ostentatious than in its so-called methods, and it is here that charlatanism can most readily intrude itself. Every little change, every pitiful modification, is proclaimed aloud as a new or an improved method." We must keep in mind that an *educational method* is a lawful, systematic, persistent, and efficient plan of work, adapted to an educational period. Devices are helpful expedients, and should be so designated.

I. **Primary Methods.** — Up to six the child's chief work is to form the acquaintance of sense objects and roughly group these objects. From six to ten the child steadily advances in objective classifications. The great activity of sense-perception and verbal memory, and the moderate activity of conception emphasize the importance of leading the child to gain a considerable store of objective concepts.

1. *Lead the child to detect resemblances and group common objects.* Take chairs, knives, doors, windows, fruits, parts of the body, colors, and so on. It is essential that the learner shall do the work.

2. *Lead the pupil to group geometrical forms and construct tables of weights and measures.* Here we

have easy and interesting work.   At every step so manage that the child will feel the joy of discovery.

3. *Lead the child to classify animals and plants.* The pupil must be led to observe animals and plants, and discern common points and make bold classifications.   This work is a perennial delight to the little ones.

4. *By easy steps lead the learner through percepts to concepts.*   In childhood self as conception acts feebly. Resemblances must be obvious, the classifications must be bold and picturesque, and names of concepts must be easy.

" The training of conception should begin in connection with sense observation.   Objects should be laid in juxtaposition and the child invited to discover their similarities of form, color, etc.   And here his active impulses may be appealed to, by giving him a confused multitude of objects and inviting him to sort them into classes. By this direct inspection of a number of things, notions of simple classes of natural objects, as species of animals and flowers, as well as of geometric forms and numbers, may be gained.   A sufficient variety of instances must be supplied in every case, but the number required will differ according to the character of the notion to be formed.   This operation of comparing and classing should be supplemented by naming the objects thus grouped, and by forming easy definitions of the more important concepts gained." *

II. **Intermediate Methods.**—Primary and high school methods in our best schools are now excellent, but intermediate methods are often remarkably defective. This stage of development does not seem to be grasped by the great body of our teachers.   The precious years of girlhood and boyhood are largely squandered.   This is the semi-scientific period.   During this period the

* Sully.

foundation for science work and language work should be deeply laid in experience.

1. *Lead the learner to make bold but accurate classifications.* Boys and girls take delight in objective analysis and synthesis, and in thus gaining objective concepts. They like to find out classifications for themselves. These efforts, wisely directed, educate conception.

2. *Lead the pupils to find out the classifications of science.* Botany, zoölogy, and geography furnish ample scope for these achievements. As pupils gain percepts first-hand, so must they gain concepts. They observe that plants and animals are related by resemblances. Through these common characteristics they think animals and plants into classes. In our common schools, it has been found highly satisfactory to devote half the school year to the ordinary geographical work, and one fourth to zoölogy and one fourth to botany. The gain is immense. This course has so much to commend it that it is likely to be followed in all our elementary schools.

3. *Lead the boys and girls to make outlines and definitions.* At this stage of development, as well as earlier, the pupil needs all possible objective helps, such as the molding board, globes, maps, charts, pictorial representations, and outlines, in addition to the objects themselves. Lead the learner to discover relations between concepts and make the outlines, as of parts of speech, classes of vertebrates, etc. Concepts must now be defined. Children define percepts by describing objects, but boys and girls define objective concepts by referring the notion defined to a higher class and

giving the characteristic difference. The pupil gains the concept quadruped through his percepts of individual quadrupeds and makes his own definition. It is easy for him to make his own definition when he gains concepts for himself. Definitions must be clear-cut.

4. *Lead boys and girls to make tables of weights and measures.* In our transition times, we must have both the common and the metric weights and measures. The pupils weigh and measure, and thus gain the percepts which they think into concepts. Reform is needed, and we should hasten the domination of the metric system.

III. **High-School Methods.**—Here but little needs to be said. This is pre-eminently the period to master classified knowledge. Conception is now fully active, and memory is at its best. Science-making develops conception.

1. *Lead the student to rediscover the classifications of science.* He now has access to two sources of information—his own experiences and the vicarious experiences of others. He finds the treasured experience of the race in books. He is now prepared to appreciate this experience and make it his own. Still, at every step, he must go back to Nature and rediscover and verify for himself. Teachers and books give him information, but his percepts and concepts must be his own.

2. *Logical diagramming educates conception.* The student first masters details. He studies objects in their relations and sums up his acquisitions in logical and exhaustive diagrams. Diagramming enables the student to discern more clearly class limits as well as class rela-

tions.   But mere aggregations are not logical diagrams.
Loose diagramming hinders rather than helps.   Diagramming by the teacher does little good.   Only independent diagramming really helps.   Few teachers can
resist wholly the temptation to do this work for their
pupils.

3. *Giving logical definitions educates conception.*
Thus the student learns to use concepts with exactness.
Words representing concepts become full of meaning.
The student thinks clearly when his concepts are clear-
cut.   In all cases each one must *make* his own defini-
tions.   Committing definitions or classifications, not
grounded in experience, does not develop conception.
" A concept is a definition and not a mental image."

Clearness of Concepts.—" When we consider that children learn
many words before they have a knowledge of the things for which
they stand, that adults often learn the use of words in a mechanical
way without concerning themselves about the exact notions which
the words should represent, that words are applied loosely, sometimes in one way and sometimes in another, that our knowledge of a
thing is frequently incomplete and inaccurate, that one man looks
at a subject from one standpoint and another from a different point
of view, we can not wonder at the confusion and misunderstanding
that often arise in the communication of thought.   Inaccurate concepts, imperfect definition of words, and difference in use of words
are the occasion of confusion in the use of language." *

4. *Conceiving and using clear-cut self-concepts educates conception.*   Young people need to explore the
mind world as well as the matter world.   Here well-
defined concepts are even more important than in matter studies.   The student must make his *self-concepts*
out of his own *self-percepts.*   The notions I have of this

* James H. Baker.

gratitude, and this, and this, are self-percepts ; but my notion of gratitude and of my capability to feel gratitude are self-concepts. Psychology is now as easy to the student as zoölogy or botany, and even more fascinating. It must be studied in the same way, only the student looks within and observes and classifies his own mental acts and capabilities.

5. *Stating clearly and using logically necessary concepts educates conception.* Necessary concepts must be thought out of intuitions of necessary realities. I gain intuitions of beauty when I feel the emotions of beauty in the presence of beautiful things. Out of my beauty intuitions I make the general notion *beauty.* Out of my duty percepts I make the concept *duty.* I think my intuitions of particular spaces into the general notion *space.*

Rules for Educating Conception.—To make these directions for conception-culture striking they are presented in this form :

1. *Study to comprehend.* You apprehend this object when you know it is a sense-object. You comprehend it when you know it in its relations. You perceive this pear—you apprehend it ; but when you think of it as fruit you comprehend it. Perceiving is apprehending ; conceiving is comprehending.

2. *Think your percepts into concepts.* The mind ascends through percepts to concepts. To stop short of this is a great mental waste. Treasuring our experiences in clear-cut concepts is true mental economy.

3. *Make your own definitions.* Unless your definitions grow out of your own experience and thought, immediate and appropriated, they will prove of little worth to you. No feature of the new education is more striking than this—pupils are led to make their own definitions out of their own experiences. This is Socratic as well as Pestalozzian.

4. *Classify for yourself.* Through your own experience you may appropriate the experience of the race ; but you are compelled to do

your own thinking. No one can discern relations for you. In the light of your own and the appropriated experience of others, you must make over again the classifications of science.

5. *Create experiences.* You will need to constantly supplement your experiences by imaginary experiences. This is a necessity in geography, and to some extent in all studies. You so combine your experiences as to virtually create new experiences.

VII. Errors in Conception-Culture.

Many educational fallacies and blunders occur in our efforts to educate conception. Some leading mistakes are pointed out. The thoughtful teacher only needs to be cautioned.

1. *Concepts before percepts.* This group of errors is most common and most baneful. The law of ascent is palpably violated. Before the child gains the *percepts* this lake, and this, and this, it is required to commit a definition of the *concept* lake. Before he gains the concrete notions of numbers he is made to commit the multiplication-table and the tables of weights and measures. This hurtful error pervades the old education. This blunder may be said to characterize the work of teachers ignorant of child-nature and ignorant of the laws of mental growth.

2. *Stopping with percepts.* Particular notions are of little value except as they lead up to general notions. Percepts are scaffolding; concepts are completed structure. Object-lessons which stop with percepts are educational mistakes. If all our teachers could understand the mental necessity of perceiving particulars in order to discern generals, and of assimilating particular notions into general notions, it would revolutionize our methods of teaching.

3. *Exclusive book work.* In geography the book is studied, but not the earth and its products and its inhabitants. In botany the book classifications are committed, but the student remains a stranger amid the plant world. In all studies definitions and rules are committed, but these are meaningless words because they are not rooted in experience.

4. *Making for the learner definitions, classifications, and diagrams.* Eat the pupil's dinner for him if you will, but I beg of you to let him do his own thinking. Lead him to work up to concepts and definitions and rules and diagrams.

5. *Neglect of conception-culture.* Thinking is conceiving, judging, reasoning. Classification, chronologically and logically, is the first step in thinking.

Few really take this step, few really think. One person in a thousand thinks up to the truth. Is it strange? Do our schools train pupils to think? Do our churches? Do political parties? It need not surprise you to find the unthinking masses drifting along in grooves made by their predecessors. A revolution is demanded. The school-room is the place to begin. The great want of the world is *thinking teachers* capable of educating a *race of thinkers.*

SUGGESTIVE STUDY-HINTS.

Helpful Books.—Psychologies which will assist you in gaining deeper insight into the nature of conception and its processes and products come first. These, such as Porter's Intellect, Schuyler's Psychology, and Sully's Outlines of Psychology, are now numerous. Helpful works treating of the culture of conception are not abundant, but attention is called to Bain's Education as a Science, James Johonnot's Principles and Practice of Teaching, E. V. De Graff's Development Lessons, and Brooks's Mental Science and Mental Culture. You will find good manuals of methods in science, in language-lessons, and in objective arithmetic especially helpful.

Letter on Conception-Culture.—You have doubtless given some attention to this subject for years; you have observed much and read much. The best thing you can do now is to put your knowledge into good shape, and embody what you know about the culture of conception in a letter to some fellow-teacher or to some young friend who seeks to become a teacher. You may also with great profit change this letter into a paper for publication.

I. **Relations of Conception and Definitions of Terms.**—Point out in cut (page 2) the position of conception in the mental economy. Show the relations of conception to sense-perception; to self-perception; to necessary-perception. Illustrate. Show and illustrate the relations of conception to memory; to imagination; to reason; to judgment. Give your own definitions of conception; of conceiving; of a concept; of education of conception. Give and illustrate the distinctions you make between *perception* and *conception;* between a *percept* and a *concept;* between a *concept* and an *image.*

II. **Importance of Conception-Culture.**—What is thinking ? What relations does self as conception discern ? Do you consider *conception*-culture as important as *perception*-culture ? Show that conception-culture increases mental vigor, conserves mental energy, makes science possible. Present an original reason for the culture of conception.

III. **Growth of Conception.**—Point out in cut (page 175) its stages of growth. Which is earliest active, perception or conception ? Do you use growth in the sense of development ? Describe the activity of conception during the *kindergarten* period; during the *primary* period; during the *intermediate* period; during the *high-school* period; during the *college* period. How may this faculty be kept vigorous even in old age ?

IV. **Laws of Conception-Growth.**—What do you mean by educational laws ? State in terms of conception the law of *effort;* the law of *means;* the law of *methods;* the law of *ascent.* Mention and explain a special law of conception-growth that you have discovered.

V. **Means of Educating Conception.**—Place on the board *Table of Conception-Culture Values.* State your reasons for the estimates in which you differ from the author. Does the culture-value of a study depend largely upon the methods of study and teaching ? What studies do all educators agree in giving a high conception-culture value ? Why ? To what studies do all assign a low value ?

VI. **Methods of Educating Conception.**—What do you mean by educational methods? Why do you refuse to call *devices* and *expedients* and trivial changes methods? What do you mean by *primary* methods of educating conception? By *intermediate* methods? By *high-school* methods? By *college* methods? State three directions to *primary* teachers. State and illustrate the four directions to *intermediate* teachers. State and explain the five directions to *high-school* teachers. Write on the board and explain the five *rules* for educating conception.

VII. **Mistakes in Conception-Culture.**—Do you count as educational mistakes all violations and misapplications of educational laws? What law is violated when the teacher attempts to teach concepts before percepts? Give examples. Why is it a serious blunder to stop with percepts? Show that exclusive oral work is a mistake. Should the teacher, the book, or the pupil make the definitions? How do you account for the neglect of conception-culture? What is the *great want* of the educational world?

CHAPTER XIV.

EDUCATION OF JUDGMENT.

THIS is the development of the power to discern truth. Relations between things are as real as the things themselves. The agreement and disagreement of our notions of things are realities. Self as judgment discerns and asserts these agreements or disagreements. When our judgments correspond with reality they are true; as when we discern and assert that the *earth is round*. Our judgments are false when they do not accord with reality; as when we say the *earth is square*. Truths are more precious than the treasures of kings. The love of truth characterizes the grand man. A sound judgment is the ability to see things in their proper relations.

I. Relations of Judgment and Definition of Terms.

The Mind is a Unit.—Its activities can not be separated by fixed lines. While the soul's various capabilities may be studied separately they can not be thought of as acting separately. The fact of the interaction of our various powers is fundamental in educational as in mental science. *Judgment must be thought of as simply the self-judging.* Judgment is re-enforced by all our other capabilities, but an act of discerning truth is essentially an act of judgment.

I. Relations.—The position of judgment in the mental economy is indicated by the cut in the margin. Like conception, its place as one of our thought-powers is unquestioned.

1. *Relations to perception and conception.* Self as *perception* gains intuitively particular notions, and as *conception* thinks these into general notions. Self as *judgment* thinks his percepts and concepts into truths. Particular and general notions are the stuff out of which judgments are made. Then, in the formation of our notions, judgment plays an important part. To think is to judge.

2. *Relations to memory.* Memory holds up before

the mind related notions that self as judgment may discern agreements and disagreements, and thus discover truth. Memory stores truths as our most precious treasures. Truths, like ideas, are assimilated, associated, and recalled.

3. *Relations to reason.* Reason takes ready-made judgments for premises and discerns their ground relations. Conclusions are simply inferred judgments. Reason contributes largely to the work of judgment-making.

4. *Relations to the emotions.* Truths discerned occasion truth-emotions. Many of the deepest joys of life come from finding out new truths. In turn, the love of truth inspires research.

II. **Definitions.**—Every one makes judgments moment by moment. So familiar are we with the sentence-making faculty that definitions are scarcely needed. Man may be called the sentence-making animal. According to popular usage, judgment characterizes good sense; as used here good sense characterizes judgment. No distinction is made between the faculty of judgment and logical judgment. We think of judgment as our truth-discerning power. The total intellect is used practically in discerning things in their proper relations, but the act is essentially an act of judgment.

1. *Judgment* is the capability of self to discern and assert truth-relations. I discern the agreement between the notions *white* and *snow*, and I make the assertion *snow is white.* As judgment self adapts means to ends and discriminates applications, but Aristotle taught that we "judge respecting things, affirming or denying one thing of another." This gives us propositions as logical judgments.

2. *Judging* is the act of discerning and asserting truth-relations. We judge when we discern the agreement as disagreement of notions.

3. *A judgment* is a product of judging. When expressed, we call a judgment a proposition, as, "She, in my judgment, was as fair as you."

4. *Education of judgment* is the development of our power to discern and assert truth. Culture of judgment makes the difference

between the weak, hesitating judgment of the child and the strong, penetrating, decisive judgment of the educated man. Judgment is our power to judge. The expression of an act of judgment is a proposition. Judgment implies the presence in the mind of two ideas and a knowledge of the relation between them. So there are three elements in the proposition—the subject, the predicate, and the relation discerned between these.

II. Importance of Educating Judgment.

For nothing should one be more thankful than for a *sound* judgment. This is the capability to see things in their proper relations. As judgment self discerns relations and finds out truth. It is something much higher than the mere proposition making power of the logician. "Sound judgment is the total intellect used practically." Happy is the man who is capable of discerning and loving truth. A good judgment is more to be desired than kingdoms.

1. *Judgment is our truth-discerning power.* Truth is more valuable than diamonds. It is the food upon which all great souls feed. The culture of judgment increases our capability to elaborate our ideas in truths.

2. *Judgments enter into our various experiences.* You acquire percepts—self as judgment is there. You gain concepts—self as judgment is there. You reason —self as judgment is there. You feel emotions of truth and beauty and duty—self as judgment is there. You choose and act—behold, self as judgment is there. Its culture increases our power to reach truth.

3. *Judgments are the stuff out of which reasons are made.* Reasons are interlocked judgments. Through judgments we reach new truths. Right judgments make correct reasoning possible. Culture of judgment de-

velops good sense, and we begin to see things in their proper relations.

4. *Good judgment is the charac-teristic of the good teacher.* The lack of good sense is the most deplorable of all intellectual defects. We say of persons, they have much learning but poor judgment. They seem to lack common sense. The teacher is called upon to decide promptly what is best, what is right, what ought to be. This is essential in the selection of the proper objects of thought for teaching; in their arrangement in the natural and logical order; in direct-ing the observation, thought, and ex-pression of his pupils; in the use of motives, in managing the school, in all his dealings with his pupils. If he judges wisely concerning all these matters, everything goes on well; if unwisely, trouble comes.

III. Growth of Judgment.

Though feeble in childhood, judg-ment ought to grow more and more vigorous as the years go by. The teacher has special facilities for the study of child-judgment. Each lan-guage-lesson is a psychological study.

1. *Judgment in childhood.* In its first years the child begins to discern truth-relations but does not assert the agreement of notions.

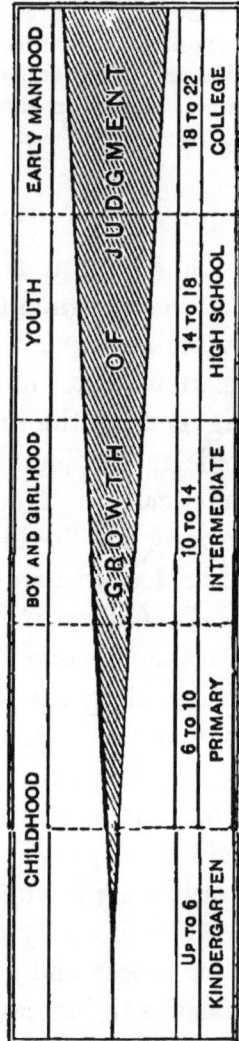

At first the child says "hot," "bad," "sweet," merely using predicates. Later it uses both subject and predicate, and says: "Cake
hot," "Boy bad," "Sugar sweet." Evidently the little ones judge.
About the third year the child begins to *predicate* the agreement of
notions, but its judgment is weak and unreliable. The rapid development of objective judgment is now remarkable.

2. *Judgment in girlhood and boyhood.* The power to discern
and assert objective truth-relations now becomes quite active. It
curbs the tendency to exaggerate. The boy has his own opinions,
and is very positive about them. The board *is* black; the tree *is*
tall; the apple *is* sour.

3. *Judgment in youth.* The capability to see things in their
proper relations is now fully active. This is eminently the period
for the systematic culture of the truth-discerning power.

4. *Judgment in manhood.* This faculty certainly becomes more
vigorous year by year to the meridian of life. When men work right
on, like Humboldt and Goethe, their judgments keep vigorous even
in old age.

IV. Laws of Judgment-Growth.

Bacon tells us that "reading makes the full man,
writing the correct man, speaking the ready man," and
might have added, *thinking the great man.* Thinking
according to law develops the weak and thoughtless
child into a Hegel or a Webster.

1. *General laws.* These may be stated in terms of
judgment as follows: (1.) Well-directed effort in discerning and expressing truth-relations educates judgment. (2.) Such subjects as call judgment into constant
and vigorous activity are best for its culture. (3.) Systematic and persistent efforts in making and using judgments develops this power.

2. *Special laws.* (1.) We must ascend through percepts and concepts to judgments, just as we ascend
through percepts to concepts. (2.) Sentence-making
develops judgment. A sentence is an expressed judg-

ment. All sentence-making consists in discerning and expressing truth-relations, and hence promotes the growth of this faculty. (3.) Perceiving judgments as true cultivates the truth-discerning power. Belief is assent to the truth of a judgment. The habit of making our own judgments and accepting them as true strengthens the capability to discern truth-relations.

V. Means of Educating Judgment.

All exercises calling into activity the truth-discerning power may be regarded as means for cultivating this faculty. No other mental power takes so wide a range. Porter says, "We can not think without judging, and that to think is to judge." At three, Aristotle judged as a child, at sixty as a philosopher. In childhood our judgments are simple, and limited to the material world; in manhood our judgments are comprehensive, and relate to all worlds.

Table of Educational Values.—Undoubtedly each study educates in some degree all our powers. Still, some studies are better than others for the culture of certain faculties because they call these faculties into freer, fuller, and more constant activity. In making the following estimates this fact is kept in mind. The estimates in column one are those of the author; in column two, those of Dr. Edward Brooks; in column three, those of Dr. W. T. Harris.

JUDGMENT-CULTURE VALUE OF	1	2	8	4
Arithmetic......................................	6	8	3	....
Geometry, algebra.............................	6	8	4	....
Language-lessons, composition........	9	7	8	....
Psychology, logic, ethics, philosophy...........	10	10	10	....
History and literature........................	9	9	10	....
Botany, zoölogy, chemistry, geography.........	8	8	7	....
Latin, grammar, and rhetoric	9	9	9	....
Reading or drawing or music.................	6	5	5	....

13

(1.) The study of mathematics gives early and constant activity to the judgment. Mathematics is a science of related ideas; nearly every process involves an act of "judgment." From the simplest thought $(1 + 1 = 2)$ to the profoundest theorem of calculus, the judgment is in constant activity. Every analysis in arithmetic, every solution in algebra, every demonstration in geometry, consists of a series of related judgments, and the student of these sciences is compelled to use constantly the faculties of relative thought.* (2.) Mathematics deals with a low order of certainty, viz., quantitative equality, but it does not deal with the logical judgment at all. For the logical judgment subsumes a particular under a general. But mathematics does not subsume, but finds dead, precise equality. The judgments of quantity are the easiest of all, and do not require much effort; they do not cultivate judgment. $2 = 2$; $a = a$; $3 < 4$; express dead equality and inequality. Compare such judgments with "Cæsar was wise in crossing the Rubicon," or "This picture is beautiful," or "This act is good." † (3.) Language-lessons, including composition, analysis, and construction of sentences and logical definitions, rank very high as means of judgment-culture. (4.) Psychology, logic, and ethics also deserve a very high place. Character-building calls judgment into constant use.

VI. Methods of Educating Judgment.

Under self-teaching and Nature's teaching man remains a savage. One does not learn to think by mere thinking. *Thinking under guidance develops the power to think efficiently.* Teaching is the art of training the learner to think. Educational methods include the work of the learner as well as that of the teacher. The teacher leads the learner to put forth his *best* efforts in the *best* ways. Methods in educating judgment are plans of work that call this power into systematic, vigorous, and persistent activity.

I. **Kindergarten and Primary Methods.**—The child judges, discerns truth-relations, but his judgments are

---

* Dr. Edward Brooks.   † Dr. W. T. Harris.

of things objective and obtrusive.   At an early age the child begins to use easy concrete sentences.   At first both the subject and the verb are omitted; later the verb only is omitted, as "Horse black," "Sister naughty." Later the child uses verbs, but continues for some time to use percepts as the subjects of his judgments, as "Rover barks," "This bird sings."   Later the child begins to use concepts as subjects, as "Dogs bark," "Birds sing."   The teaching must be *adapted* to these stages of growth.

1. *Lead the child to form his own judgments.* There is no need to hurry.   Lead the child to discern and express obvious truths ; as, the rose is red, the table has four legs, the apple is sweet.   Even at this stage the learner must be led to think for himself.   However feeble the thinking, and however easy and simple the concepts and judgments formed, well-directed effort educates.

2. *Lead the child to prize truth and form the truth-habit.*   Judgment must express actual relations. Is the apple really sour ?   Did I in reality recite well ? Is the horse in reality a quadruped ?   The truth-habit is invaluable.   The wise mother lays the foundation early and fixes the habit.   The kindergarten and primary teacher greatly strengthen the habit of truthfulness, and in this way promote the growth of judgment and at the same time develop character.

3. *Be certain that the child judges.*   Babbling is not thinking.   The child may say $3 + 3 = 6$ or the lake is round without an idea.   Lead the pupil through percepts to grasp the concepts 3 and 6, and to really discern the truth that three and three equal six.   Lead

the child, by means of concrete examples, to form for itself the concepts lake and round. It can then say intelligently the lake is round. These easy sentences will be its own judgments.

II. **Intermediate Methods.**—From ten to fourteen, the judgment is decidedly active. Girls and boys delight in forming and using judgments. Under direction they work up to mastery.

1. *Lead the learner to construct and analyze sentences.* I count composition and analysis of the English sentence of great educational value, disciplinary and practical. Each step is based on the learner's experience. Truth-relations are discerned and expressed. These sentences are expressed judgments. This is the period to master the English sentence. The old-time manner of parsing hinders, and does not help; indeed, in our time, it is avoided during this period by the wise teacher.

2. *Lead the learner to study things in their relations.* Each step is a judgment, and, when the work is properly adjusted, the pupil may be led to take the successive steps for himself. To make progress, the pupil *must* judge.

3. *Lead the learner to classify and define.* A concept is a condensed judgment, and may be expanded into a sentence. A logical definition is a judgment asserting the truth-relation between an individual and a species or between a species and a genus. Here we find geography, botany, and zoölogy of the highest value.

III. **High-School Methods.**—From fourteen to eighteen the judgment is wonderfully active, and becomes more and more penetrating and reliable. This is the fitting period for its highest culture.

1. *Lead the learner to judge for himself.* Stimulate to the utmost independent effort. At any cost manage to have the learner master problems for himself. In mathematics see that the student does the work without help. Easy problems mastered by the learner are better than difficult problems which master the pupil. In all studies stimulate students to do independent thinking.

2. *Stimulate vigorous judging.* Only sturdy effort develops power. Childish thinking gives us effeminate youths who enjoy a sensational novel, but are incapable of reading with pleasure and profit Shakespeare, or Bacon, or Kant. It may be well to dilute lessons for young pupils, but a youth needs to do hard work. Vigorous endeavor gives the penetrating judgment and develops power. Thinking makes the great man.

3. *Develop a thirst for truth.* Truth is more valuable than diamonds. Happy the student who hungers and thirsts for truth. He longs to become acquainted with things in their proper relations. He seeks to strictly conform his judgments to realities. He hates untruths as he hates sin. Love of truth has developed the world's greatest heroes.

VII. ERRORS IN EDUCATING JUDGMENT.

The old sage instructed the teachers to develop judgment rather than cram memory with crude facts. This rule is often reversed.

1. *Memory is crowded and judgment neglected.* The knowledge of persons thus treated is a crude jumble, a heterogeneous mass, a source of weakness rather than strength.

2. *Children are dragged through difficult abstract work.* The result is confusion, discouragement, and weakness. Whenever the pupil is dragged through arithmetic or algebra or physiology, he is dwarfed, not educated. Only when truth-relations are discerned with sunlight clearness does study develop judgment.

3. *Youths are fed with spoons.* Too many high-school teachers treat youths as though they were children. Now is the time for robust work. "Milk for babes but meat for men."

4. *The laws of descent and ascent are violated.* With many teachers judgments in the form of definitions and rules come before percepts and concepts. This is one of the many ways in which these laws are violated and pupils stultified.

5. *Hasty judgments are assented to as true.* We are inclined to accept the opinions of others as true without examination. Then we are so liable to judge as we *desire* without reference to reality. Prejudices often so blind us that we do not discern the truth. We should cultivate honesty and thoroughness in judging. We must really discern truth-relations before we assert them. We must discriminate sharply between opinions and truths

6. *Pupils take the statements of teachers and books without thinking.* This is a prolific source of error and of feebleness of judgment. In some way the learner must be led to judge at every step.

SUGGESTIVE STUDY-HINTS.

Helpful Books.—Compayré, in his lectures on pedagogy, treats briefly, but clearly, of judgment and its culture, as does Brooks in his Mental Culture. Locke's Conduct of the Understanding is excellent. Most writers treat of thought culture rather than of the culture of the thought powers.

Letter on the Culture of Judgment.—Lead your friend to realize the value of a cultured judgment. Have you well-defined views about the education of the truth-discerning power? Present them in your letter clearly and pointedly.

I. **Position and Definitions.**—Show by the cut, page 2, the position of judgment in the mental economy. State and illustrate the relations of judgment to perception; to conception; to memory; to reason. Define judgment; judging; a judgment; education of judgment. Illustrate the distinction you make between perception and conception; between memory and imagination; between conception and judgment.

II. **Importance of educating Judgment.**—Which do you consider the more important, the culture of memory or the culture of judgment? You may give three original reasons in favor of cultivating judgment.

III. **Growth of Judgment.**—How early does the child discern truth-relations? Illustrate the steps by which it reaches sentences. How early does the child intelligently use sentences? What is the golden period for judgment culture? How may this faculty be kept vigorous in old age? Point out the growth of judgment in several periods, as indicated by the cut.

IV. **Laws of Judgment-Growth.**—State in terms of judgment the law of *effort;* the law of *means;* the law of *method;* the law of ascent. Illustrate each.

V. **Means of educating Judgment.**—Place on the board and explain the table of educational values. Give your reasons for your estimates. Do you rank arithmetic highest? Why do you place language-lessons so high? Do you consider botany as good a means as mathematics for judgment culture?

VI. **Methods of educating Judgment.**—Prove that more depends on plans of work than on subjects. Illustrate by your method of teaching history. Give three directions for primary teachers; three for intermediate teachers; three for high-school teachers. Give your method of educating judgment.

VII. **Mistakes in educating Judgment.**—Show how the law of ascent is violated. What mistake is made about memory? Explain the mistake of dragging pupils through work which they do not understand. Point out two mistakes that you have observed.

CHAPTER XV.

EDUCATION OF REASON.

By this is meant the development of the power to discern cause-relations. Thinking is discerning relations. When we conceive we discern class-relations; as, *animal, vegetable.* When we judge we discern truth - relations; as, *God is love.* When we reason we discern cause-relations; as, *we are happy because we are good.* We conceive, judge, and reason; thus we elaborate crude notions into science.

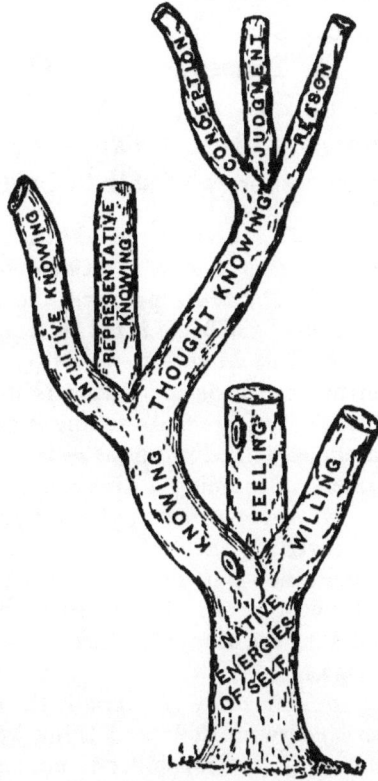

I. RELATIONS OF REASON AND DEFINITIONS OF TERMS.

Reason crowns the intellectual pyramid (see cut, page 154). We treasure rich stores of intuitions; we modify our experiences; we think our particular notions into general notions, and these into truths, that reason may have materials out of which to make science.

I. **Relations.**—Self as reason *commands* all his other intellectual powers. *Necessary-intuition* furnishes reason the necessary-truths as a fulcrum on which to place his lever to move the world. Necessary-ideas, generalized into necessary-truths, make reasoning possible. *Judgment* supplies the propositions out of which self as reason makes his arguments and in which he expresses his conclusions. Reason *serves* as well as *commands;* reason assists in the formation of percepts and concepts and judgments and ideals.

II. **Terms Defined.**—Our faculties are simply our capabilities to do acts different in kind. A faculty is merely a distinct native energy of self. Reason is the native energy of self to infer conclusions.

1. *Reason is the capability to discern new truths through related truths.* A man is rational because he discerns the reasons of things. The brute perceives the apple falling, but does not discern the *cause;* the brute is not rational.

2. *Reasoning is discerning ground-relations.* Reasoning is Inferring conclusions. Virtue is its own reward; truth-telling is a virtue; *therefore* truth-telling is its own reward. Whenever we say intelligently such words as *hence, because,* and *therefore,* we evidently reason. Reasoning is discerning conclusions.

3. *A reason is an inference from premises.* You give a reason for inverting the divisor in division of fractions, or for the course you are now pursuing. In all cases a reason includes the premises and a conclusion. One and sometimes both premises are unexpressed, but they are always implied. A *syllogism* is a formal statement of a reason.

4. *Education of reason* is the development of the power to discern cause-relations and think knowledge into system. It is the culture of the capability to understand the universe. We educate reason when we develop the power to infer new truths through related truths.

5. *Faith* or *belief* is confiding in our conclusions. We investigate to the utmost and reach conclusions. We accept these conclusions as true, trust in them, act on them. We thus study history and build science.

II. Importance of Reason-Culture.

Not to educate reason is to limit one's knowledge to his perceptions, and leave him to grope his way in a sea of inexplicable mystery. To such a one the universe is a maze without a plan, and life is not worth living. Contrast the vigorous thinker with the dawdling dreamer, and you have a striking object-lesson.

1. *Cultured reason gives one a rational universe.* As reason grows more and more vigorous, all things begin to assume proportion and harmony. Substance, energy, law; space, duration, cause; planets, suns, systems; plant, animal, man—all things fall into system, and make for us the music of the spheres.

2. *Education of reason gives independence.* The student acquires power, to investigate, and thus to discover truth for himself. He becomes a self-helper, an independent thinker, an original worker. He finds out the relations of the facts of history, discerns the logic of mathematics, and penetrates the secrets of cause and effect in the natural sciences.

3. *Education of reason gives mastery.* Educated reason is the power, and knowledge is the lever that moves the world. Sometimes, instead of mastering them, a student is mastered by geometry and chemistry. To such a student these sciences are a source of *weakness.* Mastery gives strength, and educated reason gives mastery. Knowledge mastered gives increase of power.

4. *Culture of reason multiplies the values of remembrances.* Why is it useful for us to know the past? As a guide to the future; inasmuch as the past

has been thus and so, we reason that the same will be true in the future. Without reason we would be unable to project the future. Many reasons for the culture of reason will occur to you. Does it not seem marvelous to you, this neglect of reason-culture?

III. GROWTH OF REASON.

While it is true that all the faculties grow together, it is equally true that some faculties reach full activity later than others. Of all the intellectual powers, reason acts most feebly in childhood and is the latest to reach full vigor. The easiest problems are difficult for the child; but the boys and girls easily solve much more difficult problems, and youths laugh at problems vastly more intricate. Each one is familiar with these facts, and hence with the growth of reason. "The child's first steps toward reasoning consist in making simple deductions or inferences from palpable facts by the comparison of two objects, one or both of which are present. This concrete form of reasoning is used by children from *five to twelve years of age*. But reasoning in a higher form, that in which the mind deals with the *relations* of facts established by observation

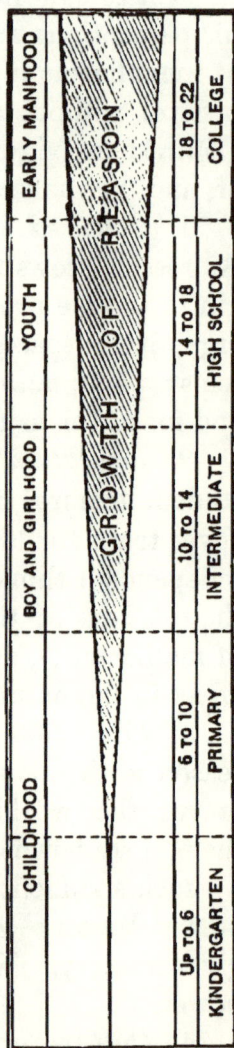

and experience, and also with the relations of abstract ideas, *rarely begins to develop before the child attains his twelfth or fourteenth year;* and then several years must be devoted to the exercise of this power before the mind can clearly comprehend that which requires purely abstract reasoning to make it known." * This faculty seldom asserts its predominance before the sixteenth year, nor does it usually reach full activity before the twentieth year. When called systematically and persistently into vigorous activity, reason grows more and more powerful up to the meridian of life, and it may be kept vigorous even in advanced old age. Plato, Bismarck, and Von Moltke have given evidence of immense reasoning power in advanced life.

IV. Laws of Reason-Growth.

As reason involves all our other powers, the laws of reason-growth must be studied in view of this fact.

I. **General Laws.**—These laws are the ways in which self must put forth effort in order to growth. These laws, stated in terms of reason, are as follows:

1. *Law of effort.* Well-directed effort in discerning cause-relations educates reason. Reasoning under guidance develops reason. From generals we infer particulars; through particular truths we discern general truths. Thus we think up to laws and create science.

2. *Law of means.* Studies which call reason into vigorous and persistent activity are valuable means for reason-culture.

3. *Law of method.* Systematic and persistent plans

* Calkins.

of work which necessitate the vigorous use of this power develop reason. Herbart speaks of school methods as the well-ordered self-activity of the pupil in investigating under the *leadership* of the teacher.

II. **Special Laws.**—Dr. Payne claims that the laws of ascent and descent in the mind-world are as comprehensive, as well established, and as widely applicable as the laws of gravitation in the matter-world. Around these laws are grouped many of the most helpful educational principles as well as some of the most hurtful educational fallacies. Plato and Aristotle taught in accordance with these laws. The new education embodies these laws in practice; the old education ignored them both in theory and practice. Working in harmony with the laws of ascent and descent educates reason. Such work calls into wise activity all the intellectual powers and tends to their harmonious development.

1. *Law of ascent.* The mind ascends through particulars to generals. It ascends through intuitions to concepts, through concepts to judgments, through related judgments to conclusions.

2. *Law of descent.* The mind descends from generals to particulars. It descends from reasons to judgments, from judgments to concepts, from concepts to intuitions. It descends from aggregates to elements, from the complex to the simple, from the vague to the definite.

V. Means of educating Reason.

Reason is self reasoning. You infer that the river is frozen because the temperature is below zero. Reason is simply your power to infer conclusions from premises. Nothing except reasoning can educate reason; but we reach power by means of knowledge. Knowledge is valuable as an instrument of mind, both as a fulcrum and lever; but mind is the power. In education knowledge is valuable as a means of eliciting mental effort, and hence as a means of culture.

Table of Reason-Culture Values.—Such studies as tend to call a faculty into most vigorous activity are the best means for its education. This we call the specific-culture value of a study. Those studies which call forth the best efforts of self as reason, have the highest reason-culture value. The values in column 1 are the author's, in column 2 those of Dr. Edward Brooks, in column 3 those of Dr. W. T. Harris. You may put your estimates in column 4 and the averages in column 5.

REASON-CULTURE VALUE OF	1	2	8	4	5
Mathematics.............................	6	10	3	....	....
Natural and physical sciences............	8	8	5	....	....
Language and literature.................	8	7	9	....	....
Psychology, logic, philosophy............	9	10	10	....	....
History, political economy, sociology.....	9	10	9	....	....

"Mathematics is a science of reasoning; nearly every one of its truths is related to and derived from some previous truth. The pupil can hardly proceed a single step in mathematics, if it is properly taught, without bringing into exercise the faculty of reasoning. This is not true in the same sense nor in a comparable degree of any other science."*

"Mathematics is usually ranked first as a means of reason-culture, but only a small proportion of our reasoning is mathematical, nor is that reasoning of a high order. Psychology, moral philosophy, history, biology, jurisprudence, philology are all superior to mathematics for educating reason and good judgment." †

"The sciences are the grand instrumentality for the education of reason. There could not be a better school for the culture of the faculties of reflection." ‡

* Dr. E. Brooks.   † Dr. W. T. Harris.   ‡ Gabriel Compayré.

METHODS OF EDUCATING REASON.

Reason is the capability of self to investigate. It includes in its operations discrimination and assimilation, analysis and synthesis, induction and deduction. It calls into its service all our other cognitive powers, and thus descends from aggregates to elements and ascends from elements to systems.

I. **Elementary Methods.**—These are systematic and persistent plans of work adapted to the development of budding reason. They are the methods of our elementary schools.

1. *Lead the child to make easy inferences.* Reason acts feebly now, but these feeble efforts prepare for greater things. Dimly the child discerns simple cause-relations in its narrow world; hence it may be led to make easy inferences and thus strengthen reason. The child burns its fingers, and thereafter avoids fire, because it infers that fire burns. All real teachers study children with intense interest. Preyer found that his boy used *why* intelligently when little more than three years old. You will be delighted to observe and foster the budding reason of the children committed to you.

2. *Be satisfied with obvious inferences.* But see that the pupil actually reasons. Reasoning alone can educate reason. Carefully guard against the hurtful policy of attempting too much. Abstract reasoning and committing logical formularies are very much out of place during this period. In many attractive ways the wise teacher incidentally leads the pupils to make bold and apparent inferences.

3. *Lead the pupils to find out.* From ten upward

the learner discerns clearly objective cause-relations.
Boys and girls are trained to tell *why*, and say intelligently, *because*. In arithmetic they give a reason for
each step. In history they are led to discover cause-
relations between events. In language-lessons they are
trained to think and to analyze thought. In botany
and zoölogy they are led to infer for themselves.

II. **Advanced Methods.**—From the fourteenth year
upward the student investigates and finds out for himself. Before this period his questions were: " What is
it ? " and " How is it ? " Now he asks also: " Why is
it ? " " Whence is it ? " and " What can I do with it ? "
Self as reason seeks answers to these questions, and systematic and vigorous endeavor to find answers develops
the thinking powers.

1. *Lead the student to investigate.* This includes
all that we mean by methods. You incite a burning
desire to know. You lead the learner to form habits
of effective penetrating thought. You train him to
discriminate and assimilate ; to analyze and synthetize ;
to induce, deduce, and reduce ; to descend from aggregates to elements and ascend from elements to systems.
For some time learners investigate under your leadership, but they become more and more independent and
self-reliant.

2. *Lead the learner to discuss.* Discussion is investigating with others. Written and oral discussion
develops penetrating and sturdy reason. Ideas fight.
Iron sharpens iron. Conflict of minds develops power.
Lawyers discuss, investigate in open court, and become
an overmatch for other men. The class-room is the
place for joint investigation. The teacher presides and

leads. Each student becomes an aggressive investigator. Each exposes the mistakes of his fellows, and clearly and forcibly presents his own views. Instead of being a place for stupid rehearsals, the class-room becomes a place of intense mental activity. The result is marvelous development of thought-power. Discussion calls forth a student's best efforts. An hour of intense conflict often does more to educate reason than years of dreaming. This is the method in which great men and great women are educated.

3. *Lead the student to so study mathematics as to develop reason.* Mathematics has been considered the best means for reason-culture; hence Benton reviewed geometry annually for many years to sharpen and keep vigorous his power to reason. For the same purpose Lincoln, after serving as a member of Congress, profoundly studied geometry. Mathematics treats of related truths. Each intelligent step necessitates reasoning. Because the work compels the student to constantly put forth effort, it develops skill in mathematical reasoning. But mastery is the essential result of good methods. We must so teach mathematics as to secure mastery on the part of the student.

4. *Lead the student to so study science as to educate reason.* Each one for himself gains elementary experience by direct insight into the sense-world, the self-word, and the world of necessary realties. The student is now prepared to appropriate the *vicarious* experience of the race. He first thinks his notions of individual things—e. g., this horse, this memory, this space; into general notions—e. g., quadruped, memory, space. Now he thinks his general notions into truths, as, man is mor-

14

tal. Finally he discerns through related truths cause-relations and infers conclusions. Through particular truths he thinks more general truths, and from general truths he infers particular truths.

5. *Lead the student to so study language, literature, and history as to educate reason.* History is a record of events, as causes and effects. Constructing for one's self a rational history of Greece or Rome or England or France is a tremendous effort of reason, and gives scope and vigor to this power. The investigation method of studying history, language, and literature calls reason into constant and vigorous exercise.

6. *The investigation method of studying psychology, logic, and philosophy educates reason.* High thinking is necessary to mastery. These tremendous fields of research demand penetrating and long-sustained thought. In grappling with these mighty themes reason attains its greatest power. Aristotle, Bacon, Hegel, stand for the great thinkers.

Mistakes in Reason-Culture.

The unthinking masses! This is the exclamation of all the ages. Individuals think, but the millions drift.

" The heights by great men reached and kept,
　　Were not attained by sudden flight ;
　　But they, while their companions slept, ·
　　Were toiling upward in the night."

Why this dearth of thinkers ? The answer comes slowly and sadly, Our schools fail to develop the art and habit of high thinking.

1. *Crowding memory and neglecting reason.* Even geometry is absorbed rather than mastered. In our

eagerness to acquire facts we do not take time to reflect. Mental indigestion and a race of learned weaklings must be the result. *Fewer facts and more mental force* will work a tremendous revolution.

2. *Feeble thinking.* The teacher lectures while the students recline on "downy beds of ease." The cardinal principle of some school-keepers is, "So manage that the student will be called upon to do nothing that the teacher can do for him." Is it any wonder the world is full of timid and feeble thinkers? The great need of our times is a host of vigorous thinkers. Better teaching is imperative. Better teachers is the world's great want.

3. *Misty thinking.* Teaching is always misty when the teacher is a misty thinker. "*Possibly* $2 + 2 = 4$." "It *may* be true that things which are equal to the same things are equal to each other." To such a teaching nothing is clear, nothing is certain. Each study is a jumble. Like teacher, like pupil. Such teaching is a sorrowful failure.

4. *Too much mathematics.* Mathematics has its place in reason-culture; but when it assumes to cover all the ground it is time to protest. The culture and knowledge given by mathematical studies are, at most, merely the preparations for exploring other fields of research. The educator must have broad views.

5. *Tediousness.* "Tediousness," says Herbart, "is the great sin of instruction." It is even more reprehensible in the school-room than in the pulpit. It is everywhere the deadly foe of thought. Then we have no right to thus afflict our pupils. You will deserve to be called a saint if you can spend a day in some schools

and not long to take the wings of the morning. The tediousness, misnamed thinking, is simply excruciating.

6. *Failure to think knowledge into system.* Things out of their relations are worthless. A finger disconnected with the hand is worthless; a hand disconnected with the arm is worthless; so also an arm disconnected with the body is worthless. Sensations not assimilated into concepts are wasted; concepts not assimilated into truths are of little value; and truths not thought into system are squandered.

SUGGESTIVE STUDY-HINTS.

Helpful Books.—Principles of Education, Practically Applied, and Methods of Teaching Arithmetic, Algebra, and Geometry, by Superintendent J. M. Greenwood, of Kansas City, Mo., are admirable and helpful books. J. A. McLellan, in his Applied Psychology, gives excellent suggestions in his presentation of the art of questioning. Spencer and Huxley have made valuable contributions along this line.

Letter on Reason-Culture.—This is a grand theme. You can afford to think deeply and write your best. You want to lead your friend to strive more earnestly to educate reason.

I. **Relations of Reason and Definitions of Terms.**—Show the position of reason in the cut, page 2; also in the cut, page 154. Show and illustrate the relation of reason and necessary-intuition; of reason and judgment; of reason and memory. Give and explain *your* definitions of *reason;* of *reasoning;* of *a reason;* of education of reason; of faith; of doubt; of unbelief. Ascend the cognitive pyramid by defining each cognitive power and its product.

II. **Importance of Reason-Culture.**—Tell why you count reason-culture so important. Explain as best you can the neglect of reason-culture. Should sex be considered in the education of reason?

III. **Growth of Reason.**—How early does the child reason? How do children reason from the fifth to the twelfth year? What do you mean by concrete reasoning? abstract reasoning? When does reason become fully active? Show that reason may be kept vigorous even in advanced old age. Why do you object to abstract work for young pupils?

IV. **Laws of Reason-Growth.**—What is meant by an educational law? State in terms of reason the law of effort; the law of means; the law of method. Explain Herbart's definition of method. State the law of ascent; the law of descent. What do you mean by the old education? by the new? Where do you class Squeers and Gradgrind? Socrates and Plato?

V. **Means for educating Reason.**—Why do you place geometry high? What studies do you place highest? Place on the board the table of culture-values, giving your estimate in column 4 and averages in column 5. Do you place geometry higher than Latin?

VI. **Methods of educating Reason.**—Show that you educate all the intellectual powers in educating reason. What kind of inferences do you lead young pupils to make? Why do you object to young children committing logical formularies? Can you lead boys and girls to investigate for themselves? Is it best to encourage them to discuss? Explain your notions of advanced methods of educating reason. What questions does the child ask? the boy? the youth? What do you mean by investigation? by discussion? How will you so teach geometry as to educate reason? science? language? psychology? logic?

VII. **Mistakes in Reason-Culture.**—Why do we say "the unthinking masses"? How do great men reach the heights? State one of the causes of mental indigestion. Why have we so many feeble thinkers? Can there be too much mathematics? What does Herbart say about the sin of tediousness? Is this the unpardonable pedigogical sin?

CHAPTER XVI.

CULTURE OF THE THOUGHT-POWERS.

THINKING is discerning relations. We discern *class*-relations—we think things into groups; we discern *truth*-relations—we think our notions of things into truths; we discern *cause*-relations—we think truths into reasons. Thinking is indicated by such terms as *dis-crimination* and *assimilation, analysis* and *synthesis, induction* and *deduction.* We *reflect,* we *consider,* we *investigate,* we *think;* we gain *insight,* we *understand,* we *comprehend;* we *infer,* we *conclude,* we *reason.*

Thinking is knowing things in their relations. A man is endowed with powers of direct insight into the world of things and their necessary conditions; but to the unthinking man the universe is a maze without a plan. Thought changes chaos into order. Everything takes shape and falls into rhythm. The sciences shine resplendent, presenting all things in their relations. . A well-ordered solar system, with the sun as its center, becomes a member of an infinite host of harmonious worlds. God, the infinite and eternal energy from which all things proceed, becomes the loving Father, and man becomes a candidate for immortality.

Thinking educates the thought-powers. "When I was a child I thought as a child, but when I became a man I thought as a man." Culture makes the difference. Child-thinking, under guidance, leads up to profound thinking. "Education implies instruction, which is twofold. On the part of the child, it is the constant building in of power and knowledge in his mind by the systematic right exertion of all his powers. On the part of the instructor, it is the intelligent stimulation, direction, and control of the activities of the child, with a view to his education. The instructor instructs only as he secures the upbuilding of the child by the child's own exertions. The two must cordially co-operate. The education of the child should begin with his life, and when, by the aid of others, he reaches that state in which he will make the best use of all his powers, he is prepared to carry on his education through life himself." *

Good teaching leads to good thinking. Is it reasonable to expect the great body of our teachers to become educational artists? "No, emphatically No," answers one of our ablest superintendents. "All that we can hope for is that the mass of our teachers will do their work passably well as directed by experts. It is consummate nonsense to expect the average teacher to learn psychology and the science of education." Is this the lesson of sixty centuries of human experience? Are the educators of the race doomed to be drudges? Must they forever grope their way? Must our teachers be mere artisans, toiling mechanically as directed by masters? It can not be. The twentieth century has great things in store for humanity. The teachers will work in the light of the thought and experience of the race. They will be as familiar with the mind-world and mind-growth as they are now with the plant-world and plant-growth; they will govern their pupils into self-government and guide them to self-guidance. Even now such teachers are becoming a mighty army. Good teaching is becoming the rule and not the exception.

Plain living conditions high thinking. Not many rich are called. Nearly all the leaders in the world of thought come from the ranks. Luxurious living makes profound thinking impossible. We commiserate the rich man, not Lazarus. Lotze and Ladd assure us that dismal failure awaits all attempts to even conceive of cerebral processes as correlated with thought-processes;

* Boyden.

but *somehow* good thinking and a good brain go together. The culture of the thought-powers, therefore, must be based on the art of right living.

Exploring the plant and animal worlds cultivates the thought-powers. Below the high school, botany and zoölogy are the very best science studies. The plan now pursued in many elementary schools of devoting the fall term to zoölogy, the two winter terms to geography, and the spring term to botany, gives admirable results. No better plan seems possible. These sciences ought to be given a large place in our schools because of their universal interest, the ease with which materials may be obtained, and the abundant opportunity for original observation, comparison, and thought. In all departments simple experiments and specimens should be studied, and not words. Only a little science should be given at any one lesson; technical terms must be avoided; scholars should be made to think with the teacher, and then by themselves under the guidance of the teacher. At first only the simplest illustrations should be used and the more common materials taken into consideration. The working teacher will manage to give easy lessons in physiology, physics, and chemistry, but will not permit these lessons to interfere with the work indicated above.

Simplifying the studies of children helps. "That education is the best, not which imparts the greatest amount of knowledge, but which develops the greatest amount of mental force. The mind must have leisure to work by itself on the materials supplied, otherwise the thinking faculties become paralyzed, and dead knowledge becomes a substitute for living. The mind becomes a passive recipient of knowledge, becomes incapable of making fresh combinations and discoveries. Cramming is the rapid acquisition of a great deal of knowledge ; education is mastering a small amount of knowledge. Cramming stultifies ; education develops thought-power." *

Thought-Lessons are Language-Lessons.—Words are not only the instruments for the expression of thought ; they are also the instruments of the thinking process. Human speech is the complement of human reason. No act of thinking is complete till its products have been set forth in words. Each lesson should be a lesson in language, because it is a lesson in thought.

"Every lesson, in all stages of learning, is given to awaken the self-activity of the child, to occasion thinking. It is only by questioning that we can determine whether the final step in the thinking process has been taken, since this step is the act of expression itself. If we are giving a simple object-lesson for the exercise of perception, we know that the child has got the idea and completed his act of thinking when he has the right word for the idea and can use it properly and promptly. If we give a lesson which demands the thinking of relations, we know that the act of thought has been performed when it is expressed in definite propositions. So, in all stages of intellectual development, the character of the mental product is shown in the character of the expression which we are able to elicit. The teacher must not be deceived by the earnest plea, 'I know, but I can not tell.' *Let the thing be clearly seen*, says Horace, *and the willing words will follow.* The un-

* T. G. Rooper.

doubted educational procedure, therefore, is : first the thought, then the oral expression of the thought, then the written expression of it.   Thus the interaction between thought and expression will finally result in the best thought possible to the mind in its presumed stage of growth." *

Apperceiving is thinking our Experiences into Unity. —Self inherits past experiences but unifies them.   The present and the past are *integrated*, and this integration is accomplished through discrimination, comparison, and selection.   This sort of bringing of things together into the object of a single judgment is of course essential to all thinking.   The things are conjoined in the mind ; the thinking them is thinking them together.†

"Apperception is that activity of synthesis by which mental data of every kind (sensations, percepts, concepts) are constructed into higher forms of relation.   It is the essential mental act in perception, conception, judgment.   *Apperception* singles out that act of mind which is common to them all—the relating activity of attention—and thus by its general application emphasizes the unity of the intellectual function as a whole.   Whenever by an act of attention mental data are unified into a related whole, this is an act of apperception ; and in its discriminating, selecting, and relating results, the concentration of attention is called . apperception." ‡ (*Study Apperceiving*, p. 89.)

* J. A. McLellan.   † William James.   ‡ J. Mark Baldwin.

PART IV.

EDUCATION OF THE EMOTIONS.

THE EMOTIONS.

Self-Emotions. (Egoistic.)

- Hope and Fear; Exultation and Despair, etc.
- Joy and Sorrow; Gayety and Depression, etc.
- Courage and Cowardice; Bravery and Timidity.
- Cheerfulness and Gloominess; Sprightliness, etc.
- Desire for { Life. Property. Power. Esteem. } Desire for { Knowledge. Beauty. Perfection. }
- Content and Discontent; Satisfaction and Regret; etc.
- Humility and Pride; Meekness and Vanity, etc.
- Etc., etc.

Social Emotions. (Altruistic.)

- Love and Hate; Friendship and Enmity, etc.
- Sympathy and Antipathy; Pity and Indifference, etc.
- Affection and Disaffection; Good-Will and Malice; Generosity and Envy, etc.
- Gratitude and Ingratitude; Philanthropy and Misanthropy, etc.
- Good-Humor and Anger; Mercy and Cruelty, etc.
- Honor and Shame; Equanimity and Confusion.
- Reverence and Scorn; Admiration and Contempt, etc.
- Etc., etc.

World-Emotions. (Cosmic.)

Truth-Emotions. (Intellectual.)
- Emotions of Curiosity.
- Emotions of Wonder.
- Emotions of Surprise.
- Knowledge-Emotions.

Beauty-Emotions. (Æsthetic.)
- Emotions of Beauty and Ugliness.
- Emotions of Humor and Pathos.
- Emotions of Sublimity and Insignificance.

Duty-Emotions. (Ethical.)
- Emotions of Right and Wrong.
- Emotions of Ought and Ought Not.
- Emotions of Approval and Remorse.
- Emotions of Merit and Demerit.
- Etc., etc.

PART FOURTH.

EDUCATION O.F THE EMOTIONS.

CHAPTER XVII.

THE EMOTIONS.

WE think; we also enjoy and suffer. We remember; we also *feel* pleasure and pain. We perceive; we also *feel* agitations and impulses. We gain knowledge; we also hunger and hope and love and desire. We call these agitations and impulses, enjoyments and sufferings, pains and pleasures, *feelings*. We know *something* and feel *somehow*. When feelings are occasioned by affections of the body they are termed *sensations*, but when they are occasioned by ideas they are termed *emotions*.

The Feelings. { Sensations. { Emotions.

Feeling, with its color-tone of pain and pleasure, enters into all conscious life. Feeling is an original mode of the operation of conscious mind. Self is *active* in feeling. Feelings are *occasioned*, and not caused. Sensor-excitations occasion sensations, sensations occasion ideas, and ideas occasion emotions. All feelings are characterized by tone, strength, rhythm, and content. *Tone* refers to the pleasure or pain of feelings. *Strength* refers to intensity of feelings: now love is gentle as evening breezes, now turbulent as the tornado. *Rhythm* refers to the time and form of feelings: anger

Characteristics of the Feelings. { Tone. Strength. Rhythm. Content.

rises and falls like the waves of the sea. *Content* refers to the activities occasioning feelings. The content may be simple, as when we behold a green surface; or complex, as when we are stirred by patriotism. No hard and fixed lines can be drawn about the different classes of feelings. In fact, a strict classification of the feelings from either the physiological or the psychological standpoint seems to be impossible.*

I. The Emotions are Feelings occasioned by Ideas.— The telegram announcing the return of your friend occasions your joy. In view of knowing, you feel. Your feelings occasioned by knowledge are called your intellectual feelings, your rational feelings, your spiritual feelings. These higher feelings are known as the emotions. Sensations are never thought of as emotions.

1. *An emotional power is a capability for a distinct kind of feeling.* I feel grateful to my friends; my native energy to feel grateful is called gratitude. I love my mother; my native energy to love is an emotional power, but loving is an emotional act. When we think of an emotion we include in the notion both the feeling and the power to feel; thus, when we think of anger, it means to us the capability to feel anger as well as the angry feeling. It is neither possible nor desirable to define strictly each one of our numerous emotions. We can, however, group our emotions and study these groups.

2. *The emotions may be grouped as self-emotions, social emotions, and world-emotions* *Self-emotions* are our personal feelings; *social emotions* are our feelings toward others;

The Emotions.
{
Self-Emotions.
(Egoistic.)
Social Emotions.
(Altruistic.)
World-Emotions.
(Cosmic.)
}

* Ladd.

world-emotions are our feelings in view of the true, the beautiful, and the good. This classification is easy and exhaustive, and is considered the best possible for educational purposes. We study with interest and profit the profound theories and complex classifications of Horwicz, Bain, Porter, and others, but we see no way to harmonize or practically apply these schemes. They hinder and do not help the teacher.

3. *Emotions are occasioned by ideas.* The term *ideas*, as here used, includes all our cognitions. Experiences, immediate and revived, awaken emotions. We speak of fond recollections as well as pleasant experiences. Ideals as well as ideas occasion pleasure and pain. Reasons occasion agitations and impulses. It is convenient, however, to designate as *ideas* whatever occasions emotions; sights and sounds are transmuted into ideas before they occasion hopes and fears.

Sensations.—These include all feelings which have their origin in the physical organism. The cravings of the appetites and the instinctive impulses appear as sensations. These are termed *animal* feelings, because they are common to man and brute; they are also called *physical* feelings, because of their physical origin. Some of these feelings are occasioned by affections of the special sensor-organs, and are termed *special* sensations; others are occasioned by affections of various organs and tissues of the body, and are termed *general* sensations. Sensations occasion ideas and ideas occasion emotions. (See Chapter II.)

II. **The Self-Emotions are Feelings occasioned by Ideas pertaining to Self.**—These are the emotions that minister to self and look to self-betterment. They are our native impulses to make the most of ourselves, and are referred to as the *personal* emotions, the *egoistic* emotions, the *self-emotions*. Ideas referring to self

awaken the self-emotions. Praise occasions joy, and
blame occasions sorrow.

III. **The Social Emotions are the Feelings occasioned
by Ideas pertaining to others.**—They are the feelings
which minister to others and look to social betterment;
they are our native energies to feel for and with others;
they are our impulses to do the most for our fellows.
These feelings are spoken of as the *social* emotions,
the *altruistic* emotions, the *sympathies*, the *affections*.
Ideas referring to others awaken altruistic emotions.
Kindness occasions gratitude and unkindness strife and
anger.

IV. **The World-Emotions are the Feelings occasioned
by Ideas pertaining to the True, the Beautiful, and the
Good.**—These are the emotions that minister to cosmic
life; they inspire us to mingle with the universe, become philosophers, artists, Christians. These are called
the *higher* emotions, the world-emotions, the *cosmic*
emotions. Ideas referring to the true, the beautiful,
and the good awaken these feelings, and hence they
are called the *truth*-emotions,

Cosmic { Truth-Emotions.
Emotions. { Beauty-Emotions. the *beauty*-emotions, and the
{ Duty-Emotions. *duty*-emotions. Emotions oc-

casioned by truth are termed truth-emotions; emotions
occasioned by beauty and humor are classed as beauty-
emotions; emotions occasioned by right and wrong are
called duty-emotions, ethical emotions, and emotions
of conscience. Conscience is self feeling duty-emotions,
as memory is self remembering; but we think of conscience as our capability to feel ethical emotions, and
we think of these feelings as emotions of conscience.
Thus conscience stands for our moral nature. Moral

education is the education of conscience, as æsthetic culture is the development of taste. Conscience is supreme in the emotion-world, as reason is in the intellectual world, and choice in the will-world. Conscience is the one imperative in the mental economy; its impulses are mandates.

V. Education of the Emotions.—When fostered, an emotion becomes refined and powerful. Power is developed by effort. Muscular power is developed by muscular effort, intellectual power by intellectual effort, and emotional power by emotional effort. The æsthetic emotions of the artist become refined and powerful because they are constantly cherished. An emotion repressed grows weaker; one who habitually represses his fiery temper acquires self-control. In educating our emotional nature we foster all ennobling impulses and repress all degrading feelings.

1. *Knowledge and emotion.* Emotion is occasioned by knowledge. Special emotions are occasioned by special kinds of knowledge. We feel because we know. Our emotions act in the light, and we reach the heart through the head. Even love not enlightened by intellect is blind and brutal. God is reason as well as love. Paul, the peerless logician, loved and cared for all the churches. In the presence of appropriate knowledge all our better emotions spring forth. We study to interest our pupils in such knowledge as will awaken and cherish the ennobling emotions.

2. *Educate the heart as well as the intellect.* Whenever we educate intellect at the expense of the heart we make a vital mistake, and we may expect our pupils to grow into cold, hard, matter-of-fact, unsympathetic, un-

15

æsthetic, and unethical men and women. We starve
the healthful and ennobling emotions in order to over-
feed the intellect; we defrand our pupils out of their
birthright to a world of love and beauty and duty. Education is the harmonious development of all our capabilities. The soul is endowed with emotions and will
as well as intellect. A person is educated when his
emotions and will and intellect are harmoniously developed. The educator seeks to develop and discipline
every energy of the soul, that the person may attain
the highest usefulness and happiness of which he is
capable.

Heart, as now used, stands for our emotional nature. In other
ages, and notably in Bible times, heart stood for the intellect, and,
like our term mind, was often used to include the entire self.
Bowels, as bowels of mercy, formerly stood for our emotional nature.

3. *Emotion-culture conditions intellectual culture.*
The intellectual emotions, including *interest in study,*
love of knowledge, the pleasure of discovering knowledge, the pleasure of pursuing knowledge, the pleasure
of detecting logical consistency, and the love of truth,
are tremendous forces in education! Well does Hamilton ask, "What can education accomplish without
an appeal to the feelings?" And then there are also
the various forms of the æsthetic sentiment and the
moral sentiment. How often does the instructor forget
to stimulate into activity these mighty forces in education, forgetting that all vigorous self-development of
the intellect is based on a large development of the
feelings!

4. *The true teacher faithfully roots the emotions into
good habits.* "While home, society, the state, and the

Church do much to mold the character of the young, there still remains a profound responsibility resting upon the teacher. After he limits the scope of his work by making due allowance for pre-natal influences and for what is necessarily done for the child by other agents, he still has an important function to perform, which grows out of the nature of his office and the continuity of the relation between him and his pupils. The molding influence of a good teacher upon the character of his pupils is beyond computation. The fundamental virtues of civil society—regularity, punctuality, silence, obedience, industry, truthfulness, and justice—are developed and impressed in a good school as nowhere else. Here the child learns to be regular in his attendance, punctual in the beginning and the ending of every duty, silent when others should speak, obedient to the rightfully constituted authority, industrious in the discharge of the duty lying next, truthful in the scope and the details of whatever he undertakes to tell, and scrupulously just in allowing others what of right belongs to them. From a man who habitually practices all these virtues what more need be demanded? And these are preeminently school virtues. These it is the business of the teacher more than of any other agent to create. Their constant practice in school is essential to his own success and that of his pupils." *

5. *Self-control is paramount in education.* Submission of the emotions to reason is essential in character-building. We foster and carry over into action all ennobling impulses, but we repress and restrain our wayward feelings. We cherish and strengthen gener-

* Larkin Dunton.

osity, but stifle envy. Education of the emotions is
subjugating them to reason. We strengthen helpful
feelings by holding in mind the ideas which occasion
them, but we weaken hurtful impulses by refusing to
entertain the ideas which give rise to such feelings.
Emotional education is developing self-control. It includes the *repression* of noxious feelings, as well as the
development of elevating emotions. In the culture of
our emotional nature we suppress hurtful feelings, just
as we suppress hurtful weeds in vegetable culture. We
repress and restrain our lawless impulses, while we cherish our ennobling emotions.

CHAPTER XVIII.

EDUCATION OF THE SELF-EMOTIONS.

By this is meant the development of the feelings
that make for self-betterment. Infinite Wisdom has
planted deep in every human heart the desire for perfection. Each one feels burning impulses to excel,
and to make the most of himself. The individual is
cardinal in the mind-world. Society is at its best when
it does the most for its individual members. A person,
a *self*, is our highest possible conception. Great men
and women are the bright stars in the firmament of
history. Education does most when it makes the most
out of *individuals*, and gives the world its Platos and its
Dantes and its Washingtons and its Wesleys.

I. **Relations of Self-Emotions and Definitions.**—The
emotions stand midway between intellect and will.

Because we feel impulses to act, our emotions are called our *motive* powers. Self as intellect *knows*, self as emotion *desires*, self as will *does*.

Relations.—Few realize the importance of the egoistic emotions in the mental economy. Teachers and parents need to study profoundly the child as an emotional being. (*In cut, p. 2, point out the position of the self-emotions. In diagram, p. 229, give the self-emotions named, and mention others.*)

1. *Relations to the appetites.* The egoistic emotions should dominate the appetites. The brute is dominated by its appetites, and lives to eat. The man should dominate his appetites, and eat to live. The appetites are animal cravings, which appear to us as organic sensations, and which look to the well-being of the body. Instinct guides the brute in the gratification of its appetites, but a man controls his appetites, subjecting them to law. We desire to make our bodies the best possible *servants* of self, and not the *masters*.

2. *Relations of the egoistic emotions to intellect.* Feelings not illuminated by intelligence are blind and brutal. Emotions are occasioned by ideas. We *feel* because we *know*. Intellect is the eye of emotion. As intellect, self finds out the laws of our physical and mental economy, and as egoistic emotion desires to obey these laws.

3. *Relation of the self-emotions to will.* Will is the effort-making power of self. We *know*, we *feel*, we *will*. Ideas pass over into emotions and emotions pass over into determinations and acts. Our desires for self-betterment lead us to so choose and act as to make the most of ourselves.

Definitions.—It is difficult to define our feelings. We all know what joy is because we experience it; but to tell what it is gives us pause. In order to define a feeling it is necessary to translate it into terms of knowing. It is doubtless best to think the emotions into groups, and to form clear notions of these groups.

1. *The egoistic emotions are our native energies* to feel in view of everything affecting ourselves. Love of life is egoistic. Self-love is the standard. The command is, " Love your neighbor as yourself."

2. *The self-emotions are the feelings occasioned by ideas affecting self.* I desire knowledge: this feeling is a self-emotion. Desire expresses both the feeling and the capability to desire.

3. *Education of the egoistic emotions is the development of the feelings that make for self-betterment.* The repression of all hurtful self-emotions is implied. We cultivate cheerfulness and repress despondency. We thus educate our emotional nature and gain self-control.

II. **Importance of educating Self-Emotions.**—That ideas may grow into character they must pass over into emotions and become resolves and acts. Right emotions are as important as right thinking.

1. *Culture of self-emotions leads to the formation of desirable habits.* Hopefulness, cheerfulness, courage, and all elevating egoistic desires, when fostered, grow into right habits. The culture of the self-emotions fosters sweetness of disposition and all noble aspirations, and likewise represses and restrains lawless impulses.

2. *Educated egoistic emotions dominate the appe-tites.* The body is the organism through which self

works. The appetites are cravings for bodily needs, and must be so satisfied as to make the body the best possible instrument of the mind. Early and always a self must control his body with its appetites.

3. *The culture of the self-emotions helps to make life worth living.* Our aims in life become exalted. The desire for excellency inspires the best efforts, and lifts one above the low and beastly. A grand life is always worth living. The joys of such a life are almost infinitely greater than the beastly pleasures of one who lives to eat and drink and dance.

III. **Growth of the Personal Emotions.**—Sensations make up a large part of child-life. The appetites are autocratic. Of all the feelings occasioned by ideas the self-emotions earliest become active. Study the child. You find that most of the egoistic emotions are active before the sixth year. Some of these feelings, such as the desire for perfection, become active later. These emotions are all very active before the fourteenth year, but some, such as hope and courage and patience, go on developing through life. The early activity of the egoistic emotions indicates the importance of the early culture of these feelings. Even in childhood these emotions must be so strengthened as to control the appetites.

IV. **Laws of Self-Emotion-Culture.**—Many teachers go on from year to year without analyzing the emotions. Their notions about the feelings are vague and shadowy. To such teachers culture of moonshine has as much meaning as culture of the emotions. Long and careful study of the emotion-world leads to the discovery of laws relating to the development of the emotions. The

teacher profoundly studies these, and labors to acquire
skill in their application.

1. *Calling the egoistic emotions into constant, vigorous, and lawful activity educates these feelings.* The
habit of feeling cheerful and hopeful develops cheerfulness and hope. An emotion grows strong when
cherished, and becomes feeble when repressed.

2. *Egoistic knowledge tends to develop the egoistic
emotions.* Biography and history lead one to contemplate self in others. The study of the superiority and
achievements of great men and women calls our self-
emotions into vigorous activity. Egoistic literature
fosters the desire to make the most of self.

3. *Carrying egoistic emotions over into acts tends
to educate these feelings.* Emotions not carried into
acts are wasted. Our emotions become strong when
they habitually become resolves and acts. We stifle
wrong feelings by refusing to act on them.

V. **Means of Self-Emotion-Culture.**—Emotions are occasioned by ideas. Judicious praise as a means of self-
emotion-culture is placed first, and wise reproof next.
Judicious praise fosters the ennobling emotions. Wise
reproof checks unwholesome and egotistic feelings.
Good companionship is of great value. Personal literature deserves a high place, and biography easily stands
highest; history comes next, and then come the best
works of fiction. Good family and school government
ranks highest. Whatever is calculated to work in us
high resolves may become a means for the culture of
the self-emotions.

VI. **Methods of educating the Self-Emotions.**—These
are plans of work that foster the helpful and repress the

hurtful self-emotions. What do we want to do? We
wish to cherish self-respect and all ennobling self-emotions, and likewise restrain all wayward impulses. We
seek to cherish all feelings that look to self-betterment,
and repress emotions that minister to self-degradation.
We stimulate hope and courage, and repress fear and
cowardice; we cherish good-humor and cheerfulness,
and repress sourness and melancholy; we foster the
desire for self-betterment, and stifle low and sinful
desires; we cherish true self-love, and repress egotism
and selfishness. How can we best do this?

Kindergarten and Primary Methods.—We spare no
efforts to improve our methods of intellectual culture,
but we scarcely even think of methods of emotion-
culture. Yet who will say that heart-culture is less
important than intellectual culture?

1. *Mother influence.* As the self-emotion twig is
bent, so the self-emotion tree inclines. Here the work
of mothers and kindergartners is of the highest importance. In fostering desires for proper food and drink
to satisfy natural appetites, in cherishing budding self-
respect, in stimulating cheerfulness and courage and
hopefulness and all uplifting desires, and in repressing
all hurtful self-emotions, the mother and the kindergartner do untold good and avert incalculable evil.

2. *Favoring environments.* As we place fine plants
and animals under the most favorable influences, so we
ought to do with the children. Favorable surroundings,
loving treatment, kind words, cheerfulness, and pleasant
employment work wonders. But the primary teacher
must do the best for her pupils, however faulty their
previous treatment. As a diseased body may be re-

stored to health, so a deformed soul may be educated
into harmony.

3. *Develop self-respect.* Show the pupil that you
respect him. Train the children to show respect for
each other. Your hearty approbation and judicious
praise will produce marvelous results. The desire to
be worthy, and the hope to merit your loving approval,
greatly stimulate self-respect.

4. *Develop a good disposition.* Hopefulness, cheerfulness, good-nature, sweetness, patience, contentment,
joyousness, enter into such a disposition. As you promote the development of these emotions you form in
the child a good disposition. Embody these excellences
in yourself, and they will appear in all your acts and
words and tones. Your example will prove magical.
You will be able to win back to health the most dis-
torted and ugly dispositions, as well as greatly improve
dispositions already good.

Intermediate Methods.—The egoistic emotions are
highly active in boys and girls, and require the most
careful direction. Many details here are not needed.
You will use a wise discretion, and so do the best you
can. Above all, you will deal directly with each pupil,
and try to make the most of each one.

1. *Develop high ideals.* In manhood we work out
the plans and work up to the ideals that pleased our
youthful fancies. How important, then, that these
plans and ideals should be worthy! At this period
boundless possibilities seem within easy reach. Wild
fancies hold sway. Ideals are likely to be low and sensual. If not elevated, they are likely to be realized in
depraved and vicious men and women. It requires the

utmost skill of the wisest educators to save the boys and girls, and to lift them up to a higher life. Leading pupils to see how ugly and unworthy these sensual and low ideals are does much to remove the rubbish and prepare the way for better ideals. Studying the lives of noble men and women stimulates our desires for superiority and greatly elevates our ideals. We need to give the young concrete lessons and line upon line. When each one is led to create for himself a worthy ideal of life, a life full of hope and courage and cheerfulness and patience and high desires and noble achievements, a foundation is laid for a grand life.

2. *So teach as to foster manliness.* Lead the pupil to conquer for himself. Each victory strengthens hope, self-satisfaction, patience, courage, and the desire for mastery. Pupils thus taught become manly and self-reliant, and grow into admirable men and women. Pupils improperly taught lack manliness. They are bullied and belittled for not doing impossibilities. Every recitation is an hour of defeat and humiliation. They become discouraged and despondent. They lose self-respect and courage and manliness. They become hopeless, dependent, incapable of effort; and they grow into gloomy, sour, dissatisfied, inefficient men and women.

3. *So govern as to rightly educate the self-emotions.* Lead the pupil to govern himself. Now his duty-emotions are active, and he can be led to do right. Now his affections are also active, and he may be led by sympathy. Pupils thus governed are orderly, industrious, cheerful, joyous, sweet, good-natured, manly. Bad government mars. Fear takes the place of hope; force, of

affection; blame, of praise; cruelty, of kindness. Pupils are driven, not led. Such government tends to foster every hateful feeling; instead of a burning desire for knowledge, hatred for forced study is created. Pupils thus governed tend to become everything undesirable; disorderly, ugly, morose, sour, cowardly, unmanly.

High-School Methods.—Youth is the trying time of life. The destinies of the many, for weal or woe, depend on self-control during this period. The feelings now become passions, and, like floods, when uncontrolled sweep to ruin. The educator relies largely on the egoistic emotions to carry the youth safely through this critical period.

1. *Stimulate the desire for perfection.* We are placed in a universe where law reigns. Our highest desire is, *perfection through law.* We desire physical perfection through conformity to physical laws. We desire mental perfection through conformity to the laws of mental growth. We desire moral perfection through conformity to ethical laws. Creative Wisdom drafts the plan of each life, and each one is endowed with a burning desire to carry out this plan by making the most of himself. The imperative *"be perfect"* throbs in every fiber of the human heart. The youth creates a high ideal of a grand manhood. This becomes his working model in building his character. Appetites and passions, like steam and electricity, must be so controlled as to make and not mar. Every low impulse must be stifled, and every noble impulse cherished. The burning desire to know the most and be the most and do the most inspires the youth to subjugate his wayward impulses.

2. *Foster the desire for knowledge.* Kindle in the hearts of the young an insatiable thirst for knowledge. Lead.them to realize that an hour with Plato or Shakespeare is better than years of giddy pleasure. Man is sometimes called the knowledge-seeking animal. The brute feels no desire for truth; it simply gratifies its appetites and is content. Man desires truth, and counts wisdom the most precious of all things. His appetites are merely his law-abiding servants. Happy the youth that hungers and thirsts for truth!

3. *Cherish a desire for beauty.* The universe is full of beauty, and we are endowed· with strong desires to enjoy it, to produce it, to be it. Beauty of form, beauty of motion, beauty of color, beauty of sound, beauty of sentiment, beauty of character; sublimity, humor, beauty; whatever guise it takes beauty tends to lift us up. Truth and beauty are twin-sisters, and co-workers to refine and elevate.

4. *Encourage the study of personal literature.* Biography does most to strengthen personal emotions. History as now written does almost as much as biography to educate the self-emotions. The best fiction exerts a powerful influence in this direction. Personal essays are of value. Such literature arouses the egoistic emotions and stimulates the desire to do what others have done and be what others have become. The youth becomes saturated with the cumulative lessons that noble manhood and high success come through self-denial, self-control, uprightness, earnestness, and perseverance.

Lead the youth to look well to the outcome of life. The fool blindly rushes on to ruin. These human wrecks that strew the pathway of time were victims of

uncontrolled appetites and passions. They are the dan-
ger-signals. Fortunate the youth who heeds these
warnings, and refuses to tread the path of folly and
death!

VII. **Mistakes in the Treatment of the Personal Emotions:**

1. *Neglect.* Few really understand the mighty influence of the egoistic emotions in the mental economy.
Rarely does the teacher even attempt the systematic
culture of courage and cheerfulness, and the desire for
self-betterment.

2. *Mistakes in government.* Appeal to fear is all
too common. The pupil is treated more as a machine
than as a self-determining person. Such management
is the worst possible preparation for life.

3. *Injudicious praise.* Egotism and selfishness come
of misdirected self-emotions. Flattery fosters these de-
formities. Judicious praise is the pure balmy air, but
flattery is the fatal sirocco.

4. *Demeaning.* The pupil is called a blockhead.
Such belittling epithets as take away all self-respect are
used unsparingly. This is monstrous. It is a great
thing in education to lead the pupil to think well of
himself, and inspire him with confidence and courage
and the desire to excel.

SUGGESTIVE STUDY-HINTS.

Self enjoys as well as knows. What terms designate our abilities
to enjoy and suffer? What does the heart stand for?

Letter.—Tell your friend about the heart-world. Make for him
a diagram of the emotions. Give him your best thoughts about the
culture of the egoistic emotions:

1. **Position of the Self-Emotions and Terms defined.**—Point out

the relations between ideas and emotions and between emotions and resolves. Define the emotions; the egoistic emotions; education of these feelings. Show the relations of the egoistic emotions to the appetites; to the intellect; to the will.

2. **Importance of Self-Emotion Culture.**—Why do you count emotion-culture important? Is intellectual-culture more important? Show that culture of self-emotions tends to good habits. Ought the egoistic emotions to dominate the appetites? Why do you consider the culture of the egoistic desires highly important?

3. **Growth of the Self-Emotions.**—What feelings are autocratic in childhood? How early do you find the self-emotions active in children? Before what year do these feelings become very active? What reasons can you give for the early culture of the self-emotions?

4. **Laws of Self-Emotion Culture.**—Does law reign in the emotion-world? State the law of effort in terms of self-emotion culture; law of means; law of methods; law of action. Mention a special law that you have discovered. What do you mean by education and culture as applied to the emotions?

5. **Means of Self-Emotion Culture.**—Why do you place judicious praise first? Which do you estimate of highest value for the culture of the egoistic emotions, good companionship or personal literature? Do you find history more helpful than biography? Give your estimate of the value of fiction in the culture of the self-emotions; of good school government.

6. **Methods of educating Self-Emotions.**—How do we educate self-emotions? What self-emotions do we cherish? What self-emotions should we repress? Is heart-culture less important than intellectual culture? What do you mean by kindergarten methods of educating the self-emotions? by primary methods? by intermediate methods? by high-school methods? State and explain four directions for primary work; four for intermediate work; four for high-school work.

7. **Mistakes in educating Self-Emotions.**—Are these mistakes vital? Why is self-emotion culture neglected? What mistakes are made in government? Explain the danger of injudicious praise; of demeaning the pupil. Why should pupils be led to think well of themselves? Mention some of the mistakes that you have noticed.

CHAPTER XIX.

EDUCATION OF THE SOCIAL EMOTIONS.

By this is meant the right culture of our feeling for others. Our capabilities to feel in view of ideas pertaining to others are our altruistic emotional powers, and these feelings are altruistic emotions. These emotions are called fellow-feelings, social emotions, affections, and altruistic emotions. All our emotional endowments are God-given capabilities, and their lawful activities are God-approved. But intelligence underlies the rational emotions, guiding these and restraining those. Feelings not thus guided are blind and brutal. Restraint is as essential as stimulus in emotional culture. We cherish love and restrain hate; foster kindness and stifle cruelty; praise generosity and disparage envy. The child thus educated grows more and more lovely.

I. **Importance of educating the Altruistic Emotions.—** Man is pre-eminently a social being. Culture of the social emotions does most to elevate human society. Savages are egoistic; Christians are altruistic. Altruistic-culture immeasurably increases human happiness. Each one becomes his brother's keeper, and is happy because he seeks to make others happy. Altruistic-culture makes for the brotherhood of man, and fits man for the companionship of angels.

II. **Growth of the Altruistic Emotions.—** In comparison with the appetites and the egoistic emotions the altruistic emotions are feeble in childhood. Quite early, however, the child manifests in some degree sympathy, jealousy, emulation, affection. Sympathy first appears as a feeling of pity or commiseration for others.   The pains first sympathized with are of course the familiar bodily feelings, such as cold, fatigue, injury, together with the simple emotional states, as fear and disappointment.   A very young child will show unmistakably the signs of dejection and sorrow at the actual sight or narration of another child's sufferings; and the lower animals, with their simple, easily apprehended emotional experiences, come in for a considerable share of this early pity.   Affection appears first in response to mother-love.   Up to the tenth year the child is largely a being of sensations, appetites, and self-emotions.   The social emotions become quite active during boyhood and girlhood.   After the fourteenth year the altruistic emotions begin to dominate, and are fully active by the eighteenth year.   From ten to eighteen is pre-eminently the period for the culture of the social emotions.

III. **Laws of Altruistic-Emotion Growth.**—Most persons go on from year to year in a hap-hazard way, entertaining the most misty notions of the emotions and their culture.   But to the thoughtful such culture seems of the highest value.   Here, as everywhere, law reigns. To educate the social emotions we must find out and observe their laws of growth.

1. *General laws.*   The great educational laws must be restated in terms of the altruistic emotions.   (1) *Law of effort.*—Well-directed efforts in cherishing the benevolent and repressing the malevolent emotions educate these feelings.   (2) *Law of means.*—Altruistic knowing, feeling, and doing are means of altruistic-culture.   (3) *Law of method.*—Systematic, lawful, and persistent plans of work which foster all right feelings

16

and repress all malevolent impulses educate the altruistic emotions.

2. *Special laws.* Each group of human capabilities has its own peculiar laws of growth which educators find out and observe. Attention is called to two important laws looking to the culture of the social emotions : (1) Feeling for and with others develops altruistic emotions. Cherishing all kindly feelings renders one warm-hearted and unselfish. (2) Doing kind acts educates the altruistic emotions. How the mother learns to love her helpless child! How the teacher learns to love her needy pupils!

IV. **Means of educating the Altruistic Emotions.**— We feel kindly emotions in view of ideas pertaining to others. Whatever tends to call forth such feelings may become a means of altruistic-culture : (1) *Favorable environments* call forth kindly emotions and suppress malevolent feelings. (2) *Kind companions* do most, as love begets love. Cruel companions arouse all hateful emotions and give us our street *gamins.* (3) *Altruistic literature* is invaluable in the education of the social emotions. Such books as George MacDonald's works can hardly be prized too highly. The New Testament is the one perfect book for altruistic-culture. (4) *Altruistic doing* gives the highest culture to these feelings. Habitually doing kind deeds develops all kindly feelings.

V. **Methods of educating the Altruistic Emotions.**— Systematically and persistently putting forth kindly feelings educates these emotions. This we can not do by simply willing it, any more than we can call back past experiences by an act of will. But we can command the ideas that occasion altruistic emotions, and hence can systematically and persistently arouse these feelings. Well-matured plans of work are essential in the art of promoting character growth.

Kindergarten and Primary Methods.—From infancy to age all kindly feelings need to be cherished and all unlovely emotions repressed. The utmost skill is needed in the management of little ones.

1. *Environments.* Throw around the child the most favorable social influences. Surroundings do much to make children kind and generous or cruel and selfish. Anna has enjoyed from infancy kindly influences—a kind mother, kind teachers, and kind companions; now she is an unselfish, kind, lovely girl. Her brother John, almost from infancy, has lived in the streets, surrounded by all vile influences, and is now a selfish, cruel, repulsive boy. Blessed is the child that grows up in the atmosphere of love!

2. *Management.* Wise management educates the altruistic emotions. The rule of love develops love. Kind treatment awakens all kindly feelings. Provoke not the child to anger. Avoid arousing hateful feelings.

3. *Manners and Morals.* Concrete lessons in manners and morals cultivate the altruistic emotions. Indeed, the enduring foundations of noble characters must thus be laid. The teacher finds here a rich and boundless field for altruistic-culture.

4. *Doing.* Deeds of kindness develop social feelings. Little acts of kindness on the part of the child develop the kindly feelings. Parents and teachers can so manage that the child will continually feel the im-

pulse to give kind looks, speak kind words, and do kind acts.

Intermediate Methods.—The waywardness of boys and girls is proverbial. During the period of transition from childhood to youth the social emotions need to be carefully cherished in order that they may dominate the appetites and selfish impulses.

1. *Kind treatment is always salutary.* But boys and girls must not be babied. The manly and womanly feeling now becoming active must be respected. As the instrument responds to the touch of the musician, so the hearts of the boys and girls respond to kind treatment.

2. *Altruistic literature is exceedingly helpful.* The men and women who live in the hearts of the millions are those who love their fellow-men. The best literature is altruistic. Such works as MacDonald's *Sir Gibbie*, Mrs. Ewing's *Story of a Short Life*, Dickens's *David Copperfield*, and Holland's *Nicholas Minturn* help wonderfully. The New Testament will always take the first place in the culture of the affections.

3. Life-lessons in manners and morals enter into the fiber of altruistic-emotion culture. In character-building these lessons need to enter into the warp and woof of thought and emotion. Kindly emotions are thus rooted into habits. Boys and girls become *gentlemen* and *gentlewomen*.

4. *Habitual deeds of kindness immensely strengthen the altruistic emotions.* Kind looks, kind words, and kind deeds that flow from kind hearts make the heart doubly kind. Kindly feelings that do not become kindly acts are wasted.

High-School Methods.—Youth is the danger period. Most offenders go astray while in their teens. Appetites and emotions become seething passions, and when uncontrolled lead to vice and crime. The pathway of life is strewn with youthful wrecks, who haunt the saloons, the gambling-dens, and the house of infamy, and who mingle in society but to corrupt and blast. The danger is appalling, but the very vehemence of youthful emotion may prove the anchor of safety.

1. *Right thinking occasions right feelings.* We educate our altruistic emotions when we think lovingly of others. How bounteous are the blessings showered upon us by our fellows, our country, and our God! These thoughts arouse within us all kindly and generous impulses. The educator puts forth his best efforts to lead generous, impressible youth in these lovely altruistic paths.

2. *Carrying altruistic emotion over into altruistic doing develops all generous feelings.* The good Samaritan carried his noble sympathies over into deeds of kindness. Jesus wept, but at the same time he called back the dead Lazarus to comfort the weeping sisters. To suffer our kindly impulses to dissipate unacted, is to squander these precious feelings and neglect great opportunities.

3. *Enlisting all our powers in the service of a noble love educates the social emotions.* " Love is the climax of the feelings, and it should comprehend all the interests and command all the powers of the mind. To do this, the objects of its devotion must be able to unite all the discriminations of the mind in harmony, and elicit all its active powers. Love of God, love of humanity,

love of country, love of children, has led to the development of the noblest lives. But when mere pleasure
becomes the end of love, it corrupts all the other powers,
and the pleasure itself at last will pall. To be worthy
to stand at the head of the feelings, love should be prepared to undertake all duties and endure all sufferings.
Attachment to anything seems a slight affair at first,
but experience reveals the deeper truth in time." *

4. *Love needs cultivation to be at its best.* Love does
not reach its best by being left to itself. It reaches its
best only by persistent culture. Youthful love is a feeble
sentiment and merely a germ of matured love. If a
love is not worthy, it were better to neglect it, and so
let it die; but if it be a worthy love, it ought to be
cherished and cultivated, that it may become the most
enobling. It is the same with love for God as with
love for our fellows ; we can not love God as we ought
unless we cultivate our love for him.

VI. **Treatment of the Unkindly Emotions.**—The thoughtful parent
and the wise teacher will here make a solemn pause. What must be
done with this host of dreadful emotions — anger, envy, jealousy,
hate, enmity, malice, antipathy, blasphemy, scorn, cruelty, ingratitude, contempt, revenge ? Unrestrained, these feelings make for
harm. They hurt, and do not help. They are malevolent emotions,
which tend to bitterness, strife, revenge, rivalry, murder, war. They
fill all lands with wails of woe. No panacea for the treatment of
these dangerous emotions can be given, but parents and teachers
and society can do much to alleviate the evils. Each one can learn
to restrain these feelings :

1. *Avoid their excitation.* " Parents, provoke not your children
to anger." Study how not to arouse hateful feelings. When continually excited these feelings grow into hateful passions ; but when
not excited they become feeble by non-use.

* G. H. Palmer.

2. *Repress malevolent emotions.* We cherish kindly feelings but repress unkindly emotions. We smother anger as we do devouring flames. We stifle malice and envy, and cruelty and selfishness. We discourage in every way all hateful feelings, and thus repress and weaken them.

3. *Restrain hateful emotions from becoming hateful acts.* These feelings have a remarkable tendency to become acts, and thus multiply their intensity. Cain's anger became angry words and murder. We can not always avoid these evil emotions, but we can restrain them from becoming acts. Every such act of restraint is a victory that tends to weaken as well as curb hurtful feelings.

4. *Overcome hate by love.* We have a thousand reasons for loving where we have one for hating. Think of these and read of these. By cherishing all kindly feelings we overcome hateful impulses.

VII. **Mistakes in educating the Altruistic Emotions.—** Human well-being is promoted by the culture of these feelings. Neglects and blunders here cause deepest woe, and human history tells the tale.

1. *Neglect.* Men explore dark continents, but fail to explore the human heart. We take infinite pains to educate reason, while we suffer the noxious weeds of hateful emotions to grow luxuriantly and smother out love. Surely the culture of the affections is not less important than the culture of the intellect.

2. *Misdirection.* Even love is degraded by becoming a slave to appetite. Thus the most ennobling emotion becomes a dangerous egoistic passion. Our affections are most precious, and deserve to be so directed as to work the noblest ends.

3. *Waste.* Your sympathies do not lead you to action. You sympathize with Lazarus, but leave the dogs to lick his sores. Altruistic emotions which do not in some way become resolves and acts are squandered.

4. *Reading too much emotional literature.* Many thus waste their sweetness on the desert air, and become poor indeed in real sympathy. Expect not kindness from the constant reader of emotional literature. One who lives in an imaginary world and finds no pleasure in relieving real suffering ceases to be a practical philanthropist. Whenever and wherever you feel kindly impulses, see to it that these emotions become generous resolves and deeds of kindness.

SUGGESTIVE STUDY-HINTS.

Letter. The social emotions and their culture is a fruitful theme. Nowhere do we approach closer to the source of human happiness. You can write a thoughtful, earnest letter to your friend. The culture of the social emotions demands our best efforts.

I. Give your definition of the altruistic emotions; of the culture of these feelings. Is sympathy developed among brutes? Are savages altruistic? How does altruistic-culture make for human happiness? Give three reasons for the culture of the social emotions.

II. What feelings are most active in childhood? What social emotions become active earliest? Trace the growth of sympathy. Describe the growth of the altruistic emotions during boyhood; during youth.

III. State in terms of altruistic emotion the law of *effort;* law of *means;* law of *method;* law of *sympathy;* law of *doing.* Tell about a special law relating to altruistic-culture that you have discovered.

IV. What do you consider the best means for altruistic culture? Give your estimate for this purpose of environments; of companionship; of altruistic literature: of altruistic doing. What book do you place highest? Mention other valuable works.

V. What do you mean by methods of educating the social emotions? by Kindergarten methods? by primary methods? by high-school methods? Give some directions for the culture of the social emotions during childhood; during boyhood; during youth.

VI. How should we treat the unkindly emotions? Why should

we avoid exciting these feelings? What are the effects of repressing these emotions? Why should we restrain hateful emotions from becoming hateful acts?

VII. Why do teachers neglect altruistic-culture? Do you consider the education of the social emotions as important as the education of memory? Show some of the ways in which our social feelings are misdirected and wasted. Why do excessive novel-readers become hard-hearted? State some of the mistakes that you have noted in altruistic-culture.

CHAPTER XX.

EDUCATION OF THE TRUTH-EMOTIONS.

THE student is in love with truth. When we speak of the true, the beautiful, and the good, we mean by *the true* the realm of knowledge. Truth is agreement with reality—as true biography, true history, true science. Wisdom is philosophic truth. The wise man discerns the deeper truths of life and walks

Truth-Emotions.
{
Wonder.
Curiosity.
Desire for truth.
Love of truth.
Etc., etc.
}

in the paths of wisdom. The fool, though learned, despises wisdom and walks in the paths of folly. Culture of the truth-emotions is the development of the love of truth. The delights we feel in view of truth are our truth-emotions. We feel joy when we solve the hard problem, for the answer is true. Every step upward is a delight, for it is the mastery of a new truth. We hate the false, and love the true. We desire the true, and feel disgust for all shams and pretenses and falsehoods.

I. **Relations of the Truth-Emotions.**—So strikingly

are these feelings related to knowing, that they are sometimes called the intellectual emotions.

1. *The truth-idea is intuitive.* By direct insight we gain the truth-idea. We stand face to face with the true as with all necessary realities. We gain the truth-idea just as we gain the space-idea and the time-idea and the cause-idea. Before I can say that this or that statement is true, I must have the truth-idea.*

2. *Discernment of truth occasions truth-emotions.* We are so constituted that discovering truth and contemplating truth and using truth give us high delight. Open-eyed wonder, intense curiosity, joy of discovery and conquest, desire for knowledge, love of truth, spur us on from infancy to age.

3. *The truth - emotions are feelings occasioned by truths discerned.* Emotions are feelings occasioned by ideas. The peculiar emotions we experience in the presence of truth are termed the truth-emotions. The child explores the wonder-world of matter; the youth explores the wonder-world of mind; the man explores the wonder-world of philosophy ; the immortal explores the wonder-worlds of God's wisdom. The boundless delights occasioned by new discoveries are truth-emotions.

4. *Education of the truth-emotions is the development of the love of truth.* Truth is more precious than diadems, for it is the food of the soul. We do most for others when we lead them to love the truth. This is cardinal in education, and must determine matter as well as method.

II. **Importance of educating the Truth - Emotions.**— The most despicable of all characters is the man who

* See pp. 36 and 80.

"loveth and maketh a lie." " You are a liar" is counted
the greatest possible insult.   We class the slanderer
with the murderer.

1. *The love of truth characterizes the noble man.*
Compare Washington and Napoleon.   A truthful man
is the noblest work of God.   From infancy up the love
of the true and the hatred of the false must be in-
grained.

2. *The love of truth characterizes the science-maker.*
He earnestly seeks to know the truth, the whole truth,
and nothing but the truth.   All misleading theories, all
bias, all lies and half-truths, are torn away.   He seeks to
stand face to face with realities, and find out truth.

3. *The love of truth is the fountain of perpetual
youth.*   The joy of finding new truths keeps the soul
forever young.   This is the pleasure that never cloys.
There is an ever-increasing joy in beholding new truths.
The pleasures of exploring an infinite universe, when a
billion years have passed, will be but a beginning of the
joys in store for those who love truth.

4. *The love of truth exalts and ennobles.*   It leads
us to think the thoughts of God after him.   It rewards
us as we ascend higher and higher.   Think of the joys
of Newton, when he discovered the laws of gravitation;
of Copernicus, when he discerned the true theory of the
solar system ; of Franklin, when he found out the identity of electricity and lightning.   Love of truth gives
surcease from sorrow.

III. **Time to educate the Truth - Emotions.**—How
early the child feels these emotions can only be con-
jectured.   It is certain that very early the child suffers
when deceived.   Equally early it must enjoy in some

degree truthfulness. But truth-emotion is feeble in childhood. Still, the joy of discovering new truths early fills the cup of the young. In these early years the truth-habit must be developed. As the years multiply the love of truth deepens, and the philosopher feels a boundless pleasure as new and grand truths burst upon him. Clearly, these emotions need to be cultivated from infancy to age.

IV. **Laws of Truth-Emotion Culture.**—Reasoning educates reason, and enjoying truth educates truth-emotions. 1. *Cherishing truth-emotions develops these feelings.* We lead pupils to feel joy in the presence of truth, and pain in the presence of the false. 2. Whatever calls the truth-emotions into vigorous activity may become a means for educating these feelings. All studies may be made the means of cultivating the truth-emotions. 3. Systematic and persistent plans of work that call the truth-emotions into vigorous activity tend to develop these powers. 4. *The habit of truthfulness fosters the truth-emotions.* Truth becomes precious, and falsehood hateful.

V. **Means for educating the Truth-Emotions.**—The truth-element is coextensive with intelligence. Cognition is finding truth. Truth-ideas occasion truth-emotion. Truth in nature, in science, in history, in everyday life, may be made the means of educating these emotions. Character-building is the best means for this culture. The Bible, the wonderful gallery of characters true to the life, is incomparably the best means for cultivating the truth-emotions.

VI. **Methods of educating the Truth-Emotions.**—Leading the child or youth to systematically and persistently seek truth for the love of truth and the enjoyment of truth educates the truth-emotions.

1. *So teach as to develop a love of knowledge.*   Naturally, the appetency for knowledge is keener than the appetite for food.   How often you have seen a child leave its food untasted to listen to a story or to see the passing show!   Pupils wisely taught, hunger and thirst for knowledge.   No grades, or examinations, or threats, or punishments are needed to spur them on.

· 2. *Cherish the pleasure of discovering truth.*   You remember the story of Archimedes.   So teach, that your pupils every hour may feel like crying "Eureka!"   This is the charm of the Socratic method.   This is the characteristic of good teaching.

3. *Cherish truth-telling.*   Telling lies is cowardly and base and hateful.   The pupil should be led to loathe falsehood, and turn from it as from carrion.   Truth-telling is brave and manly and lovely; it should be rooted into habit.   The best boys and girls and men and women are truthful.   Every day you can press this lesson home.   Our school readers furnish cases.   Our literature is replete with examples.   Do you sincerely love truth?   You will find ways to cherish the truth-habit.

4. *Foster truth-doing.*   Christ said, " I am the truth."   The martyr cries, " I can die, but I can not deceive."   Paul, the chained prisoner, " reasoned of truth," and made monarchs tremble.   How brave, how true was Luther!   We almost worship one who embodies truth in every look and word and act.   How noble! how grand!

VII. **Mistakes in the Culture of the Truth-Emotions.**

—All plans of work that suppress or fail to stimulate the truth-emotions are educational mistakes.

1. *Unwilling tasks are educational blunders.* When you force a child to prepare a lesson, you foster a distaste for knowledge. In giving lessons, lead your pupils to feel that you are doing them a favor—giving them the opportunity to gain truths. Work is composed of tasks, while play is made up of games. Tasks are as necessary as work, but our pupils must be willing workers.

2. *Repulsive work is an educational blunder.* In some way you must create an interest. How many girls loathe mathematics because the study was made repulsive! Even the hardest work may be made interesting.

3. *Burdensome work is a mistake.* Let the child eat too much food, and it will loathe food. Burden the boy's memory continually with undigested facts, and he will come to loathe study.

4. *Failure to foster a love for truth.* The student studies for grades and a diploma. How few study because they really desire to find out the truth! Instead of being a perpetual joy, school life, too often, is a grinding drudgery. The student has no heart in it. Dear teachers, do you love truth? Then I know you will so manage as to get your pupils in love with truth. Tell your friend how to do this in your letter on the culture of the truth-emotions.

5. *All shams are hurtful.* Deceptions and misrepresentations are grave mistakes. The deceiver as well as the deceived suffers loss. The faith that trusts comes of truthfulness.

CHAPTER XXI.

EDUCATION OF THE ÆSTHETIC EMOTIONS.

By this is meant the development of our capabilities to appreciate and enjoy the beautiful, the sublime, and the humorous. As beauty predominates, these emotions are called the *beauty*-emotions. Sublimity and humor are treated as forms of beauty. Our capabilities to feel in view of the beautiful, the sublime, and the humorous are known as the æsthetic emotions. *Taste* is the capability to feel æsthetic emotions. The term *taste*, used in this sense, occurs constantly in literature and life. Self as intellect beholds beauty, and as æsthetic emotion appreciates and enjoys beauty. Beauty is ever concrete. We perceive beauty in things beautiful. Self as imagination creates beautiful ideals. Our notions of beautiful things, immediate and remembered, awaken our beauty-emotions. We command and educate these emotions by commanding the ideas which occasion them.

I. **Æsthetic Emotions in the Mental Economy.**—The cut, page 2, and the diagram, page 209, symbolize the position and relations of the æsthetic emotions. Self as intellect creates as well as perceives beauty. Art and poetry and music are æsthetic creations. Beauty-ideas excite beauty-emotions, and beauty-emotions move self to create and realize beautiful ideals.

1. *The beauty-idea is intuitive.* When we become acquainted with beautiful things we become conscious of the beauty-idea. Before I can say, "Yonder sunset is beautiful!" I must have the beauty-idea. The beau-

ty-idea is a necessary-idea, and is gained by direct insight.*

2. *The beauty-emotions are feelings occasioned by ideas of beautiful things.* Things are beautiful; we are endowed with native energies to feel beauty-emotions, and we experience emotions of beauty in the presence of beautiful things.

3. *Æsthetic emotions are feelings occasioned by æsthetic ideas.* The æsthetic emotions are the beauty-emotions, and include emotions of beauty and ugliness, emotions of sublimity and insignificance, and emotions of humor and pathos.

4. *Taste is the capability to feel æsthetic emotions.* Taste is commonly used as the power of self to appreciate and enjoy the beautiful. We speak of the good taste of cultured persons and the bad taste of uncultivated people. Taste stands for æsthetic emotions.

5. *Education of the æsthetic emotions* is the culture of our powers to appreciate and enjoy the beautiful, the sublime, and the humorous. Education makes the difference between the barbaric taste of the boor and the refined taste of the artist and the man of culture.

II. **Importance of Æsthetic Culture.**—The worlds of the true, the beautiful, and the good are co-ordinate. We are endowed with powers to understand, enjoy, and become a part of these glorious worlds. Æsthetic culture takes rank with intellectual culture. In our times its importance is unquestioned.

1. *Æsthetic culture exalts and refines.* Contrast a prize-fighter and Tennyson. The one is destitute of æsthetic culture, and is low, coarse, brutal; the other,

* See Intuition, pp. 36 and 80.

through æsthetic culture, has become a part of the beauty-world. Contrast the Greeks and Romans with African savages and Australian Bushmen. The elevating effects of æsthetic culture are truly marvelous.

2. *Æsthetic culture immeasurably increases human happiness.* Education is designed to fit us for the highest happiness of which we are capable. Æsthetic culture prepares us to enjoy a universe of beauty. It attunes the human heart to thrill with joy in the presence of beauty in all its myriad forms.

3. *Æsthetic culture fortifies against low vices.* One who enjoys the beauties of Nature and poetry and song and holiness learns to despise degrading vices. Love of the beautiful opens the heart to all good influences and closes it to all the grosser vices.

III. **Growth of the Æsthetic Emotions.**—These feelings are feebly active in our early childhood and grow with our physical growth. Physical beauty attracts the young. Soon the child learns to enjoy simple melodies and simple poetry. At every step in education care should be taken to cherish these feelings. From the age of fourteen to eighteen is considered the period especially favorable for the development of the higher æsthetic emotions. Through life these emotions must be kept active. The aged men and women whose æsthetic emotions are active and strong are still young.

IV. **Laws of Æsthetic Emotion-Growth.**—As thinking promotes the growth of reason, so the enjoyment of beauty promotes the growth of the beauty-emotions.

1. *General educational laws.* These are here stated in terms of the æsthetic emotions. Wisely enjoying the beautiful, the sublime, and the humorous develops the

17

æsthetic emotions. Whatever tends to call into vigorous activity the æsthetic emotions may be made the means for educating these feelings. Systematically and persistently calling into vigorous activity the æsthetic emotions educates them.

2. *Special laws.* Æsthetic emotions have their own peculiar laws of growth. The educator searches out these laws and works in harmony with them. (1) Efforts to create beautiful ideals educate the beauty-emotions. The highest beauties of many realities are assimilated into one ideal. (2) Efforts to realize our beauty-ideals cultivate our beauty-emotions. The beauty - emotions of the artist, the poet, the musician, and the teacher grow stronger and stronger.

V. **Means of educating the Æsthetic Emotions.**—The worlds of beauty and sublimity and humor furnish abundant food for the æsthetic emotions. From the rich stores the teacher selects the fittest : 1. *Physical beauty*—of form, of color, of motion, of sound, etc. 2. *The fine arts*—drawing, molding, painting, sculpture, architecture, landscape and flower gardening, etc. 3. *Vocal culture*—music, reading, elocution. 4. *Æsthetic literature* — poetry, fiction, æsthetics, essays, rhetoric, composition. 5. *Beauty of character* — truthfulness, kindness, honesty, good morals, gentle manners, etc. 6. *World studies*—astronomy, philosophy, religion, etc.

VI. **Methods of educating the Beauty-Emotions.**—A mind develops normally when excited to right and many-sided activity. Beauty, sublimity, and humor occasion the activity of the æsthetic emotions. Cherishing these feelings and calling them into systematic and persistent activity educate these emotions.

Kindergarten Methods.—The intangible influences of beauty silently minister to soul-growth.

1. *Beautiful environments cultivate the beauty-emotions.* The scenery, the flower-garden, the spreading meadows, the blossoming orchards, the golden fruit, the shady groves, the running brooks, and the songs of birds, awaken all beauty-emotions in the hearts of the little ones. Beautiful school-rooms and lovely school-grounds minister to æsthetic culture. The kindergartner, like the wise mother, surrounds the little ones with an atmosphere of beauty.

2. *Kindergarten play-songs and all rhythmic movements cultivate beauty-emotions.* In fact, beauty is obtrusive in all the kindergarten arrangements. Beauty of motion has a fascination for children which the kindergarten exercises gratify.

3. *Making pretty things educates taste.* The little ones are kept busy drawing, molding, cutting, building, making. They try to make beautiful things. The beauty-emotions thus pass over into actions.

4. *Doing prettily educates the beauty - emotions.* "Pretty is that pretty does." Kind acts are beautiful. Truthfulness is beautiful. Selfishness is ugly. Cruelty is ugly. All wrong doing is ugly. Beauty of character is the highest form of beauty.

Primary and Intermediate Methods.—All the beauty-emotions are now moderately active, and should be cultivated as assiduously as the intellectual powers. Love of objective beauty is very active during this period.

1. *Make the surroundings beautiful.* Your school-room, like the home and kindergarten, should be a thing of beauty. A few pictures, a few flowers, will

help much.   Then, your school-grounds should be made
as beautiful as a picture.   Enlist pupils and patrons in
this æsthetic work.

2. *Lead the pupils to the habit of beauty of position
and movement.*   Graceful positions in sitting and standing, graceful gestures, and beauty of movements in tactics, in walking, in gymnastics, in play, educate the
beauty-emotions.

3. *Lead the pupil to produce beauty.*   Writing,
drawing, and molding are excellent æsthetic exercises.
Drawing has probably contributed most to the advancement of æsthetic culture.

4. *Vocal music and good reading educate the beauty-
emotions.*   Vocal music should be made prominent in
all our elementary schools.   The reading should be as
beautiful as the music and the drawing.

5. *Enlist the children in easy æsthetic literature.*
Read to them easy. poems and pretty stories.   Have
them commit and recite memory-gems and write pretty
letters.   Lead them to read beautiful literature.

6. *So manage that the beauty-emotions will become
pretty-acts.*   Good conduct is beautiful, but bad conduct is ugly.   Good words and gentle manners are the
highest forms of beauty.   Generosity is beautiful, but
stinginess is ugly.   Gentleness is beautiful, but rude-
ness is ugly.   Truth is beautiful, but falsehood is ugly.

High-School Methods.—During youth æsthetic emotions are intensely active.   This is the golden period
for their highest culture.

1. *So teach æsthetics, rhetoric, composition, and literature as to educate the æsthetic emotions.*   The student learns to enjoy the beautiful in literature.   The

plays of Shakespeare become as charming as the most beautiful music. The sublime epics, Paradise Lost, the Iliad, and Job, becoming as fascinating as galleries of art. The student begins to produce as well as to enjoy beautiful literature.

2. *The student must so study and practice the fine arts as to feast the æsthetic emotions.* All can draw, most can sing, and some can read. Each one can excel in at least one æsthetic art. Art criticism is an excellent exercise. At a small cost each high school may secure photographs of the works of the masters. In the world of beauty the soul becomes refined and exalted.

3. *The student must be led to luxuriate in the beauties of science, and language, and philosophy.* Dry facts are respectable considerations, but the beauty of truth, of design, of system, of infinite wisdom, that we discover at every step, exalts and ennobles us.

4. *Beauty of holiness is the superlative of beauty.* *Whole* means physically whole, healthy; *holy* means morally whole, healthy, sound. Physical beauty comes of physical health. So beauty of character comes of moral wholeness. God is beauty, for he is the Holy One. The holy men and women of olden and modern times are the beautiful characters that adorn human history and exalt human nature. Our highest endeavors are, to become holy, and to realize in ourselves the beauty of holiness. The art of developing holy characters is the finest of fine arts. Beauty of conduct is the climax.

VIII. **Mistakes in educating the Æsthetic Emotions.** —Educators do not always realize the many-sidedness of soul-life, and the necessity for all-round culture. In-

tellect is often highly educated, to the neglect of heart-
and will-culture.   In connection with the æsthetic emotions many educational mistakes are made.

1. *Error of the utilitarian.* " Thousands for utility,
but not a dollar for ornament!" exclaimed the *practical*
man of the school board. " Teach my boy arithmetic,
but do not waste his time with music, and drawing, and
gymnastics," was the injunction of the dollar-wise parent.
No wonder that the old schoolmaster, thus instructed,
tried to crush all the beauty-emotions out of children by
mountains of facts.   Modern education, with the motto
"Utility and beauty," is rapidly remedying this fundamental mistake.

2. *Error of the œsthete.*   The æsthete considers æsthetic culture the principal thing.   Both the ethical and
the practical are undervalued.   Solid culture is replaced
by the study of the fine arts.   The old-time " Ladies'
boarding - school " embodied this ruinous error.   Coeducation has worked wonders in correcting these
extremes, but very much remains to be achieved by the
coming teacher.

3. *Error of the mathematician.* Mountains of math-
matics crush out the beauty-emotions.   Sometimes it
is grammar, and sometimes Latin.   One's specialty is
made to so absorb the time and energies of the pupil
that no place is left for æsthetic culture.   " I have no
time to teach music and drawing," said a teacher who
required the pupils to devote two hours daily to arithmetic.

4. *Error of the Philistine.* A teacher who lacks
imagination and æsthetic culture trudges on mechanically, scarcely aware that there is a beauty-world.   Un-

der such teachers pupils grow up with little poetry to enrich their lives in God's world of beauty.

SUGGESTIVE STUDY-HINTS.

Helpful Books.—Our literature is rich in works treating of the æsthetic emotions and their culture. Excellent manuals for music, and drawing, and elocution, and gentle manners, are numerous. The teacher who loves the beautiful will work close to nature and art, and will lead her pupils into the paths of beauty, and sublimity, and humor.

Letter. The culture of the æsthetic emotions is a delightful theme on which to write. Take time and write thoughtfully. Try to enlist your friend in this forward movement.

1. *Place of the æsthetic emotions in the mental economy.* Point out the relations between intellect and æsthetic emotions; between these emotions and will. How does æsthetic culture affect manners? morals? Are brutes endowed with these emotions? Define æsthetic emotion; æsthetic culture; taste.

2. *Importance of æsthetic culture.* Why do you rank æsthetic culture with thought-culture? Show how æsthetic culture refines; exalts; increases human happiness; saves from degradation. Give three original reasons for æsthetic culture.

3. *Growth of the æsthetic emotions.* Tell what you know about the activity of these emotions during the kindergarten period; during the primary period; during the intermediate period; during the high-school period; in manhood; in old age. How early do the little ones manifest beauty-emotions? What do you consider the golden period for æsthetic culture?

4. *Laws of æsthetic culture.* Illustrate the law of effort; the law of means; the law of method; the law of creating beauty. Do ideas *cause* emotions? Is *self* active in beauty-emotions?

·5. *Means for educating the æsthetic emotions.* Place on the board your estimates of the educational value in æsthetic culture of drawing; of music; of good reading; of poetry, etc.

6. *Methods of educating the beauty-emotions.* Give four directions for kindergarten æsthetic culture; four directions for primary culture; four directions for intermediate culture; four directions for high-school work. How do environments help or hinder? What

literature do you count best? May pupils be trained to write beautiful compositions?

7. *Mistakes in educating the æsthetic emotions.* Explain the error of the utilitarian; of the æsthete; of the Philistine. What mistakes have you noticed in æsthetic culture?

CHAPTER XXII.

EDUCATION OF CONSCIENCE.

By this is meant the development of the duty-emotions. "*I ought*" is the highest impulse of the soul. "I can starve, but I can not steal." "I can die, but I can not betray my country." "Burn me if you will, but I can not deny my Saviour." Such is the language of the educated conscience. Moral education is the education of conscience.

I. CONSCIENCE IN THE MENTAL ECONOMY.

Conscience is to the moral universe what gravity is to the world of matter. Gravity regulates worlds, and conscience regulates moral beings. In all the arena of human thought no other theme has for us such thrilling interest as the education of conscience.

I. Intellect and Conscience.—Self as intellect *knows* right, and self as conscience *feels* impulses to do right. Knowing duty occasions duty-impulses. Conscience is the moral impulsion in man. Conscience *moves* to right as invariably as the needle points to the pole.

1. *The duty-idea is intuitive.* A moral being stands face to face with a moral universe. We gain the duty-idea by direct insight, just as we gain the cause-idea and

the time-idea and the space-idea. Bound up in each rational act is the duty-idea. Self as necessary-intuition perceives the duty-idea in a moral act, as he perceives the cause-idea in a physical act. We gain intuitively the concrete ideas of right and wrong, of ought and ought not, of merit and demerit. These ideas are necessary, self-evident, universal.

2. *Self as intellect finds out the right.* " I ought to tell the truth," is a moral judgment. All judgments are intellectual products, and differ merely as to subject-matter. Moral judgments are simply judgments concerning right and wrong. We must find out what is right in the same ways in which we find out what is true in science. The space-idea is intuitive, but the truths of geometry are thought-products. The duty-idea is intuitive, but ethical truths are thought-products.

3. *Self as conscience feels impulses to find out the right.* We desire to know duty. "*Find the right,*" is the first imperative of conscience. In the search for moral truth intellect is at its best. *Be sure you are right.* This is your highest intellectual duty. Arrive at your moral judgments with the utmost care. Mathematical judgments are important, but moral judgments · are infinitely more important.

II. **Conscience and Law.**—Conscience is the native energy of self that makes for righteousness. Righteousness is rightness, and, everywhere and always, right is accordance with law. Moral laws regulate the moral universe just as physical laws regulate the physical universe. Self as intellect finds out moral laws in the same ways that he finds out physical laws. Intellect finds out the laws of love : " Love God supremely," and

" Love others as you love yourself." Your impulse to
obey these laws is an imperative of conscience. Self as
intellect may be mistaken, but self as conscience infalli-
bly feels the impulse to do what is believed to be right.
Conscience is the law-obeying energy of the soul.

III. **Appetites and Conscience.**—Duty-emotions dominate all other impulses. Conscience is the only imperative of the soul. Duty-emotions are impulses to do
right—to do what we think we ought to do. Conscience commands all our intellectual powers to find out
duty ; commands will to choose and do what we believe
we ought to do. The clamoring of the appetites and
passions is hushed in the presence of the imperative of
conscience. " It is my duty," silences all other considerations. " It is wrong," arrests every unlawful impulse.

IV. **Will and Conscience.**—Choose and do the right,
is the ultimate imperative of conscience. Conscientiousness is habitually doing what we deem right after
the most searching investigation. You have used your
intellect to the utmost to find out the law. You believe it your duty to work for prohibition. Now your
conscience moves you to do all you can to abolish the
saloon. When you do this you act conscientiously.
But to close your eyes at noonday and declare there is
no sun, is not conscientiousness but rather willfulness.
Paul persecuted conscientiously, but he calls himself
the chief of sinners because he had refused to investigate. When we know we are right, we move boldly
forward even in the face of danger and death.

V. **Culture of Conscience.**—Educating conscience is
so developing our ethical emotions that our duty-im-

pulses become practically imperative.   Between the man
who habitually does what he intelligently believes to be
right, and the *policy* man, there is an immeasurable distance.   Each was endowed with duty-emotions, but the
one has educated his conscience, while the other has
repressed and dwarfed his moral impulses.   Compare
Paul with Napoleon, or Luther with Richelieu.

VI. **Conscience, or the Ethical Emotions.**—Our feelings occasioned by our duty-ideas are called *ethical*
emotions, *duty*-emotions, emotions of conscience.   *Conscience is our capability to feel ethical emotions.*   Self,
as intellect, gains ethical ideas; self, as conscience, feels
ethical emotions in view of ethical ideas; self, as will,
does ethical acts in view of ethical ideas and ethical
emotions.   Strictly, conscience is self feeling duty-
emotions, but for convenience we use the term con
science to represent ethical emotions, as well as the
capability to feel these emotions.

We do not think of conscience as an entity, nor of
an act of conscience as an isolated act.   Each ethical
act is an act of the entire self.   Self feels ethical emotions in view of ethical judgments, and, in view of these
judgments and impulses, determines and acts.   As the
impulse to right is the dominant activity, we say that a
moral act is an act of conscience.   Self as conscience
feels ethical emotions, and the native energy of self to
feel rightness is termed *conscience*.   In this sense conscience is a capability, a power, a faculty of self.   Education *develops* but does not *create* conscience.   Culture
renders the moral impulses more and more powerful as
incentives to conduct.   However diverse their theories,
most writers practically accord with these statements.

II. Necessity for Moral Culture.

Reason *may* be educated, but conscience *must* be cultivated. Without some moral culture a man becomes a monster. It is the education of conscience that fits us for the companionship of men and angels. Moral education is superlatively important.

1. *Conscience-culture leads to the grandest manhood.* The ultimate product of moral training is a human being, under the direction of an enlightened conscience, habitually striving to do his full duty to himself, his fellow-beings, and his God. This is the educational climax. A conscientious man is truly the noblest work of God.

2. *Conscience-culture gives self-control.* It subjects the lawless appetites and passions to law. It makes one law-abiding. The Chief-Justice of England says, " Temperance, self-control as to the drink-habit, would close three fourths of all the prisons in the world." Self-indulgence makes demons, and fills our prisons, our brothels, and our gambling-hells. Conscience-culture gives self-control, and dethrones appetite and passion.

3. *Conscience-culture leads to the highest happiness.* Happiness everywhere is a result of obedience to law, as misery is a result of violation of law. "Happy are the pure in heart." " Happy those who hunger and thirst after righteousness."

4. *Conscience-culture makes life worth living.* It lifts up society, and makes our impulses pure and ennobling. It makes men and God our friends, and gives us the universe to enjoy forever. " He who overcomes shall inherit all things."

"There are men who do not know that when they tutor the magnetic needle they are tutoring currents that enswathe the globe and all worlds. There are men who do not know that when they tutor conscience they are tutoring magnetisms which pervade both the universe of souls and its author. Beware how you put the finger of special pleading on the quivering needle of conscience, and forbid it to go north, south, east, or west; beware of failing to balance it on a hair's point; for whoever tutors that primordial, necessary, universal, infallible emotion tutors a personal God" (Joseph Cook).

III. Growth of Conscience.

The brute has no respect for moral law, for it is destitute of ethical insight as well as of ethical emotion. The child at a very early age feels duty-impulses, but these impulses are feeble, and fall far short of being practically imperative. The mass of mankind are ethical infants all their lives. Soon the little one sees dimly the law of obedience to parents, and feebly feels the duty-impulses to obey. This is the budding of conscience, and needs to be fostered with infinite care and tact.

The duty-impulses become moderately strong during boyhood and girlhood, but need constant watchfulness to see that they become acts. Train the young to do habitually what they believe to be right, and conscience will grow strong.

Conscience becomes highly active and commanding in youth. This is the golden period for its systematic culture. The youth loves and obeys law because it is right.

Conscience rightly educated grows more and more powerful to the end of life; it becomes the imperative soul-energy. It makes a man mighty to conquer. One righteous man shall chase a thousand guilty ones, for—

"Thus conscience does make cowards of us all."

Good Conscience and Bad Conscience.—These are misleading expressions. Conscience is always good. When Paul persecuted Christians to the death, he said, "I did it in *good* conscience, for I thought I ought." He simply acted conscientiously. When we act conscientiously we say we have a *good* conscience, but when we act unconscientiously we say we have a *bad* conscience. It is every way better to say *we* are *good* when we obey conscience, but *we* are *bad* when we disobey conscience. Conscience always moves us to resist the wrong and choose and do the right, Conscience is always good. We are responsible not only for what we know, but also for what we ought to know. Those that have few opportunities shall be beaten with few stripes.

IV. Laws of Conscience-Culture.

Like memory and reason, conscience grows by use. Every time you gladly act conscientiously you increase the vigor of your ethical emotions. The laws of conscience-culture are as well defined as those of imagination-growth. The duty-impulses constantly move us to find out and do the right. (1.) *Obeying these impulses strengthens conscience,* and disobeying them weakens conscience. (2.) *Whatever tends to strengthen the ethical emotions may be made a means for cultivating conscience.* (3.) *Systematically and persistently seeking to find out duty,* and doing what we believe we ought to do, educates conscience. Ethical emotions carried over into acts become powerful. (4.) *Habitually doing what you believe to be right educates conscience.* As reasoning makes one strong to reason, so feeling and doing duty make one ethically strong. (5.) *Habitually doing what you believe to be wrong enfeebles conscience.* The duty-impulses become too feeble to influence action, and the transgressor ceases to ask, "Is it right?"

V. MEANS OF CONSCIENCE-CULTURE.

Well-directed effort in finding out moral law and doing what we believe right, educate conscience. A world of duties to learn and do is the limitless field from which to choose the means for conscience-culture. It seems almost needless to attempt to enumerate.

1. *The family is primary.* Loving parents teach the laws and make it easy to obey. As the child learns to walk by walking, so it learns to do right by doing right. The family fosters all good impulses.

2. *Good companionship stands next to the family.* The influence for weal or woe of associates is tremendous. When your associates love and live up to law, you find it easy to do right; but when your associates are lawless you *drift* into lawless habits.

3. *Good literature ranks very high.* "The Bible," says Huxley, "is incomparably the best means for moral culture." When we realize that the loving Father gives laws for our good, we find it easy to obey. When we know that an approving conscience is the smile of God, we have the highest possible motive to do right. The New Testament is the one perfect ethical code, and the life of Jesus is the one perfect ethical model. The best ethical literature is of inestimable value. No one knows how much he is influenced by what he reads. Pure literature is of priceless value. On the other hand, vicious literature does incalculable harm in weakening all moral restraints.

4. *Congenial occupation deserves special mention.* Poor, weak human nature finds it hard to battle against temptations that come of idleness or uncongenial occupation.

5. *The Sunday-school and church are powerful means for conscience-culture.* Here millions of the best men and women put forth their best efforts to get duty into the hearts and lives of the young.

Scientific ethics touches not the masses. Nothing can ever take the place of Christian ethics as the means of conscience-culture.

6. *The school and college exert a powerful ethical influence.* They give purpose and direction to youthful effort. They keep the young busy and interested. They give deeper insight into the tendencies and outcome of courses of action. In the absence of school-life the best youths may drift into evil habits.

VI. METHODS OF EDUCATING CONSCIENCE.

Conscience is self feeling duty-emotions. Its imperatives are, *find* duty, *choose* duty, *do* duty, *rejoice* over duty done, and *grieve* over duty not done. Methods of educating conscience are systematic and persistent plans of instruction and training that tend to make these imperatives effective. Conscience is the capability of self to feel duty-emotions. As used in life and literature, the term conscience is the synonym of ethical emotions and ethical acts. It is so used in this work. Self as conscience feels the impulse to investigate in order to find out duty. Self as conscience feels the impulse to choose duty as understood. Self as conscience feels the imperative, "I ought to do what I believe to be right." Self as conscience feels a glow of satisfaction in view of duties done. Self as conscience feels remorse in view of law violated. Conscience is the moral faculty. It is the native energy of self to feel rightness. Moral education is the development of conscience. A man is educated intellectually when he becomes capable of putting forth his best cognitive efforts. A man is educated morally when conscience dominates all other feelings and becomes the controlling imperative in the mental economy. Such a man earnestly strives to find out and do every duty to self, to others, and to God. He feels his highest joy in loving and obeying law. A plan of life that systematically and persistently calls ethical emotions into effective activity is a method of educating conscience. Ethical emotions do not count unless they terminate in ethical actions. Every time you resist a temptation or perform a duty you strengthen conscience.

I. **Kindergarten and Primary Methods of educating Conscience.**—These are methods adapted to the moral education of the little ones. Like the thinking powers,

the duty-impulses act feebly in childhood. The fostering care of parents and teachers is peculiarly needed to
cherish the budding ethical emotions. Some one has
shrewdly said, " Moral education should begin with the
grandparents."

1. *Develop the duty-idea.* Like the number-idea,
the duty-idea is intuitive. As the child works up to
number-ideas through concrete examples, so the little
ones work up to duty-ideas through duty-experiences.
Early duty-lessons must be easy, and as concrete as early
language-lessons. The duty to obey parents is earliest
developed.

2. *Make duty lovely.* The loving parents are the
first to lead the little ones to joyous obedience along the
paths of love. The loving teacher leads the little ones
in the same paths. The child is led to think of God as
the loving Father and of heaven as a happy home. Thus
duty becomes to a child joyous and lovely, and naughti-
ness sad and hateful.

3. *Lead the little ones through object-lessons to law.*
The hourly occurrences are the best lessons. Little
stories are excellent. Example is irresistible. As in
arithmetic and music, the child moves up through practice to law.

4. *Train the little ones to do what they think they
ought to do.* Only voluntary effort educates. In some
way the child must be led to choose and do right. It
may not know why, but it is right because mother says
so. Children as well as philosophers must take much
on faith in those they trust. It is worth everything to
train the little ones to the habit of right doing.

5. *The education of conscience is positive.* It is

right to feel grateful and kindly. It is duty to tell the truth and obey parents and teachers. So thoroughly impress the positive virtues that the child will acquire the habit of making its duty-emotions ethical acts. Keep before the child its duties. The negatives should seldom be mentioned. In teaching penmanship the ideal form and not the blunders is kept constantly before the pupil. In teaching morality we need to pursue a similar course.

6. *Throw around the little ones a moral atmosphere.* Suffer them not to be tempted above what they are able to bear. Make it easy for them to do right. When they go wrong, gently lead them back to the path of duty. Spare no vigilance in cherishing the duty-habit.

II. **Intermediate Methods of educating Conscience.—** These are methods of moral culture adapted to boys and girls. In all lands, in nearly all communities, are to be found sturdy moral characters—men and women kind and true and good. How have these moral heroes developed golden characters? Ask Mark Hopkins and Miss Willard; ask Job and Elijah; ask Jesus. Take the lessons you learn into your school-room and teach them to your pupils.

1. *Give practical lessons in morals.* Lessons from life are most impressive. It is important that boys and girls should gain clear-cut moral notions. Duty must be made as clear as axioms. Hence these lessons must be specific. Generalizations do little good.

2. *Lead boys and girls to respect and obey human laws.* These become real object-lessons. Parental requests are laws of the family. Requests of teachers are

laws of the school. Legislative acts are laws of the State. Congressional acts are laws of the nation. Instill reverence for law. Cherish the impulse, " I ought to obey the law." See to it that duty-impulses become acts. The pupil will thus grow into a law-loving and law-abiding citizen.

3. *Develop the habit of right doing.* It is of the utmost importance that boys and girls should habitually do what they believe they ought to do. Thus conscience is efficiently educated, and a sturdy moral character is developed. I wish I could sufficiently emphasize this thought. We must not suffer pupils to fall into the habit of doing what they consider wrong, and thus weaken conscience and build bad characters.

4. *Foster a taste for æsthetic literature.* As we keep poison out of food, so must we keep base literature away from the young. The best literature is æsthetic. We must manage to have the boys and girls read only the best. In our times this is no easy task. We must so educate our pupils that they will choose pure literature as they choose wholesome food.

Character-Growing.—Methods of conscience-culture learned in the school of experience help most. "From my own life's experience I know the necessary ingredients of character and the importance of it, above all knowledge. I have learned, also, not to expect too much. I never yet made a stingy child generous from impulse, or an improvident child prudent at all times; but the fact that both faults have been in a measure overcome encourages me to persevere. I work in every possible way for these essentials: Honesty in every detail; contempt of mean little ways; respect for each other's rights and mine; habits of industry and order, application and perseverance—the sum total of all being *self-control.* The amount of knowledge they acquire gives me little concern. With the experience of so many years I am bound to teach them with a greater or less de-

gree of excellence. Although teaching and I understand each other
as a whole, each year develops some new trait that has to be studied
and adapted. Whatever success I have had is due to the study of
the individual, added to my natural aptitude. I have either no
method or all methods. Whatever helps, I seize upon, keeping
always in mind the development of power in the child. My idea
of intellectual power is ability and desire to obtain knowledge
with accuracy and rapidity and certainty, and to use it effectively.
My idea of moral power is intellectual power with the supreme love
of right and the ability to realize the ideal life in the actual life. I
have always made character-growing my highest aim. By assimilating my best experiences and the experiences of the best moral
educators, I have tried to form perfect character-ideals. I have
always given my best endeavors to the work of leading my pupils to
realize these ideals in their own characters." *

III. **Advanced Methods of educating Conscience.**—
These are methods of moral education adapted to youth
and early manhood. They need to be thorough and
powerful.

1. *Self-control from principle is cardinal.* Youth
is the period of mighty impulses that move the world.
Now is the time for danger - signals. The appetite
for drink and other perverted appetites must not be
permitted to sweep away the foundations of character.
In youth all the feelings are intensely active. Shall
we leave our youths to throw conscience and duty to
the winds and sow their wild oats? After a few gay
and giddy years of lawless gratification of their appetites and passions, will they return to a life of duty and
purity? Survey yonder battle-field of the mad passions
after the battle. Where, oh, where are the armies of
the glorious youths you saw enter? Alas! alas! most

---

* These are the precious utterances of one who is evidently a great
teacher, but whose name the author at present is unable to give.

of them have fallen to rise no more. Those stragglers you see are individuals called back to the path of duty by mother-love and the early education of conscience. The vast proportion of these prodigal sons and daughters will never return to their father's house. There is absolutely no safety but in self-control. Early and always foster self-control from a conviction of duty.

2. *Conscience must dominate youthful action.* Only thus can our youths be saved and a noble manhood insured. Conscience is now very active and its impulses imperative to youths who from infancy have been trained to the habits of right doing. By all possible means the dominion of conscience must be maintained through these years of hope and danger.

3. *Ethical studies must be made prominent.* Ethics is the science of duty, and applied ethics is the art of right living. Youth is the time to gain large views of our relations and duties. Now each one needs to create an ideal character as a life model. Moral law, the beauty of goodness, perfection through right living, happiness as the consequence of lawful living, are lessons that must be inwrought into the very fiber of the soul. Applied ethics, the art of right living, the greatest of all arts, is freighted with the well-being of the individual and the race.

4. *Ethical literature must have the first place.* Huxley tells us that the Bible is incomparably the best means of moral culture. God is our loving Father, and in the words of Herbert Spencer is, "the infinite and eternal energy from which all things proceed." * Jesus

---

* *Which* not *whom.* Spencer does not think of the absolute as the lov-

is the Perfect One. The Bible is God's best gift to man, and is intended to guide him in the way of truth, duty, and everlasting life. The works of authors like Shakespeare and Dickens and MacDonald, are rich ethical treasures. Young people need to constantly drink at these pure fountains.

5. *Pure and wise associates are indispensable.* A generous and confiding youth is easily led by those he loves. Probably four out of five who go to the bad are misled by vicious associates. " Evil associates corrupt good morals." On the other hand, good and wise associates do most to educate conscience and lead their companions in paths of duty.

6. *Punishment is a moral necessity.* Its purpose is to lead the wayward back to the path of duty and keep them in it. " The way of the transgressor is hard." All offenses call for punishment. When we violate hygienic laws we suffer. When the child violates home laws it is punished. When we do wrong we suffer remorse and are punished by the disapproval of loved ones. The parent and the teacher and the State and God visit on the transgressor the suffering necessary to reformation. We punish in love, in order to get the transgressor right and keep him right.

An approving conscience is the smile of God; remorse His frown.

VII. Mistakes in educating Conscience.

A world full of degraded human beings is the result of failures in moral education. The millions would

ing Father, but as the infinite and eternal energy. He holds that the absolute is not personal.

be better men and women but for the deplorable mistakes in the most important field of human culture. A good man or woman is the noblest work of God, and a bad man or woman is the most deplorable work of man.

1. *Neglect of moral culture.* The murderous plea, "I am not my brother's keeper," suffers the masses to drift in the ways of folly and sin. Then, parents and teachers and preachers and friends do not always with untiring purpose inculcate duty.

2. *Failure to remove sources of corruption.* States wisely quarantine against deadly epidemics. Saloons, houses of infamy, gambling-dens, and *"variety"* theatres corrupt our youth and breed moral pestilence. Not to suppress these sources of corruption is a grievous blunder. These immoral pest-houses should be closed to youth.

3. *Precept without training.* Only doing right educates conscience. No amount of precept will save. The great mistake everywhere is the failure to carry precept over into practice. Moral lectures and moral sermons are good, but they become effective only when they become ethical emotions and ethical acts. Planting the corn is well, but cultivation is better. In moral education, example and training must accompany and supplement precept. The golden moral chain is made up of right ideas, right examples, and right training.

4. *Failure to control our thoughts.* It is true that the current of our thoughts deeply affects our conduct and character. It is equally true that this current is largely under our control. We can make the stream of thought clear and wholesome, as we can make it

muddy and impure. When we think on the true, the honorable, the just, the pure, the lovely, the reputable, our ethical emotions become imperative.

SUGGESTIVE STUDY-HINTS.

ETHICAL EMOTION-CULTURE.

I. **Helpful Books.**—We are rich in choice works helpful in ethical culture. It seems unfit to mention two or three out of so many. Comegy's Primer of Ethics, Robinson's Principles and Practice of Ethics, Hopkins's Law of Love, Cook's Conscience, Rosenkranz's Philosophy of Education, Howland's Practical Hints for Teachers. Dunton's Moral Education, and Everett's Ethics for Young People, are admirable works. Our literature abounds in good ethical works.

II. **Letter on Conscience-Culture.**—Lead your friend to realize the nature of moral education. Go into details, and show just how you would promote the growth of conscience. Send a copy of your letter to some journal for publication. Such productions will prove valuable. What you find helpful may help others.

III. **Conscience in the Mental Economy.**—What do you mean by conscience ? Is conscience a cognitive or an emotional power ? Compare conscience and gravity. Show the relations of intellect and conscience. Prove that the duty-idea is intuitive. Show that moral judgments are products of intellect. Does conscience impel us to investigate in order to find out duty ? Show the relations of conscience and the appetites ; the self-emotions ; the will. Is conscience a moral guide ? In what sense is conscience infallible ? What do you mean by the education of conscience ? by a weak conscience ? by a strong conscience ? What distinction do you make between conscience and the ethical emotions ?

IV. **Necessity for Moral Culture.**—Why must conscience be educated ? Prove that conscience-culture tends to a superior manhood. How does conscience-culture give self-control ? Prove that moral education leads to happiness. Is an immoral life worth living ?

V. **Growth of Conscience.**—Why has the brute no regard for moral law ? How early does the child gain the duty-idea and feel duty-emotions ? Explain what you mean by a feeble conscience.

Do many persons remain ethical infants all their lives? Trace the growth of conscience from infancy to manhood. Explain the meaning of the expressions *good conscience* and *bad conscience*. Are these expressions misleading?

VI. **Laws of Conscience-Culture.**—State in ethical terms the law of *effort;* law of *means;* law of *methods;* law of *habit.* Prove that acting unconscientiously enfeebles conscience. Does conscience seriously trouble great criminals?

VII. **Means of Conscience-Culture.**—Give your reasons for putting the family first. What do you think of good companionship? of good literature? of congenial occupation? of the Sunday-school and church? of the Bible? What does Huxley say about the Bible?

VIII. **Methods of educating Conscience.**—What is conscience? How do we educate conscience? How will you develop duty-ideas? Why must duty-lessons for children be objective? Why must duty be made lovely? How will you train children to the habit of doing right? How are grand moral men and women made? Why should duty-lessons be practical? How will you lead your pupils to respect and obey law? Why should right doing be rooted into habit? How will you foster a taste for ethical literature? Show that self-control is better than kingdoms. Why should conscience dominate? Give your reasons for making ethical studies prominent. Do duty-ideas tend to duty-acts? What do you consider the primary office of punishments?

IX. **Mistakes in the Education of Conscience.**—Why is it that we have a world full of degraded human beings? Do you think the moral education of the race is possible? Why do we so neglect ethical culture? Prove that prohibition helps. Show that example and training are as necessary as precept. State your own experience in promoting character-growth.

PART V.

EDUCATION OF THE WILL–POWERS.

THE MENTAL POWERS.

- **The Intellect.**
  - Perception.
    - Sense-perception.
    - Self-perception.
    - Necessary-perception.
  - Representation.
    - Memory.
    - Phantasy.
    - Imagination.
  - Thought.
    - Conception.
    - Judgment.
    - Reason.
- **The Feelings.**
  - Sensations.
    - General sensations.
    - Special sensations.
  - Emotions.
    - Self-emotions.
    - Social-emotions.
    - Cosmic-emotions.
- **The Will.**
  - Attention
    - Attracted.
    - Voluntary.
  - Choice, or Self-determination.
  - Action.
    - Reflex.
    - Instinctive.
    - Impulsive.
    - Purposed.

A mind is a unit. Its activities can not be separated by fixed lines. While the soul's various capabilities may be studied separately, they can not be thought of as acting separately. The fact of the interaction of our various powers is fundamental in educational as in mental science. Milton taught that "in the soul are many lesser faculties that serve reason as chief." But a faculty must not be thought of as an *entity;* self is the entity, and his faculties are his capabilities to do acts different in kind. Nor must the faculties be thought of as acquired *facilities;* education develops but does not create faculties. We must think of the faculties as the native energies of self. Each self is endowed with native energies to know and feel and will. The capabilities of self to do acts distinct in kind are called his activities, his powers, his faculties. But no mental act is simple. Each act of self is an act of the entire self. The dominating activity characterizes and *denominates* the act; as, when *reason* is the dominant activity, we say the act is an act of self as *reason.*

CHAPTER XXIII.

THE WILL-POWERS.

THESE are our effort-making capabilities. Self as intellect *knows* something; self as emotion feels somehow; and self as will makes some intentional effort. All mentality is knowing, feeling, and willing. Take away from our mental lives knowing and feeling, and the residue is willing. Will enters into each mental act. Analyze any of your acts: you find that *attention* conditions knowing; that *ideas* occasion emotions; that ideas and emotion occasion *choices;* and that choices occasion *actions.* Intention, purpose, liberty, characterize will, but will is simply *self willing*, and may be defined as the native energy of self to make intentional effort.

Will *is not* to be conceived as an activity in itself. As a concrete reality, will is active intelligence stimulated by emotion, or active emotion directed by intelligence. Will must have material to work upon—an object to be willed; and such material can be obtained only from intelligence and emotion. All education, in a sense, is education of will. The education of intelligence is an exertion of will in directing intelligence to particular objects; the education of emotion is an exertion of will for the suppression of feelings that are inimical, and the stimulation of those that are favorable to the well-being of man.*

Will *is* to be conceived of as a capability of a self to put forth intentional effort. Each one is aware that he purposely concentrates his efforts, prefers one thing to another, and intentionally executes his purposes. This is mind in liberty; this is will. As we voluntarily attend, and choose, and act, will is to be thought of as standing for the powers of attention, choice, and action.

I. **The Will-Powers.**—We usually think of will as our power of self-determination, because choice is pre-eminent in willing. But in order to know or feel or do, we must *concentrate* our efforts—must *attend.* In order that we may achieve, we must *execute*—must *act.* We thus see that self puts forth voluntary effort in three distinct ways: in attending, in choosing, and in acting. Practically, *attention, choice,* and *action* are now generally recognized as our will-powers. The educator thinks of the learner as a self who can attend,

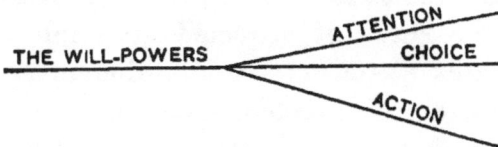

choose, and act, as well as know and feel. This insight is of great value. Will stands for *attention, choice,* and *action.* It ceases to be the vague, mysterious, metaphysical thing that has wrought such confusion.

II. **Attention is the Power of Self to focalize his Efforts.**—It is " the self-governing intelligence applying itself to what it wills."

" Attention is the actual self-direction of the mind to any object external or internal." " The activity of the soul which effects the

* J. Clark Murray.

concentrating and focusing of its efforts is called attention." "Attention is the concentration of the activities of the mind by the
power of the will." "The greater or less energy in the operation of
knowing is called attention." "The essential achievement of the
will is to attend to a difficult object, and hold it fast before the
mind." "Effort of *attention* is the essential phenomenon of will."
" In attention we find the first exhibition of will; it is the beginning
of all control over the mental life, and may be defined as the power
to voluntarily concentrate mental effort." "Attention is an act of
will, and may be defined as the power of concentrated voluntary
effort." "Attention is the power of command over our thoughts,
and thus over our feelings." "Attention is the power to concentrate
effort, and fix the mind persistently on an object or group of objects,
and to resolutely exclude from the mental view all irrelevant objects."
Such, substantially, is the teaching of all psychologists. Attention
is a will-power, just as perception is an intellectual power.

1. *Attention is voluntary concentration of effort.*
I purposely exclude other themes and fix my mind on
this topic. I do this intentionally, as it is my *wish*
to grasp the wonderful truth that " *self attends voluntarily.*" We speak of attracted attention, and sometimes call this *non-voluntary* attention or *reflex attention.* Thus, an unexpected sound or touch or sight
attracts our attention. *Insistent* ideas also attract our
attention, and are sometimes hard to banish. Persons
with little will-power drift, having their attention drawn
hither and thither. *But attention proper is always
voluntary.* Many things may conspire to divert my
attention, but I resolutely exclude them, and keep my
mind fixed on the subject in hand. When we think
and speak of attention we mean voluntary attention.
Culture converts the attracted attention of the child
into the purposed attention of the youth. Education
makes attention completely voluntary.

2. *Attention enables us to master difficulties in detail.* "Attention is an act of will. The mind is directed to certain objects before it. When these are numerous, they appear dim and indefinite; but when we give attention to any one object, it stands out distinctly from the others." * As we become acquainted with many persons, one by one, so we master, step by step, the most complex subjects by concentrating our powers on each step in succession.

3. *Attention is our capacity to prolong and change effort.* You keep the problem before you until mastered. You keep your mind on the lesson until it is learned. You then rest and turn to another lesson. At will we concentrate, prolong, and change the direction of our efforts.

The Potencies of Attention.—The psychologist sometimes amuses himself by defining each of the mental powers in terms of consciousness. An equally valuable exercise is the defining of each capability of self in terms of attention. Such exercises effectually dissipate the error of supposing that the so-called faculties are isolated properties of which the mind is composed. The young psychologist will need to guard against going to the opposite extreme, in supposing that each activity of self is merely a phase of consciousness and a potency of attention. A deeper insight into the mental economy reveals to you a self endowed with energies, different in kind. Awareness is one of these energies, and attention is another. You *attend*, that you may remember, and you are *aware* that you attend and remember; but memory is not attention, nor is it awareness.

III. Choice is the Native Energy of Self-Determination.
—Choice is the pre-eminent will-power, and is usually thought of as a synonym of will. "Choice is the capability of free election in view of cognitions and emo-

* Dr. McCosh.

tions." "Without intellect there is no *light;* without feeling there is no *motive;* without motive there is no *choice.*" "Choice is the power of rational self-determination in consideration of motives." "When two courses are open to us, choice is our power to decide to take one rather than the other." "Choice is simply the self-determining power of the soul." "Choice is mind in liberty, and is the power of preference." "Choice is the determining power in human action. When but one course is open, self adopts it. When several courses are open, self as choice determines in favor of one." "Choice is the capability to decide what action to take." "Choice is the power to elect one of two or more alternatives in view of motives rationally apprehended." "Choice is the ability to make up one's mind in the presence of rival claims." Thus speak the great psychologists.

1. *Self is free to choose.* Ideas occasion emotions, and ideas and emotions occasion choices. Self-activity characterizes mind. Mental acts are occasioned but not caused. The idea of personal liberty is an intuitive idea. That we are free to choose is clearly a necessary truth. On this truth rests the science of duty. Persons are praised and blamed, rewarded and punished, because they are free and hence responsible. All men know that they can choose as they please. No one ever thinks of choice as necessitated except when constrained so to do by metaphysical dogmas. A being not endowed with liberty of choice is not a person.

2. *Motives occasion choices.* Incentives to choice are termed motives. These include reasons for choice, and are the ideas and emotions which move us to de-

19

termine. What was your motive? We often ask ourselves as well as others this question. What induced you to pursue that course? Even the least cultured ask this question. Rational choice is deliberative self-determination. Motives are inducements to choose.

3. *Ideas, desires, choices.* Ideas are fundamental. We must know before we can desire. We keep a thought before our minds until it awakens a desire and thus induces a determination. Often ideas fight and emotions conflict. The idea of happiness through the lawless gratification of the appetites fights with the idea of happiness through obedience to law. The desire for sensual pleasure conflicts with the ethical desires. The house of mirth allures, while the house of mourning appeals to our noblest emotions. Self as choice terminates these fearful battles by *determining* to do right. Ideas occasion emotions, and emotions as active desires move us to choose. We resist unworthy desires, and determine in favor of ennobling desires.

Self Determines.—I determine for myself. As I am rational, I deliberate before deciding. For good reasons I adopt this plan and reject that. I am autocrat: in view of these conflicting ideas and emotions I determine. I am free: I am conscious that I can stay or go. I am master: motives are mere considerations that I make strong or weak at will. I am responsible: I myself, uncompelled, chose to act thus; I know I could have chosen differently. I am a person: I am a self-acting, self-conscious, self-determining being. I am immortal: I am in touch with the Infinite Will.

IV. Action is the Native Energy of Self to execute his Determinations.—Volition, executive power, executive volition, action—these are the terms used to designate our power to carry choices over into acts. Rational *action* is the capability to purposely execute determinations. "Volition is born of choice, and is the power to carry out our choices." "Volition is will in action, and is the consummation of self-determination." "Action is the mental execution which follows resolution." "Executive volition is the ability to carry choices over into acts." "Volition is our power to command all our capabilities to unite in the execution of our purposes." "Volition is the overt act of will." "Action is the power to exert force in the line of rational choices." Action is the capability to do what we determine to do. Action is self executing his choices.

Reflex-Acts, Impulsive-Acts, Rational-Acts.—In the animal economy movements which immediately follow feelings, and where there is no rational choice, are termed automatic, reflex, instinctive, impulsive. Such acts are unpurposed and non-voluntary. Infinite Wisdom has so planned that more than nine tenths of our acts are of this kind. Habitual acts tend to become automatic. These unpurposed acts require comparatively little expenditures of energy. We are thus enabled to direct almost our entire energies to purposed and directed effort.

A Rational Act is the Intentional Execution of a Rational Choice.— You have before you several interesting books which you desire to read. In what order will you read them? After careful consideration, you determine to read this book first; this, second; and so on. You now proceed to execute your purpose by reading the books in the order you determined on. *Action*, in its strict sense, is the capability to execute purposes. Thus, Napoleon was a man of action, and Bismarck a man of great executive power.

1. *Self reaches the outer world through his physical organism.* Sensation and movement are the connecting links between self and the not-self. It is impossible for us to manifest any thought, feeling, or purpose except by bodily movements. The look, the gesture, the

spoken or written word, come of bodily movements. Self as action commands all his mental and physical abilities in the execution of his purposes. The reflex organism—marvelous mechanism!—is the ready servant of the will. You determine to write a letter, and in the execution of your purpose you grasp the pen and write. Ganglia and nerves and muscles respond to your slightest volitions and automatically carry on the work. How? No one knows. Self as will originates movements in the motor ganglia; these movements induce molecular waves, which vibrate through the motor nerves to the muscles. The muscles contract and relax, and thus produce the necessary movements. A mind is self-acting, but how does it create motion? How does the singer call into play the right muscles in the necessary degree of tension to produce the song? How do you converse? We here touch the unknown. Is it also the unknowable?

2. *Repetition converts purposed action into habits.* From infancy you have been trained to pronounce correctly and speak properly and act politely; now you do these from habit, without thought and without purpose. Wonderful! Wonderful! Habit is the great conservator of mental energy.

3. *Executive power is the capability to bring about results.* Alexander was a man of wonderful executive power, but Aristotle excelled him. The one changed the map, the other the thought, of the world. Executive power is the ability to achieve. It is the ability to organize and direct. You will demonstrate your executive ability by making the most of yourself and doing most for others.

CHAPTER XXIV.

EDUCATION OF ATTENTION.*

By this is meant the development of our power to devote ourselves wholly to one subject. The fact that we can become able to do this is fundamental in education. Rosenkranz counts this conception of attention the most important principle in pedagogy. Great achievements are possible to one who can concentrate all his energies upon his wisely chosen field of work.

I. **Relations of Attention to other Activities.**—Will is voluntary and purposed effort. There are clearly three movements in acts of will: (1) Self *selects* a special field and devotes himself to it: this is will as *attention*. (2) Self, in view of various considerations, *determines*: this is will as *choice*. (3) Self *executes* his determinations: this is will as *action*. Attention in some form and in some degree enters into each mental act.

1. *Attention as related to choice and action.* We can study these powers separately, but we know that self attends while he determines and acts. Each of these activities supplements the others, but the act of concentrating your mind on one thing is essentially an act of attention.

2. *Attention as related to intellect.* Self as attention concentrates his cognitive energies and thus gains mastery. Effective thought is in the ratio of attention. Compare an act of reverie with an act of investigation. We attend, that we may know.

3. *Attention as related to emotion.* We attend to

* See chapter on Attention, in Elementary Psychology.

things that interest us, and attention intensifies our
emotions. Joy and hope grow brightest when we
direct our attention to them, and anger quickly dies
when we turn our attention to charity.

ATTENTION AND CONSCIOUSNESS.—Self is ever doing acts of knowing, feeling, willing, and is ever aware of doing these acts. This constant conscious activity is thought of as a mental stream, and is sometimes represented as a river. The central current represents the field
of *clear* consciousness; the sluggish stream on either side represents
the field of *obscure* consciousness; the eddies and pools and sprays,
along the shore, represent the field of *sub-consciousness;* and the
land from which flow innumerable brooklets represents the field of
unconsciousness. Could the river contract and deepen its current at
will, and constantly change its direction to suit itself, it would admirably represent the self-acting mind. Self purposely selects his field
of effort, and concentrates his energies upon it: this is the central
current, the field of clear consciousness. Self attends indifferently
to things bordering the field of clear consciousness: this is the field
of obscure consciousness, represented by the sluggish waters on either
side of the current. But it is not well to carry the figure too far.
It is certain that we are conscious in the degree that we attend.

II. **Terms defined.**—No psychological term is in more
common use than attention. Its meaning is clear even
to the child.

1. *Attention is the power of self-concentration.* As
attention, self selects one special field and refuses to be
diverted from it. We turn away from everything else, and
concentrate our entire energies on the subject selected.

2. *Attracted or non-voluntary attention* is the spontaneous attention given to whatever surprises or attracts
us. The child turns without purpose from object to
object.

3. *Voluntary attention is determined self-concentration.* This is attention proper. You *intentionally*

devote yourself to the preparation of the history lesson. You purposely fix your mind on the geometry lesson. You voluntarily bring to bear all your powers on the lesson in psychology. Voluntary attention is purposed concentration.

4. *Versatility is the ability to change.* Napoleon gave himself wholly to the business in hand; when this was finished, he turned instantly to the next business. Thus, he tells us, he was able to dispose daily of a prodigious amount of work. Self as attention changes the direction of his efforts.

5. *Education of attention is the development of the power to purposely focalize effort.* When a child, you could give slight attention only for moments; now you can give complete attention for hours. This wonderful growth comes of well-directed effort, and is called education or culture. You have developed your power of attention.

III. **Importance of Attention-Culture.**—We are endowed with the capability to select our field of work and with the power to concentrate our energies on one point at a time; we are able to master difficulties in detail. The capability to attend is the exponent of mental efficiency. As we develop our power of attention, we increase in geometrical ratio our mental efficiency. The culture of attention is pre-eminently important, because—

1. *Mental growth depends on attention.* Dreaming does not educate. Drifting does not develop power. The dawdling student remains a weakling. As my arm grows stronger and more skillful when I use it vigorously, so my reason becomes more and more powerful

when I persistently give my best efforts to investigation.

2. *Complete attention gives to each capability its
maximum of power.* It makes perception complete,
memory almost infallible, and thought penetrating.
Take two persons having equal natural abilities: the
one who can give complete attention accomplishes many
times as much as the one who can only give partial attention.

3. *Complete attention illuminates.* The lens concentrates the sun's rays. The focal point becomes the
center of light and heat. Attention focalizes thought
and emotion, and the mental focal point becomes
the center of mental light and interest. Everything
in the focal point stands out with sunlight clearness.

4. *Culture develops attention into a habit.* The
child attends feebly and but for moments. You lead it
to repeat the effort day by day. Soon it develops the
power to attend more closely and for longer periods.
But, what is more important, it acquires the studious
habit. As the years advance the learner habitually devotes himself completely to the matter in hand. This
habit distinguishes students from dreamers, and efficient
men and women from triflers.

5. *Teaching is the art of educating attention.* "If
the teacher's art is to be summed up briefly, it may be
described as the art of developing the power of fixing
the attention." * Were the object of school the development of the habit of *inattention*, some teachers would
be a remarkable success. Visit our schools, our lecture

* N. C. Rooper.

halls, our churches: you find one man in a hundred who can give his *entire attention* for an hour. Fellow-teachers, are we to blame? What can we do for the ninety-and-nine?

IV. **Growth of Attention.**—The educators who have led all forward educational movements lived for years in the closest relations with children. Teachers, you have studied, day by day, the living, playing, loving, learning child. What great practical lesson have you learned? You have closely observed the budding and growth of each of the intellectual powers. You have watched with profound interest the growth of the helpful emotions. Now you will make a special study of the child as will. You find that bright objects and musical sounds *attract* the *attention* of the infant. This is the beginning of will-activity. Preyer tells us that his boy gazed *attentively* at his image in the glass when but sixteen weeks old. You find that the little three-year-old in the kindergarten can attend feebly but for moments; therefore you try to make the kindergarten work as attractive and almost as varied as the plays of children. At six you find that the child can give moderate attention for a brief period, and hence can *begin* to study. You find it necessary to continue to attract attention through the primary years; but you notice that attention becomes more and more voluntary. The child begins to attend *intentionally*, and also begins to resist *distractions*. You observe that your *intermediate* pupils can give much closer attention and for a longer time. Voluntary attention is now quite active, and the pupils can really study. You find that the *youth* who has been properly educated can give almost complete attention for a long period. Hence it is that the high-school student is capable of great things; but the college student is capable of deeper and more prolonged attention, and hence of greater things. Finally, you observe that the men and women who excel in every field of high achievement are the ones capable of intense and prolonged attention. Thus you have discovered for yourself the growth of the power to concentrate effort. You are now prepared to study the laws of this growth.

V. **Laws of Attention-Growth.**—The child is led but the man is a leader. Effort made lawfully develops the vacillating child into the man of iron will. You study to express the great educational laws in terms of attention.

1. *Law of effort—Each act of determined attention increases the power to attend.* Attention is highly developed when one can concentrate all his energies for the achievement of an end.

2. *Law of means—Studies which demand close and continued attention are best for developing the power of self-concentration.* In the study of mathematics the learner *must* attend in order to make any advancement. This is true of all studies, but beginners realize this fact most in the study of arithmetic.

3. *Law of method—Plans of work that secure vigorous, systematic, and persistent concentration of effort educate attention.* Not much more can be said. You so manage that your pupils habitually do their best, and thus develop greater and greater power of attention.

Some of the most helpful lessons in teaching may be condensed as special laws of attention-growth.

4. *Attention through interest.* Interest is fundamental in the mental economy. Children and adults attend to the things which interest them. The teacher creates interest and thus attracts and strengthens attention. You find it hard to give attention to what does not interest you. How then can you expect children to do this? Glad attention educates.

2. *Concentrated effort must stop short of exhaustion.* Intense attention is the most exhausting of all mental activity. The little ones can attend but for moments. In the primary grades lessons must be brief,

and exercises demanding close attention be followed by play or restful work. As the years go by, the pupils become capable of greater and more prolonged attention, but at all ages this law must be heeded.

3. *Attention can be kept fixed only as it is kept moving.* Storm-centers, in the mental as in the physical world, are never stationary. You keep your mind on the subject because you pass from point to point. You hold the attention of your pupils because you lead them on step by step. Stationary attention is impossible.

4. *Attention through determination.* You determine to master a difficult theorem in geometry. To this end you concentrate your energies upon the theorem. You determinedly resist distracting influences. When you find yourself relaxing or wandering, you bend your energies anew to the task. You will not relax your efforts until the victory is won. This is attention at its best.

VI. **Means for educating Attention.**—Kindergarten work is wonderfully attractive and marvelously varied, and so is well calculated to strengthen the child's attention. Arithmetic is counted an excellent means for attention-culture during the primary and intermediate periods. During the high-school period, algebra and geometry are considered the very best means for developing attention. Botany and zoölogy deserve to rank high as a means of attention-culture. Much more, however, depends on methods than on subjects. Each study may become of high value as a means of educating attention.

VII. **Methods of educating Attention.** — These are plans of study and teaching that call attention into vigorous, systematic, and persistent activity, so as to develop the feeble attention of the child into the profound attention of the man. *Attracted* attention is converted into *voluntary* attention. Voluntary attention is so exercised as to become more and more powerful. Now, we *attract* the attention of the little ones. Later, we so interest the children that they give purposed attention for a little time. Year by year we lead our pupils to give closer and closer attention for longer and longer periods. Thus we so educate our pupils that they become capable of concentrated thought. Attention becomes a habit, and gives thoughtfulness and steadiness to purpose. Our methods are our ways of achieving these results.

VIII. **Kindergarten and Primary Methods of educating Attention.**—The child is very largely a thing of sense and impulse and action. Its ideas are sense-ideas. Its impulses pass over directly into acts. As the bee flits from flower to flower, so the child hastens from object to object. The wise teacher sees the child as it is, and so adapts the work as to develop its feeble powers.

1. *Attract attention.* To do this will often tax your utmost ingenuity. What ideas has the pupil gained? In what things does the child feel an interest? You begin with these. The little girl loves flowers, but gives no heed to numbers. Ask her to bring you ten flowers. You must manage to connect the number-lesson with these flowers. The little boy seems stolid when you try to teach him arithmetic, but you find that he takes a lively interest in animals. You now give problems about animals, and the stupid boy becomes interested and attentive. Kindergarten work is admirably planned to gain the attention of the children, and to develop attracted into purposed attention. Similar work, to a less extent, is greatly needed in most primary schools.

2. *Lead the child to do as well as know.* You man-age to have the child *try* the orange by each sense, and to *mold* a clay orange, and to *draw* a picture of the orange, and to *make* a little composition about the orange. You thus lead the child to fix and hold its attention upon an object. In these ways you convert attracted attention into voluntary attention. Kinder-garten and primary work must very largely consist in doing.

3. *Sustain attention by constant movement.* The orator holds the rapt attention of his audience by pre-senting, in succession, different phases of his subject. Successful writers understand and act on this principle. Study the lessons given by the Great Teacher ; how perfectly he embodies the law that *attention can be kept fixed only as it is kept moving !*

4. *Create and sustain interest.* The story, the ob-ject, the doing, interest the children when intimately connected with their experiences. *Attention through interest is the great law.* Even the most cultured find it difficult to hold the attention upon a subject devoid of interest. How, then, can you hope to keep the attention of the children when your lessons are to them dry and irksome? It is giving interested attention that strengthens the power to concentrate effort.

5. *Make it easy to attend.* Look to the physical comfort of your pupils. As far as possible, remove disturbing influences. Take the children when they are fresh. Make the exercises sparkling, lively, short. The earnest attention you thus secure will repay you, and will prove invaluable to the children.

6. *Give yourself wholly to the lesson.* So order

your school that the pupils will govern themselves. Study the lesson from the standpoint of the learner. Throw into the lesson your enthusiasm. Enter into the very spirit of the children. Give the exercises your undivided attention. You will in this way secure the complete attention of your pupils. One such lesson is worth more than a score of the dawdling kind.

IX. **Intermediate Methods of educating Attention.**— Attention is now largely voluntary. The pupil intentionally attends in order to accomplish some purposed end. The heart throbs with higher and wider interests. Thought and conscience and choice begin to count for much in the mental life. *Work* now gradually takes the place of the *play*-lessons of childhood. The girls and boys learn to really study. Attention and its cultures mean much more now than in childhood. How can we best promote the growth of attention during the intermediate period?

1. *Secure the most favorable conditions.* Vigorous health and physical comfort are of first importance. Light, temperature, seats, exercise, clothing, food, sleep, greatly affect the capability to attend. Quiet and the absence of everything calculated to distract attention must be secured. *You* retire to your quiet and comfortable studio to do your thinking. Then give your pupils, as far as you can, the same advantages. You thus make it easy to attend.

2. *Create great interest.* At no other period is this so essential. Boys and girls are intensely alive to their environments and to their personal interests. You must make the school-work more interesting than all other

things. Whatever else you do or fail to do, you must create and sustain interest, and thus secure attention. Now is the time to awaken permanent interests by cherishing the enobling desires.

3. *Cultivate right habits of study.* Train your pupils to try to keep their minds wholly on the lesson. They must learn to refuse to turn aside. If the attention wanders for a moment, they must determinedly bring it back. The greatest thing you can do for your pupils at this period is to develop in them right habits of study. The essential feature of all effective study is complete devotion to the subject.

4. *Lead your pupils to victory after victory.* Lead them to run down a truth with as great an interest as they run down a rabbit or a fox. So manage that each one solves the problem and finds out the classification. These victories intensify attention, and change the listless pupil into a real student.

5. *Enlist your pupils in worthy endeavors.* Boys and girls without high purposes are apt to be wayward and listless. During this period pupils are liable to squander their time and their energies. A worthy purpose, as the purpose to graduate, will often work wonders, converting the careless girl and the wayward boy into attentive students.

X. **High-School Methods of educating Attention.**— Youths ought to be capable of concentrated and prolonged effort. The students in the high-school must be able to give determined attention. The youth who can bend all his energies to his studies can accomplish something; but the youth who can not or will not do this will prove a failure. Above all, the high-school should

develop the powers of attention and investigation. Ex
amine the students in a hundred high-schools. You
discover that less than half of these give earnest attention to the work, either during recitation or study
hours. You find a still smaller proportion capable of
independent investigation. Surely better results may
be secured by better high-school methods.

1. *Educate attention by cherishing the spirit of
mastery.* Less ground must be covered. The *best*
must be selected. Each pupil is to be inspired with the
spirit of mastery and persistently trained in the *methods*
of mastery. The recitation hour is one of united and
determined effort to master the topic. The teacher
leads, and the pupils do their best. Each one is deeply
interested, and all give the utmost attention. The plan
of work wisely leads to mastery, and prepares the way
for future and greater victories.

2. *Educate attention by fostering wider interests.*
Cherish the longings of youth to explore the world
without and the world within. Lead your pupils into
the enchanting fields of literature and art. Enlist them
in work for human good. In a world so grand, in the
midst of these boundless interests, with so much to enjoy and so much to do, appetite and passion seem insig-
nificant. Mighty resolves now become plans of action.
That they may achieve, students now habitually resist
distractions and allurements, and focalize their energies
on their studies.

3. *Educate attention by holding it in class-work.*
Good teaching secures and holds attention. The eye
must not wander nor the attention flag. Three centuries have scarcely improved the plan given by Co-

menius—the greatest educator of the seventeenth century. He formulated the following:

Rules for gaining and keeping Attention.—The substance only is given.

1. *Bring before the class things interesting and profitable.* This is golden, and may well guide the teacher.

2. *So present the subject as to awaken and sustain interest.* You will thus secure and keep the attention.

3. *Suffer not the eye to wander.* You can hold attention so long as you can keep each eye fixed on yourself or on the object studied.

4. *Represent everything to the senses.* Place something on the blackboard. Use objects when you can. In some way appeal to the senses.

5. *Ask appropriate questions.* This is indispensable. All attend when any one may be called on at any moment.

6. *Hold each member of the class responsible.* Call on them promiscuously. When one fails to answer satisfactorily, call on another without repeating the question.

7. *Train the members of the class to ask questions.* They are interested and will naturally seek deeper insight.

4. *Rules for attention-culture.**** The capability of self to concentrate his efforts is strengthened by acts of attention. How to get and keep attention is the constant study of the teacher. How to develop the power and habit of attention is the ever-present thought of the educator. The following brief rules may assist by way of suggestion:

1. *Secure attention through interest.* You *must* know your pupils. Child-nature must be to you an open book. You *must* know the subject. The subject must in every way be *adapted* to the learner.

2. *Favor attention by good management.* Secure the most favor-

---

* SYMPOSIUM.—Have the rules written on the blackboard. Arrange for a short essay on each rule. Discuss. Round tables and symposiums are valuable educational expedients.

20

able conditions for study. Physical vigor is highly important. Freedom from interruptions and from distracting influences is necessary.

3. *Win attention by good elocution.* The orator never needs to ask attention—he wins it. So it should be with the teacher.

4. *Hold attention by keeping it moving.* The focal point of attention is the storm-center of mental energy. Storm-centers are never stationary. The theatre and the circus hold the attention by *movement*, as do the historian and the novelist and the teacher.

5. *Stimulate attention by success.* You lead your pupils to so attend and work as to gain victory after victory. Nothing stimulates effort like success.

6. *Inspire attention by pointing the way to achievement.* The pupils who lead their classes are the ones who give the best attention. The men and women who lead in every field of human achievement are those who most completely concentrate their efforts. Newton assures us that he excelled because he gave his attention exclusively to the topic he was studying. Dickens tells us that he owed his success to patient, toiling attention. Napoleon ascribed much of his superiority to the habit of attending wholly to one thing at a time. Attention is the royal road to achievement.

XI. **Mistakes in educating Attention.**—Attention is *intentional* concentration of effort. The attentive pupil voluntarily devotes himself to the lesson, and purposely excludes everything else. *Attention through interest and interest through determination* is the great law of teaching. Violations of this law are educational mistakes.

1. *Compulsory attention does not educate.* All attempts to force attention are blunders. "Mind your books, or you will catch it!" was the panacea of the old schoolmaster. "Get your lessons, or I will grade you down," is the one expedient of the half-way-teacher. Fear of the consequences of neglect may spur the pupil to voluntarily give some attention, but this is a low

motive, and the culture of attention thus secured is comparatively slight. Then fear is a great consumer of the mind's energies. The fear of low marks and of failure in examinations is a source of great educational waste.

3. *Doing the work for the pupil does not educate.* Self-exertion develops power. Making the work so easy that the pupil does not need to attend closely is a great mistake. At every step the learner should be led to do his best. Aim to secure *complete* attention.

3. *A divided teacher makes a listless class.* It is a mistake to try to do two things at once. You must make your school self-governing, so that you may give your entire attention to the class. In no other way can you hope to interest your pupils and hold their undivided attention.

4. *Going on with the lesson without the attention of the class injures teacher and pupil.* Stop. Now you have attention. Hold it. You must have resources to meet emergencies. Don't become vexed. Tell some story. Draw something. Enlist your pupils in a discussion. Propose some plan. In no case go on without attention.

5. *Resting satisfied with partial or spurious attention is a great mistake.* This is a disastrous educational blunder. Feeble attention means feeble knowing and feeble feeling and feeble willing. Excellence comes of complete attention.

SUGGESTIVE STUDY-HINTS.

Helpful Books.—Our literature is growing rich in its literature of attention-culture. Among many excellent productions may be

mentioned : Securing and Retaining Attention, by James L. Hughes;
Chapters on Attention-Culture, in Lessons in Psychology, by J. P.
Gordy; Chapters on Attention, in Sully's Outlines of Psychology;
Training of the Attention, in James Mark Baldwin's Handbook on
Psychology. Our educational journals probably present the best
articles on this subject. I have found the articles by George P.
Brown especially helpful.

Letter.—You will now present to your friend *your* plan for
educating attention. You have studied the child. You are now
familiar with the physiology and the psychology of attention. You
have considered what others have said about cultivating attention;
now you are prepared to write valuable thoughts to help your
fellow-teachers.

I. **Attention in the Mental Economy.**—Show that attention is a
will-power. Name and define each of the will-powers. Illustrate
by a river the relations of attention and *consciousness.* Give examples indicating that memory is in the ratio of attention. Point out
the relations between attention and intellect; between attention and
feeling; between attention and choice.

II. **Terms defined.**—Give your definition of attention; of attending; of educating attention. Give the etymology of the word attention. Illustrate the nature of attention by the lens. Analyze an act
of attention. Give the distinction you make between *attracted*
attention and *purposed* attention. Is attention always voluntary?
State the distinction you make between attention and consciousness.

III. **Importance of Attention-Culture.**—Prove that attending conditions knowing. What makes the difference between revery and
investigation? Show that acquisition and memory are in the ratio
of attention. Does mental growth depend on attention? Why may
teaching be considered the art of educating attention?

IV. **Growth of Attention.**—Have you closely observed the growth
of child-attention? How early is *attracted* attention indicated?
How early do children really give *voluntary* attention? From your
observation describe the growth of attention during the kindergarten period; during the primary period; during the intermediate
period; during the high-school period. Illustrate growth by ability
to master more difficult problems during each succeeding period.
May attention continue to grow to the meridian of life? May it be
kept vigorous in old age? Give examples from life.

V. **Laws of Attention-Growth.**—State in terms of attention the law of *effort;* law of *movement;* law of *determination.* Give an illustration of each law in terms of your own experience.

VI. **Means for educating Attention.**—How does kindergarten work strengthen attention? Why do you count arithmetic of highest value as a means of educating attention? You may place on the board a *table of attention-culture values.* Give your reasons for the value you assign to algebra; geometry; geography; language-lessons; composition; botany; Latin; drawing; vocal music.

VII. **Methods of educating Attention.**—Make a distinction between a *law,* a *means,* and a method; illustrate. How do Kindergarten and primary methods differ? Give and illustrate three directions for kindergarten work; three for primary work. How do intermediate and primary methods differ? State five directions for cultivating attention during the intermediate period. How do high-school and intermediate methods differ? Present five directions for high-school work. Place on the board and explain the rules of Comenius for securing attention during the recitation. State the author's rules.

VIII. **Mistakes in the Education of Attention.**—Show the error in forced study; in doing the work for the pupil; in the appeal to fear; in a divided teacher; in going on without attention; in partial attention; in spurious attention. Mention other mistakes of this kind.

CHAPTER XXV.

EDUCATION OF CHOICE.*

By this is meant the development of the power of self-determination. Education of the will gives self-control and decision of character. Character is organized choices. Culture of will is character-building, or rather character-growing. Choice crowns the trinity of selfhood—*self-activity, self-consciousness,* and *self-determination.*

* See chapter on Choice in Elementary Psychology.

I. Choice in the Mental Economy.—Will crowns mentality. *I will* is the sovereign act of self. Self as *will* has for his *servants* his body, his intellect, and his feelings. With his servants thoroughly disciplined, the sovereign self goes forth to conquer a world, a universe.

1. *Deliberation.* As sovereign, self as will calls into council his intellectual powers. He deliberates; he investigates; he considers. The alternatives are weighed. Self determines in the light of reason.

2. *Impulsion.* The feelings *impel, move, urge, incite* self to choose. The appetites *clamor* for gratification. The passions *demand.* The ennobling desires *appeal* to reason. Love *pleads.* Conscience *presses* duty. "Peace! Come into the court of reason," is the mandate of the sovereign. Feelings *impel* but do not *compel.* Feelings are subjected to reason, and the sovereign self determines.

3. *Determination.* Self as will determines. We feel impulses; we consider all the inducements; we determine. Determination is the sovereign act of self. From the decision of self as choice there is no appeal. *Reconsideration* is a voluntary act; self is sovereign.

4. *Action.* Self executes his determinations. We carry over into action our purposes. We do what we make up our minds to do. Self as action is the history-maker. The man of action is the man of executive power.

II. Terms defined.—Choice stands for will. You think of attention, choice, and action as the will-powers; but choice is pre-eminent. Most men think of will as the capability to determine. This is its usual meaning in literature. Will, choice, and power of self-determination are ordinarily used interchangeably; but when we need precision we use the specific terms.

1. *Choice is the power of self-determination.* The following definitions are all good: "Will is mind in liberty"; "Choice is the power of preference"; "Choice is the capability of self to decide in view of motives"; "Choice is the native energy of self to determine."

2. *Motives are inducements to choose.* Self as intellect considers the motives, and, after deliberation, self as will chooses. A weak motive is a slight inducement to choose, but a strong motive is a powerful incentive to choice. A *high* motive is an unselfish motive. Motives occasion choices.

3. *Freedom is liberty in choice.* I am free to choose. Nothing more can be said. Each one is conscious of freedom. But for misleading theories, no one would even conjecture otherwise. Circumstances, feelings, and considerations occasion choices, but do not cause them; self is the cause.

4. *Education of choice is the development of decision of character.* This characterizes all great men and women. The power of prompt self-determination is grand. Culture develops the vacillating child into a Bismarck or a Beaconsfield.

III. **Importance of educating the Will.**—We have tried to realize the need to cultivate the several capabilities of self. The culture of each power is important, but it is safe to consider of superlative importance the development of decision of character.

1. *Determination is the secret of success.* "What a man achieves is simply a question of will." This utterance of Beaconsfield is exemplified by his illustrious career. "The impossible becomes realization to the man of indomitable resolution." The resolute pupil solves every problem. Culture of will develops the power of determination.

2. *Culture of choice gives decision of character.* It develops the hesitating, vacillating, unreliable child into the decisive, persistent, reliable man. Culture of choice develops the power to determine promptly and adhere

firmly to a purpose. These traits grow into habits, and characterize the man.

3. *Education of will makes for righteousness.* Self as conscience impels to right, but self as will determines. Culture of will develops choosing and doing right into habits. The girl, the youth, the woman becomes strong to resist temptation and do right. Moral character is developed.

IV. Growth of the Self-determining Powers.—You remember. You trace the growth of *your* will from childhood to the present. An hour of introspection is invaluable. You now observe with new interest and deeper insight others' wills. You trace the growth of the self-determining power as seen in others, from infancy to age. You now study with absorbing interest the records of the observations made by psychologists of all schools. You try to grasp the facts reached by extra-spection as well as those reached by introspection.

1. *Child-will is remarkable for its weakness.* The native energy of self-determination is feebly manifested when the infant is but a few months old. "The first deliberate movements," says Preyer, "take place only after the close of the first three months." Many weeks pass before the child manifests purpose and choice. When three years old, will, as attention, choice, and action, is feebly active In the kindergarten the child is dependent, docile, tractable, obedient credulous. Kindergarten exercises are adapted to strengthening the weak will of the child. In the primary period, the child is less docile and less dependent. Purpose and determination are now manifested, but the child is vacillating and easily influenced. Primary work must be so adapted as to cultivate the weak will of the pupil.

2. *Boy-will and girl-will are remarkable for waywardness.* Self-determination asserts itself and resists restraint. The boy has a will of his own, and is not always disposed to listen to reason. Though will has grown stronger, the pupil is weak in the power to adhere to a purpose and resist temptation. The wise culture of will is now doubly important.

3. *Youth-will is remarkable for its vigor.* The youth attempts the impossible with the vigorous determination of a Napoleon to

cross the Alps. The youth enters upon his work with a determination that brooks no failure.

4. *Man-will is remarkable for decision and tenacity.* The man enters upon his life-work with firmness of purpose, and adheres to it with unswerving tenacity.

V. Means for Choice-Culture.—From infancy to age, during almost every waking moment, we *prefer*, we *choose*, we *purpose*, we *make plans*, we *decide*, we *determine*. These acts tend to develop choice. Whatever calls rational self-determination into vigorous activity may be made a means for strengthening this power.

1. *Hard study* is doubtless the best means for educating self-determination. Compare the student with the idle youth. The dawdler is weak, incapable, inefficient; the student is mighty to conquer. Hard study develops will-power and makes men.

2. *Discipline*, family and school, is of very high value for choice-culture. Self-denial, self-control, and cheerful obedience to law and lawful authority become life-habits.

3. *Biography and history* rank high as a means of will-culture. The men and women who made history, possessed mighty wills. As the youth studies these records, his determination to excel becomes stronger and stronger.

4. *Good literature* tends to develop *good* will, and *bad literature* tends to strengthen *bad* will. *Good ideas* tend to become *good purposes* and good acts; *bad ideas* tend to become *bad purposes* and bad acts.

5. *Good companionship* is of inestimable value in will-culture. The friend who leads his companions to choose for themselves, and choose wisely, is a treasure.

The egotist who chooses for his associates, and the person who leads them into temptation, are unfortunate companions.

6. *Ethics and religion, after all, stand first.* Their motives are the highest. Purposes reach into eternity. Acts of will are infinite in their bearing. Conduct prepares the self for a position among the eternal tenantry of a boundless universe.

VI. **Laws of Self-Determination Growth.**—Choosing for one's self educates the capability to choose, just as judging educates judgment. The great educational laws apply to will equally with emotion and intellect, and may be stated in terms of choice.

1. *Law of effort*—Determining with promptness and adhering to purposes with firmness educate choice.

2. *Law of means*—Whatever leads one to habitually determine for himself may become a means of developing choice. A world of possibilities is the unlimited means for will-culture.

3. *Law of method*—Plans of work that require constant self-determination educate will. The learner is systematically led to form purposes and to persist in them. Efficient methods of study are such plans of work.

Laws relating specifically to the culture of will are of great practical importance. (1.) *Purposed action educates will.* A voluntary act is one done with a view to some end. Even in the kindergarten, the child is continually led to do acts to reach ends. (2.) *Forming settled determinations educates choice.* When everything has been considered, a decision must be made, and must not be changed except for good reasons. You will discover other helpful laws, but the laws given will guide you in your efforts to educate the will.

VII. **Methods of educating Choice.**—Great attention has been given to methods of educating the intellectual powers, and splendid results are secured. But comparatively little study is devoted to will-culture. Methods

of educating perception and memory and reason are
lessons in every institute, but lessons on methods of
developing decision of character are rare. Yet all admit the superlative importance of conduct.

VIII. **Kindergarten and Primary Methods of educating
Choice.**—The child is led to deliberate and choose. Its
little choices are respected. When the child deliberates
and chooses wisely, it is praised and rewarded. When
it goes wrong from impulse, it is left to suffer the consequences, and so led back to the path of duty. The
child is led to assume light responsibilities and to prove
itself trustworthy. The little ones are led to try to reach
precision in gymnastics, music, drawing, and manners.
Kindergarten work is wisely arranged to promote the
growth of choice. Primary work may safely follow
similar lines. That children may be led to achieve pro-
posed ends, the means as well as the ends must be made
interesting.

IX. **Intermediate Methods of educating Choice.**—These
are plans of will-culture adapted to the intermediate
pupils. The wise teacher often stands in wonder before
his class of boys and girls. New phases of their nature
are constantly bubbling up. This is the most trying
period for the teacher and parent, as well as the most
critical period for the pupil. Only general suggestions
can be given. Each teacher must work out and follow
her own plans.

1. *Leave the pupil to choose.* No one but self can
choose. You can do much for your pupils, but you can
not choose for them ; nor would it educate will if you
could. The act of choice must be the act of the pupil.
An entire chapter is needed here.

2. *Train pupils to study vigorously.*   It becomes a habit to choose study rather than play.   Then each moment devoted to study requires a tremendous effort of will.

3. *Lead pupils to consider.*   This habit is invaluable.   Hasty action is responsible for most crookedness and crime.   "I did not think," is the standing excuse of boys and girls.   They do not stop to consider but act from impulse.   Here is the danger.   The pupil who thinks before he acts seldom goes far wrong.

4. *Train pupils to choose the right.*   There may be more fun in playing truant than in going to school, but the one is wrong and the other is right.   By all means the pupil must be led to choose the right.

5. *Train the pupil to resist temptation.*   Temptations will come, and the pupils must be educated to overcome them.   The truant is tempted to lie: he must not.   In time of peace prepare for war.   Prepare the pupil for the hour of trial.   Boys are sorely tempted to smoke and gamble and drink.   These habits mean ruin.   Self-control must be fostered and the boys saved.

X. **High School Method of educating Choice.**—Will is highly active in youth, and this is the time for its higher culture.   To control seething appetites and passions requires a penetrating intellect, a heart full of all ennobling emotions and an iron will.

1. *Habitually determining in view of high motives, educates choice.*   Cognitions occasion the practical emotions, and these lead on to action; but self as choice decides to act or not to act, and also what action.   Deliberate choice weighs inducements to act.   Appetites and passions clamor for gratification.   The still small voice

of conscience commands, " *Do right.*" Self as intellect considers. In view of the considerations self as choice determines. In the midst of wise counselors there is safety, and there is safety in deliberate action. Hasty and impulsive action brings woe. We must not yield to the first impulse of desire, nor form hasty resolutions, but must reflect, must weigh the *pros* and *cons* before determining. Feelings must yield to reason.

2. *Habitually subordinating low and selfish impulses to the higher emotions and to reason, educates choice.* This is self-control. The appetites clamor for strong drink with its Pandora box of human ills. But the brave youth spurns low and selfish and debasing gratifications. The pure, the lovely, the beautiful, the good fill his heart with joy, and lift him up to a higher and grander life. *I ought* weighs more with him than palaces of pleasure. Greater is the man who controls himself than he who gains battles. It requires more self-determination to resist temptation than to face danger.

3. *Resisting temptation strengthens will.* Yielding weakens. Those poor, weak, fallen wretches can not now resist. There is no safety but in early resistance. The first glass makes the drunkard, for yielding once leads on to yielding again and again, and the youth becomes a slave to his appetite. How difficult the task of lifting up the fallen ones! These unfortunates are slaves to habit. They have yielded until they have lost the power to resist. Must they perish? No; oh, no! We must rescue them by removing temptation, and fostering the little manhood left. Resisting temptation strengthens will. There is absolutely no safety but in

resistance. Resisting once gives greater strength to resist again. Habitually resisting temptations to lie and
steal and cheat and to unlawful gratification of the appetites, develops will-power. Contrast a prize-fighter
with John Wesley. The one has habitually yielded to
every base impulse and is a low and brutal fellow. The
other resisted temptation and cherished every ennobling
virtue, and became a lovely, grand man.

4. *Discipline resulting in self-control educates will.*
The earnest efforts to be regular, prompt, decorous, successful, and moral, immensely strengthen will-power.
These efforts are every way encouraged. To this end
school life is better than home life. But some one
fails. Now the discipline of suffering becomes necessary in order to stimulate the power of self-control.

5. *Persistent effort to realize perfection educates
will.* Your ideal is a perfect character : to realize this
ideal you constantly put forth your best efforts. You
determinedly follow lines of work calculated to develop
such a character. You vehemently repress thoughts,
feelings, and acts calculated to mar your ideal. The
boundless possibilities of self, and the consciousness of
capabilities to realize these possibilities stimulate self-
determination to the utmost.

XI. **Mistakes in educating the Will.** — Character-
building is pre-eminently the mission of the teacher.
The Greek educational ideal of character was the perfect
individual ; the Roman ideal was the perfect citizen ;
but the educational ideal of the twentieth century will
be the perfect *individual* self and the perfect *social*
self.

1. *Neglect.* Our normal schools and teachers' associ-

ations fail to give sufficient practical emphasis to *conduct*. Our methods of intellectual culture are becoming scientific and artistic, while our methods of educating the emotions and the will remain crude and inefficient. Folly and crime keep the race in a state of semi-barbarism. Great character-builders, like Arnold of Rugby, are still phenomenal.

2. *Our training is too largely negative.* We restrain rather than develop. We teach language *positively*, by leading our pupils to *use* our language properly; we have abandoned the *negative*, false-syntax method. We teach penmanship *positively*, by leading our pupils to aim at ideally perfect forms; the *negative* method of parading mistakes has been abandoned. The same is true of orthography and reading and music and gymnastics. Only in character-building do we retain the old, hurtful, negative method. This, too, should speedily give place to positive will-training.

3. *The extremes of rigid and loose control are blunders.* The rule of "Do as you please" is scarcely less hurtful than the rule of "Must." The child is free, and should be induced to choose wisely. We throw around the young every favoring influence, and do everything to develop the habit of self-control. But, from the nursery to the university, we foster free choice and thus strengthen the power of self-determination. We seek, at every step, to develop the habits of self-control and self-government.

4. *Good-will is not cultivated.* Napoleon had an iron will but not a good will. Kant tells us that the absolutely good is good-will. Certainly it is good-will that we want to strengthen. School incentives, I fear,

do not always tend to develop a good will. This is
vital.

5. *Breaking the child's will is a cruel blunder.*
This is the mistake of the ignorant and stupid; and
who can tell the ruin it has wrought? We cherish and
strengthen good-will by leading our pupils to choose
good. Good ideas awaken good emotions and thus occasion good choices. By interesting the young in good
ideas we lead them to choose good.

SUGGESTIVE STUDY-HINTS.

Helpful Books.—Libraries have been written about the will.
"Am I free to choose, or is my choice necessitated?" This is the
question of the ages, and has enlisted the best thought of the race.
But these myriad volumes are not calculated to help much in the
culture of the will. Education of the Will, in Rosenkranz's
Philosophy of Education, is excellent. Many good things may be
gleaned from works on ethics. Good articles on will-culture are
now beginning to appear in our educational journals.

Letter. You may greatly interest your friend by treating practically of the culture of the power of self-determination. You will
do good by recasting your letter and sending it to some paper for
publication.

I. **Self-Determination in the Mental Economy.**—State your view of
the relations of will and intellect; of choice and emotion; of choice
and action. Diagram and explain *deliberation, impulsion, determination, action.* Are you at liberty to prefer one thing to another?
Give some proofs.

II. **Terms defined.**—Give your definition of *attention;* of *choice;*
of action; of motives; of weak motives; of strong motives; of high
motives; of low motives; of freedom. What do you mean by the
education of choice? Illustrate.

III. **Importance of Will-Culture.**—What has determination to do
with success? Does will-culture develop decision of character?
How does will-culture make for righteousness? State two additional reasons why you consider will-culture superlatively important.

IV. **Growth of Choice.**—State your recollections of the growth of your power of choice. Tell results of your studies of will-growth in others. What have you gained from books? Describe child-will; boy-will; youth-will; man-will; will of the aged.

V. **Means of Choice-Culture.**—Explain the value of hard study; of discipline; of good literature; of good companionship; of biography; of ethics. Make a table of choice-culture values.

VI. **Laws of the Growth of Choice.**—State in terms of choice the law of effort; the law of means; the law of method. Write out two special laws that you have discovered.

VII. **Methods of educating Choice.**—Describe the kindergarten ways of developing choice; primary ways; intermediate methods; high-school methods. Should we be as systematic and persistent in the culture of will as in the culture of intellect?

VIII. **Mistakes in Will-Culture.**—What will be the educational ideal of the twentieth century? Do we neglect will-culture? Why is negative will-culture counted a mistake? Illustrate. What is the golden mean between rigid and loose control? Do school methods sometimes develop *bad* will? Why do you protest against breaking the will of the pupil?

CHAPTER XXVI.

EDUCATION OF ACTION.

ACTION stands for doing. We act when we do what we make up our minds to do. We execute our purposes. Education of action means the development of executive power. We have men of thought like Plato, and men of action like Hannibal. Our ideal man is at once a man of thought and a man of action. Paul, the peerless thinker, was also the peerless worker.

As Will, Self attends, determines, acts.—We carry out our plans; we execute our purposes; we make our determinations acts. We are endowed with the capability to make our purposes *acts*. *Action* is

21

the native energy of self to execute his determinations. It is the executive power of the soul. I determine to write a letter: writing the letter is self *acting*. I determine to solve the problem: solving the problem is self *acting*. I determine to teach a class in Sunday-school: teaching the class is self *acting*. Self, in executing his purposes, commands all his resources of body and mind.

I. **Action in the Mental Economy.**—Mental activity culminates in action. Sensations occasion ideas; ideas occasion emotions; ideas and emotions occasion determinations; determinations occasion *acts*. You know, you feel, you resolve, you *do*. You learn that your sick neighbor is in need: you pity; you determine to relieve his wants; you now *act* in ministering to the suffering one. The unity of the self is strikingly exhibited in action. Self determines, and, in executing his purpose, he marshals all his energies of mind and body. Like the commander of a disciplined army, self hurls all his forces into the effort to win the battle. Intellect gives wisdom; emotion gives impulse; will gives purpose and concentration; but in the execution of purposes *action* dominates. Self is intent on achievement, and exerts all his powers to accomplish his purposes.

Purposed Action.—Movement is action in its general sense, but there are many kinds of movement. Mechanical movement is termed *mechanical* action; reflex movement is termed *reflex* action; impulsive movement is termed *impulsive* action; instinctive movement is termed *instinctive* action; and purposed movement is termed *purposed* action. Action, as here used, is *purposed action*, and includes all intentional doing. Whatever we do in executing our determinations is termed *willed* action. Brute movements are *impulsive* and not rational acts. Impulse passes over into action without the intervention of deliberative purpose. Only rational beings—self-acting, self-conscious, and self-determining—are capable of doing purposed acts. It is *purposed action* that we educate. We develop the energy to execute purposes.

II. **Terms defined.**—A mind is endowed with capabilities to act in various ways. The one self does these acts, and so we think of a faculty or power as merely a capability of a self. Self as will executes.

1. *Action is the native energy of self to execute his determinations.* All forms of carrying out plans are termed *action*. The man of action is the man of executive power. The terms *action, execution, volition,* and *executive power* are used interchangeably. Action is simply our capability to execute our purposes. I know, I feel, I plan, I *execute*.

2. *Education of action is the development of the executive power.* This culture develops the habit of executing our plans with promptitude and vigor. It makes the difference between the efficient man of affairs and the dreamer. The feeble purposed actions of the child are the buddings of executive power that may rule an empire.

III. **Importance of the Education of Action.**—The road to failure is paved with unexecuted purposes. Decisive opportunities unimproved are forever lost. The tide must be taken at the flood. The power and habit of decisive and effective execution are invaluable.

1. *Action-culture makes the scholar.* The boy and youth who continually form *projects* of study which they never execute are failures. They grow up to be men of *projects* and not of deeds. Only students who learn to execute with iron will their plans of study can hope to be crowned.

2. *Action-culture organizes success.* The pupil who gets into the habit of succeeding becomes the successful man. Doing leads to better doing.

3. *Doing doubles capability.* The inspiration of achievement works wonders. Inactivity dwarfs, while activity makes giants. Somehow doing what wo plan to do makes us mighty to conquer.

4. *Action is a large part of life.* Much of our lives is physical action, as talking, walking, singing, eating. Physical action is almost the entire life of the child. Most of our adult life is execution of purposes. We can thus realize the immense importance of so educating action as to lead to achievement.

5. "*Physical education means an economy of force,* for the reason that every movement is intrusted to the muscle best fitted to the end in view. If inaction, or the defective action of an organ, causes atrophy, it must follow that its frequent activity promotes increased development. This is true of the brain and of all the nervous elements used in physical movement. Not only is it true that the nervous system has a share in the organic changes made by physical exercises, but it is as true that the psychical faculties are strongly influenced. The will is developed and improved by a systematic command of muscle, and this increase of will-power is a large factor in the growth of character." *

IV. **Growth of Action.**—The child is a bundle of activities. The infant strikes and kicks and sucks and cries. These instinctive and reflex movements prepare the body for purposed action. Preyer observed willed action during the fourth month. Certainly we discover the germs of purposed action before the child is six

* Miss Clara Conway, Paper read before the National Council of Education.

months old. But the remarkable feebleness of child-will is nòtorious. Hence the surprising credulity, docility, obedience, tractableness, and dependence of children. This weakness also explains the impossibility of mesmerizing little children. Hypnotism is conditioned by continued attention, which is impossible to the young child.

The child acts from impulse rather than from purpose, but culture changes impulsive action into purposed action. The boy and girl learn to think before they act. Action is now becoming effective and achievement gives unmeasured pleasure. The executive power is highly active in youth, and reaches full activity in early manhood.

From the sixth to the fourteenth year is eminently the habit-forming period. The pupil must be led to do until doing is rooted into habit.

V. Means for the Education of Executive Volition.—These are so abundant as to embarrass the teacher. We must choose wisely.

1. *Kindergarten-work* is mostly action. How admirable the exercises are planned to promote the growth of spontaneous action into purposed action! The child intentionally represents realities and works to accomplish something.

2. *Gymnastics, school tactics, and good plays*, are all valuable for action-culture. Pupils get into the habit of executing purposes, and of working in harmony with others.

3· *Molding, carving, making things, drawing, and penmanship*, are admirable for action-culture. Our manual-training schools emphasize the value of these exercises.

4. *Music, reading, conversation, and composition*, are wonderful promoters of the growth of willed action. Spelling, pronunciation, expression, deserve special mention.

5. *Manners and morals* justly take precedence during the primary and intermediate periods.

6. *Study* ranks high during the high-school and college periods.

The student works to a programme and continually executes his resolves.

7. *Biography and history* are of high value. The achievements of others inspire us for achievement.

VI. Laws of Action-Growth.—No one objects when we say, " We learn to do by doing." "Art is long," and only repetition gives skill and forms habits.

1. *Executing purposes educates action.* Not making plans, but *executing* plans, develops the executive power. We gain executive ability by determinedly carrying out our purposes.

2. *All lines of work that demand the constant execution of purposes may be made the means of action-culture.* We have an infinite store-house from which to select. Doing intentional *acts* educates action. Executing determinations develops our executive power.

3. *Plans of work that require the systematic, persistent, and effective execution of purposes educate action.* " Few things are so repulsive as to see a conceited teacher with some pet hobby trying to convince children that the text-book is, and all previous teachers have been, wrong, and he alone has the ' best ' way. There are good ways, there are better ways, but I know neither man nor woman in all my range of acquaintance who has the *best* way in education, general or specific. I am quite confident that the best will not be discovered in my day." * However, we may modestly *strive* after the best. Vanderbilt told the ambitious youth that he had made money by working hard and saying nothing. Teachers may safely pursue this course : seek the best ways, and let results speak for you.

* A. E. Winship.

VII. **Primary and Intermediate Methods of educating Action.**—These are plans of work which lead pupils to habitually execute their purposes.   Self as action executes his own purposes.   Systematically and persistently executing purposes educates action.   Primary and intermediate methods are plans of school work adapted to pupils from six to fourteen years of age.   This is termed the habit-forming period.   The right culture of action is now of the utmost importance.

1. *Lead the pupil to do.*   Knowing comes before doing.   The pupil, in view of knowing and feeling, determines and acts.   A purposed action implies knowing and emotion.   Just here we need to pause and try to gain a deeper insight.   The child in reality begins to do when its knowledge is shadowy, and when it is not easy to distinguish impulsive action from purposed action.   Doing, it is certain, leads to better knowing and better doing.   You lead the child to *test* the apple by each sense, and to mold it and to draw it.   These purposed acts cultivate the power to act and also help the child to gain a better knowledge of the apple.   May we not thus harmonize, on a higher plain, the expressions, " We learn to do by knowing "; " We learn to do by doing " ; and, " We learn to know by doing " ?

2. *Lead the pupil to form good habits.*   This includes a large section of your work.   You manage to have the pupil keep on acting *properly* until good manners become fixed habits.   You lead the pupil to go on *doing right* until right doing grows into a firm habit.   You lead the pupil to continue spelling correctly and pronouncing correctly and composing correctly until these acts grow into life-habits.

3. *Lead the pupil to form the habit of succeeding.*
Give your pupils work that they *can* do, and then manage to have them do it. They will thus get into the habit of succeeding. You need to foster pluck. Pupils *will* accomplish what they undertake. They must know no such word as fail. The habit of succeeding, now acquired, becomes a life-habit.

4. *Appreciate success.* The veteran minister, as well as the infant just taking its first step, is strengthened by judicious praise. The little successes of the child deserve warm appreciation, as do the greater successes of the girls and boys. Without this appreciation on the part of the parents and teachers and associates, few pupils ever amount to much. Care must be taken to praise earnest effort and real success in such ways as will lead to greater effort and greater success without exciting vanity.

VIII. **High-School Methods of educating the Executive Power.**—The faltering child has become the determined youth. The aimless boy has become a student with a purpose. Now is the time to develop the iron will. The impulsive and daring youth, amid all tempests, must be educated to adhere firmly to his purposes and determinedly work out his life-plans. How may parents and ministers and friends and teachers help? How may the youth develop great executive power?

1. *Work to a programme.* The railroad has its time-table and the school has its programme. No less does the individual need to have a systematic plan of work. The programme is a wonderful conservator of mental and physical energy. The successful men that reach a grand old age owe much to system. Working

to a programme gives tenacity of purpose and greatly strengthens the executive power. It is the way to success. The writer has induced hundreds of youths to form the habit of working to a programme. "To this habit I owe my success," is the cheering testimony received from scores. I see no other way in which you can do so much for your students as in educating them to make and to follow good plans of work.

2. *Approve good work*. This is the teacher's glad office. Many a mother has made a noble man out of her son by her warm appreciation of his achievements. Many a wife has made a great man out of her husband by her approval of his noble acts. Your pupils, encouraged by your smiles of warm appreciation, will do any amount of work. Hearty approval is better than instruction. Icebergs may do for lawyers, but they will not do for teachers.

3. *Study systematically*. Hard study develops willpower as nothing else does. It develops *attention* because it is the concentration of effort. It educates self-determination because it is the constant exercise of choice. It educates action because it is the determined execution of purposes. But the student must study systematically. Spurts do not help much. Studying vigorously, day after day, and adhering to a well-digested programme, strengthens the executive power as nothing else can.

4. *Foster the habit of succeeding*. Success is bringing about desired results. Every problem the student solves is a success. Every lesson the youth masters is a success. Every temptation resisted or duty done is a success. It is infinitely important to youths to get into

the habit of succeeding. Nothing succeeds like success. The balky horse will not try. The student who failed yesterday and to-day will not try to-morrow. The habit of failing weakens even hope. Our students must not fail.

IX. **Mistakes in educating Action.**—The teacher seeks insight. Child-nature and child-growth are studied with tireless interest. Everything tending to promote healthy growth is fostered, and everything tending to retard or mar is avoided.

1. *Action-culture is neglected.* The development of rational self-activity is primary. How often this is forgotten in our zeal to impart knowledge! Right habits are more important than a knowledge of fractions. Studies are means of calling forth effort and thus developing power. Culture must be many-sided. Will and emotion, as well as intellect, must be educated. Each lesson, in some way, must educate the entire child. Exclusive intellectual culture is a fundamental error.

2. *Pupils are permitted to fail.* In the average school, half the pupils fail day after day. The blundering recitations, through which they are *dragged*, do not help. The fatal habit of failing becomes a life-habit. This must not be. The work must be such as the pupils *can* do, and they *must* be led to do it. Success in easy work is immeasurably better than failure in hard work. The habit of succeeding must be ingrained.

3. *Action is not rooted into habit.* The educational waste resulting from this neglect is enormous. How much of mental waste is saved when the child early forms the habit of truth-telling! What we do habit-

ually we do easily. How inexpressibly important it is
that all right habits be fixed early in life!

4. *Bad habits are not eradicated.* Girls are suffered
to go on sipping wine; boys are suffered to go on
smoking the fatal cigarette. Bad habits are like dis-
eases: they must be eradicated before good habits can be
formed. We must lead our pupils to stop doing wrong,
and thus break up bad habits. We must lead them to
begin doing right, and keep on doing right, and thus
establish good habits.

5. *"Breaking a child's will is not the way to educate it,* any more than breaking a stick is the way to
bend it; when it is once broken, there is nothing left
to bend. It is never right, whether at home or at
school, to make a child give in through mere terror.
Education presupposes sympathy. Terror kills sympathy. The parent or teacher who makes a child
afraid of him, puts that child out of his reach. It becomes forever impossible for that parent or teacher to
educate that child. He may force him to recite lessons,
and compel him to obey commands; but that confi-
dential leading of mind and will into larger fields and
wiser ways in which true education consists is utterly
impossible. A rule maintained by terror is a reign of
death, whether in home, or school, or state."*

6. *Injudicious praise is a mistake.* Talented young
ministers and teachers are often spoiled by flattery, as
are hundreds of bright boys and pretty girls. Un-
merited praise is poison, and its product is the vain
egotist. Judicious praise is always helpful, and should
take the place of sarcasm and fault finding.

* President W. D. Hyde.

SUGGESTIVE STUDY-HINTS.

Letter.—Your letter to your teacher-friend about the education of action will be full of helpful suggestions. You feel deeply the necessity for reform in our methods of educating the will. You will strongly urge this.

I. **Position of Action in the Mental Economy.**—Point this out in cut, page 2, and in diagram, page 284. Trace sensations up to ideas, up to emotions, up to determinations, up to actions. Illustrate.

II. **Terms defined.**—Give your definition of action; of purposed action; of executive volition; of the executive power; of the education of action.

III. **Importance of Action-Culture.**—Why do you consider the education of action very important? How does it affect scholarship? What has it to do with success? How does it bear on capability? How much of life is action?

IV. **Growth of Action.**—What kind of activity makes up most of the child's life? How early does the child manifest purposed action? How does reflex and impulsive action become willed action? Describe the growth of action during the kindergarten period; during the primary period; during the intermediate period; during the high-school period; during the college period. What do you consider the habit-forming period?

V. **Means for the Education of Action.**—Point out how kindergarten-work helps. What value do you give to gymnastics? to drawing? to music? to manners? to study? Place on the board your table of action-culture values.

VI. **Laws of Action-Growth.**—State the law of effort in terms of action; the law of means; the law of method. What does Dr. Winship say about methods? What does Vanderbilt say was his method of acquiring wealth?

VII. **Primary and Intermediate Methods of educating Action.**—What do you mean by primary methods? by intermediate methods? by high-school methods? by college methods? Point out the relations between knowing and doing. How will you lead your pupils to form good habits? How will you get your pupils into the habit of succeeding? How does judicious praise help?

VIII. **High-School Methods of educating the Executive Power.**—Show the benefits of working to a programme. How does approving of good work help? Give some of the benefits of studying systematically. Why should the habit of succeeding be fostered?

IX. **Mistakes in educating Action.**—Why do we neglect action-culture? Show the bad effects of permitting pupils to fail. Point out the waste resulting from the failure to root action into habit. Why should bad habits be eradicated? Is it a mistake to try to break the child's will? Mention some of the evil effects of flattery.

CHAPTER XXVII.

CULTURE OF THE WILL.*

The purpose of will-training is character.   By character is meant those established and fixed tendencies that are so strong as to give direction to conduct.   Loyalty to conviction characterizes high character.   "The crowning purpose of education is to make the will follow the lead of conviction in all matters involving the idea of duty.   The moral will is the significance, so to speak, of all the other activities of the mind.   Institutional life is the moral will as it has realized itself.   The ethical ideal is actualized in human society to the extent that it is common to the particular members.   The principle of conduct in the ethical world is what is known as the moral law.   This law is the universal conviction that every act of each particular member of the ethical whole should be such that when it is made universal—that is, becomes the act of all—it will return upon the doer to bless and not to curse him.   In this way the institutional world becomes a ministration of

* In this chapter quotation-marks are omitted where changes have been made, as the authors are not responsible for the form in which their thoughts are here presented

grace; each citizen receiving in return for every good deed the good increased a thousand-fold." *

The will is the self-determining energy of the soul. It is our power to choose those courses of action which we will follow, and reject those from which we will refrain. It is the faculty of the soul to initiate activity. Acts of the self as will are volitions; they are *choices* when we *determine* on one of two or more courses, but they are *executive* volitions when we *do* as we determine. The self is *free* in willing; is endowed with the power of self-determination. Every one is aware of this We are conscious of our own liberty of action. A *person* literally does as he pleases, and says truly, "I *will*" and "I will not." The self can not be compelled to will. We are conscious of freedom in willing.

The self as will determines in view of motives. The considerations which occasion choices are termed *motives*. Cognitions and emotions *move* self to determine. We lead others to determine and act by placing motives before them. All government and all plans for human elevation are based on the psychological truth that one person can influence the voluntary conduct of another. The educator seeks to place before his pupils the *highest* motives. *Cosmic* motives are the highest; *altruistic* motives are the next highest; *selfish* motives are low; *malevolent* motives are the lowest. The highest group of cosmic motives is the ethical. These are the emotions of an enlightened conscience prompting to right doing. Who is not at times aware of rising *above self*, and even above the promptings of

---

* George P. Brown; paper in the National Council of Education.

all forms of *love*, and acting solely from a sense of duty ? *

All education is, in a sense, education of will. All excellence developed by education is of the nature of habit. Will-culture places the cope-stone on the whole educational building. It determines the character which forms the guerdon or the doom of every man ; for character is a completely developed will.

Education builds on the rock of established truths, and leaves theorists to harmonize at their leisure. An action done with a view to some end is a willed action. In early life voluntary acts are largely muscular movements, as in writing, drawing, singing, reading, or practicing music. It is important to insist on the right muscular adjustment from the very first lesson. Right habits are thus formed.

Volition implies more than a cognition of an act to be performed, more than an emotion impelling to its performance. Cognitions and emotions are indispensable prerequisites of volition, but will is the *fiat* that transforms cognition and emotion into *purpose* and action. The immense importance of will-culture is apparent. Half the race fall short of reasonable possibilities because they lack *energy of will*, and not for lack of clear intelligence or delicate sensibility.

Education of the will develops decision of character. It becomes a habit to determine promptly and to adhere to purposes with unalterable decision. Indecision weakens innumerable lives. Decision of character may be developed by adopting, in our educational methods, specific plans of work for will-culture. All

* Moral Education, by Larkin Dunton, in Education for April, 1891.

educators admit this as a theory, but most fail to carry
it out in practice.   School discipline, it is true, does
much in the right direction, but it alone is insufficient.
What is wanted is a discipline which the individual im-
poses on himself.   Any human being who firmly controls himself in the face of a great temptation, and who
persists in executing his purpose in the midst of fearful difficulties, is drawing upon the universal fountain
of spiritual power, and assuredly he shall have his reward.*

Work, and therein have Well-being.—" *We acquire the virtues by
doing the acts*, as is the case with the arts too.   We learn an art by
doing that which we wish to do when we have learned it; we become builders by building, and harpers by harping.   And so by doing just acts we become just, and by doing acts of temperance and
courage we become temperate and courageous.   Both virtues and
vices result from and are formed by the same acts in which they manifest themselves, as is the case with the arts also.   It is by building
that good builders and bad builders alike are produced; by building
well they will become good builders, and bad builders by building
badly.   It is by our conduct in our intercourse with other men that
we become just or unjust.   So, too, with our animal appetites and
the passion of anger; for by behaving in this way or in that on the
occasions with which these passions are concerned some become temperate and gentle and others profligate and ill-tempered.   In a word,
the several habits or characters are formed by the same kind of acts
as those which they produce.   Hence we ought to make sure that
our acts be of a certain kind, for the resulting character varies as
they vary.   It makes no small difference, therefore, whether a man
be trained from his youth up in this way or in that, but a great difference, or rather all the difference." †

"This is the ineradicable, forever-enduring gospel: work, and
therein have well-being.   All true work is sacred; in all true work,

* Education of the Will, by J. Clark Murray, in Educational Review
for June, 1891.
† Aristotle, in his Ethics.

were it but true hand-labor, there is something of divineness.
Labor, wide as the earth, has its summit in heaven.   Produce; produce; were it but the pitifulest infinitesimal fraction of a product,
produce it in God's name.   'Tis the utmost thou hast in thee; out
with it, then.   Up, up! whatsoever thy hand findeth to do, do it with
thy whole might.   Work while it is called to-day; for the night
cometh, wherein no man can work.   Two men I honor, and no third.
First, the toil-worn craftsman, that with earth-made implement
laboriously conquers the earth and makes her man's.   Toil on, toil
on; thou art in thy duty, be out of it who may; thou toilest for the
altogether indispensable, for daily bread.   A second man I honor,
and still more highly: him who is seen toiling for the spiritually indispensable—not daily bread, but the bread of life.   Is not he too
in his duty?   If the poor and humble toil that we may have food
must not the high and glorious toil for him in return, that he may
have light, have guidance, freedom, immortality?   These two, in
all their degrees, I honor; all else is chaff, which let the wind blow
whither it listeth." *

Getting boys and girls to do right.   There are two
ways by which we may endeavor to get boys and girls
to do right.   One way is to fill their minds with rules;
another way is to train the will in habits.   The second
is a much harder thing to do, but it is the only effective
way.   There is no text-book on the subject, and it is
impossible to write one.

The education of the will can not be introduced into the curricu-
lum as a new requirement.   It must be entirely free and uncon-
strained.   Unless the impulse to do it is already in the teacher's
heart, no enactment of the school committee can put it into the
school.   I can not tell you how to do it.   You must work it out for
yourselves as opportunities present themselves.   I can simply call
your attention to its importance, and indicate some very general
lines on which you can proceed.
The best field for this education of the will is in the home; for
there life is most simple and real, contact is most intimate, and de-

* Thomas Carlyle.

22

sires and passions express themselves with least restraint. Next to
the home comes the school. Next to father and mother stands the
teacher. The pastor, the Sunday-school teacher, the employer, the
writer, the lecturer, may each do something in this moral training.
But the teacher has the best chance of them all, if he only has the
will and the skill to use it.

The test of a man's education is the quality of work that he can do,
not the quantity of information that he can remember. Mere memorized information in the mind of the scholar is as worthless as undigested food in the stomach of an athlete. The development of
strong intellectual muscles and steady moral nerves is the end and
aim of education.

Train the pupils in the schools to do the work there given
them to do with promptness, neatness, and order—with all their
might and to the best of their ability; and you will do your part
toward fitting them for any sphere of life; making them ready to
take hold of any kind of honest work, and qualifying them to assume the duties and responsibilities of membership in the social and
industrial order, and of citizenship in church and state.*

The education of the will. This, in the broader
sense, means the whole of one's training to moral and
prudential conduct. In the narrow sense, it means the
development of the power to *initiate* movements tribu-
tary to desired ends and to *inhibit* irrelevant impulses.
The longer one attends to a topic the more mastery of
it he has. The power of voluntarily bringing back a
wandering attention over and over again is the very
root of judgment, character, and will. An education
which develops this power is the education *par excellence*. The more interest pupils have in advance in the
subject the better they will attend. Induct them in such
a way as to knit each new thing on to some acquisition
already there, and, if possible, awaken curiosity, so that

* The Education of the Will, by President W. De Witt Hyde, in
Popular Educator.

the new thing shall seem to come as an answer to a question pre-existing in the mind. I count myself among those who consider will as an original spiritual energy.*

Rewards and Punishments.†—The Father endowed us with the power of self-determination, and He always leaves us free to choose. The expression of will in free choice is the highest expression of personality. God holds sacred the personality of every man. He sets before us life and death, but leaves us absolutely free in the exercise of our will-power. He has so constituted things that happiness comes of right choices, and misery follows wrong determinations. The rewards and punishments are declared in advance, but we do the choosing. God never forces our choices.

As our Father deals with us, so we should deal with our pupils. The privilege of personal choice should be sacredly guarded. While we must use all proper influences to induce our pupils to choose aright, we should never, never, never force their choices. All good comes through right choices, and all evil comes through wrong determinations. The rewards and punishments are declared in advance, but the pupil does the choosing. In training the will we hold out alternatives, but the final responsibility of a choice, with its consequences, rests with the pupil.

   * Prof. William James.   † H. Clay Trumbull.

PART VI.

THE ART OF TEACHING.

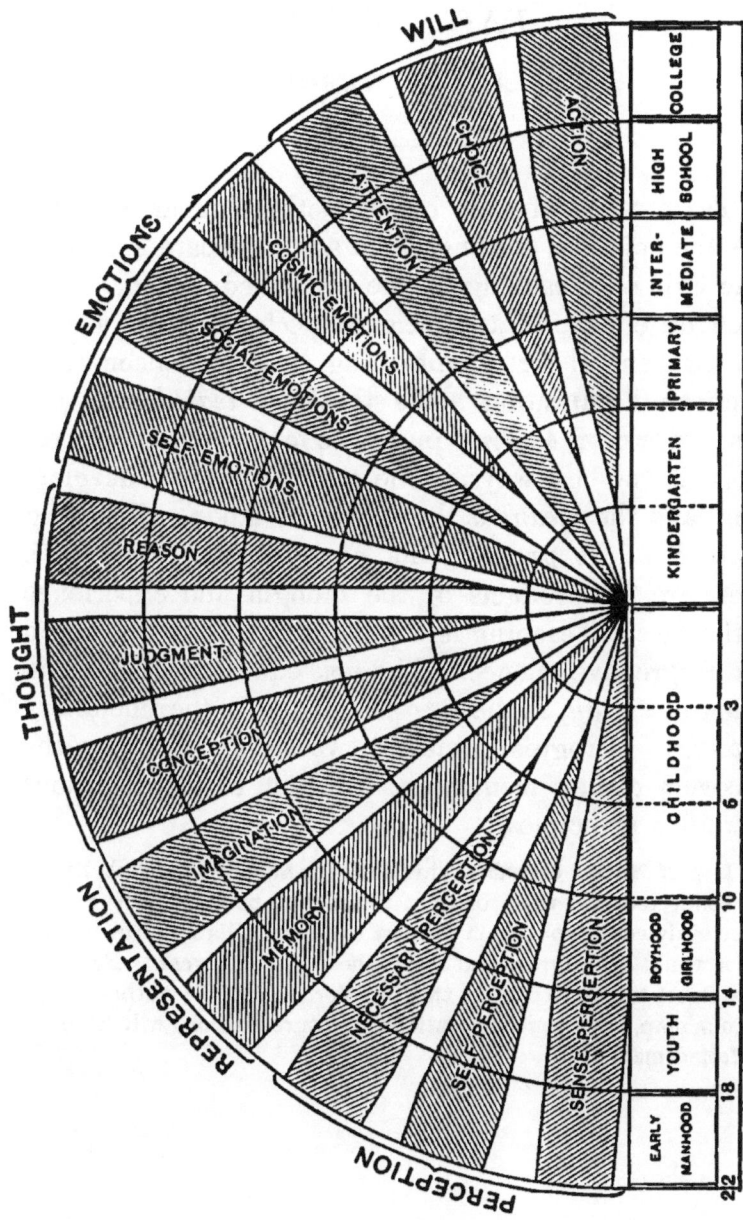

MAP OF MENTAL GROWTH.

PART SIXTH.

THE ART OF TEACHING.

TEACHING is the art of promoting human growth. It is the art of so guiding effort as to prepare for complete living. Teaching is the art of education, and is based on education as a science. *Pedagogy* is a convenient general term, embracing both the theory and practice of education. We think of *teaching* as the actual work of *leading* pupils to put forth their best efforts in the best ways. The *end* is complete development, and the *means* is the course of study. Teaching has its *laws*, its *processes*, its *periods*, and its *methods*. These are the products of the thought and experience of the race. Teaching is a *progressive* art as education is a progressive science. The *new* education is the education of *to-day*, as the *new* chemistry is the chemistry of *to-day*. Progress comes in two ways : (1) From the discovery of new principles ; (2) from new applications of known principles.

Map of Mental Growth.—This device is an effort to symbolize in one connected view the growth of the mental powers. This growth is certainly continuous from infancy to the meridian of life, but the *artist* would *arrest* growth at about the eighteenth year! Reader, I must trust to you to correct this blunder. Send the author a copy of *your* map, with your suggestions. Future editions will have the perfected map.

Educational Evolution.—Bound up in the human germ are all the possibilities of manhood. Education is the development of the possibilities of this germ Each human germ is a self in embryo. Educational *evolution* is the development of the native energies of the self. All the capabilities of the man are feebly active in the child ; education *develops* native power, but does not *create* capabilities. Each self is endowed with the same elemental energies ; in all the.ages no new capability has been added. Education simply means the growth of the feeble child into the strong man, equipped for the battle of life. Teaching is the art of promoting this growth.

CHAPTER XXVIII.

LAWS OF TEACHING.

All good comes through law. The Infinite Lawgiver is the Infinite Good. The wise man is happy because he finds out and obeys law, but the fool is miserable because of his ignorance and waywardness Law voices the eternal fitness of things, and is the articulated lan guage of energy.

Growth through lawful self-activity is the central idea in the science of education. Around the central idea are grouped the great facts of mind and mental growth. These fundamental truths are termed educational *principles* and educational *laws*. These, stated in terms of art, are *guiding* truths, are *laws of teaching*. Lawful self-effort educates ; ways of securing such effort are here called

The Nine Laws of Teaching.

I. Be what you would have your Pupils become.— This is the granite. Weak, wayward, uncultured per-

sons, though versed in all the methods, can not educate.
Teachers of culture and character, of head-power and
heart-power, will find ways to educate. Superior manhood is infinitely more important than superior methods.
Our teaching pyramids crumble because they are not
based on the granite. Teachers need to be strong, true,
manly. They need to be men and women of faith and
hope and love. Worthy teachers do everything to make
the most of *themselves*, that they may do most for their
pupils. It is an education to be for years a pupil of a
great teacher.

The Laws of Teaching.

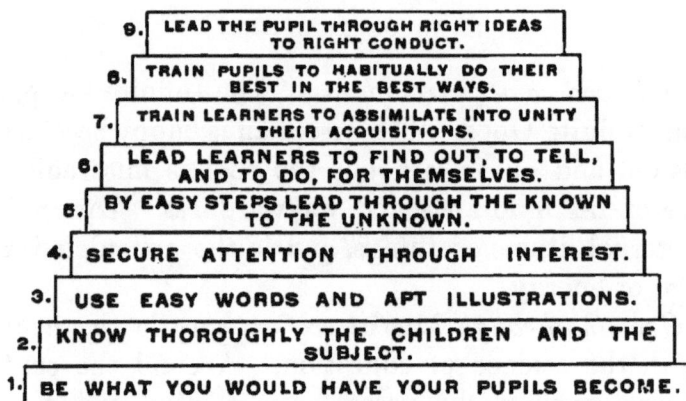

9. LEAD THE PUPIL THROUGH RIGHT IDEAS TO RIGHT CONDUCT.

8. TRAIN PUPILS TO HABITUALLY DO THEIR BEST IN THE BEST WAYS.

7. TRAIN LEARNERS TO ASSIMILATE INTO UNITY THEIR ACQUISITIONS.

6. LEAD LEARNERS TO FIND OUT, TO TELL, AND TO DO, FOR THEMSELVES.

5. BY EASY STEPS LEAD THROUGH THE KNOWN TO THE UNKNOWN.

4. SECURE ATTENTION THROUGH INTEREST.

3. USE EASY WORDS AND APT ILLUSTRATIONS.

2. KNOW THOROUGHLY THE CHILDREN AND THE SUBJECT.

1. BE WHAT YOU WOULD HAVE YOUR PUPILS BECOME.

The Pyramid.—I am indebted to Dr. J. M. Gregory for the idea. I
found his Seven Laws of Teaching helpful in my normal classes. The attempt is here made to present some of the most important laws of teaching
in logical sequence in the form of a pyramid. Dear teacher, reconstruct
the pyramid to suit your views, and write a paper on each law. What an
interesting symposium could be arranged for a reading circle or summer
normal school by placing the pyramid on the board and having a short,
spicy essay on each law! Suggestive summary statements are of great
value.

II. **Know thoroughly the Child and the Subject.**—The first mandate of pedagogy is, *"Know yourself that you may know the child."* The teacher is but a child of larger growth. The second mandate is, *"Live close to the living, growing, loving child."* With infinite interest you study your growing pupils as the botanist studies the growing plants. You gain insight and inspiration, which fits you for the joyous work of leading your pupils up to a higher and better physical, mental, and moral life. *"Know thoroughly what you try to teach"* is the third mandate of pedagogy. You have studied, as best you could, *many things.* You have tried to gain a general view of the realm of knowledge. Now you *concentrate* your efforts. You aspire to a thorough knowledge of the branches you propose to teach and of their relations to mental growth. Under the guidance of eminent teachers you now study profoundly the child and the subject from the standpoint of the educator. Under the direction of skilled teachers you gain by *practice-teaching* skill in teaching. Thus prepared, you will enter the school-room as an artist, and will be able through years of toil to prove yourself a master-workman.

III. **Use Easy Words and Apt Illustrations.**—Sunlight clearness characterizes the best teaching. Sit at the feet of Jesus while he teaches his disciples. Follow Socrates through the streets of Athens as he practices the Socratic method. Listen to the masters of assemblies as they hold spell-bound the waiting thousands. Read the best in literature. You find that the great teachers of mankind observe this law. Because of the failure to observe it, more than half of all attempts at teaching is waste labor. Could teachers be led to practice this rule, it would almost double the efficiency of the teaching force of the world.

IV. **Secure Attention through Interest.**—Attention is the condition of knowledge as well as of mental growth. We voluntarily attend, but we choose to give attention to the things which interest us. The efficient teacher in some way awakens and sustains interest, and thus gains and holds the attention of her pupils Her pupils are *happy*, and they do more in a week than the unhappy pupils of the stupid teacher do in a month. Herbart counts *tediousness* the great educational sin. He might have termed the *teacher-habit* of stupidity, dullness, dryness, and tediousness, the unpardonable *teacher-sin*.

V. **By Easy Steps lead through the Known to the Unknown.**—The learner *must* take the steps. The teacher guides effort, but pupils ascend, round by round, by their own efforts. It is a great thing in education to adjust and adapt the work so that the pupils *can* take with joy each advanced step. It is a greater thing to lead them to take these steps. This is the art of teaching. You make the learner's present attainments the basis. Through what your pupils know now you lead them to find out new things. This law stands for a large part of the work of the teacher as an instructor.

VI. **Lead Learners to find out, tell, and do for Themselves.**—Self-effort under guidance educates. The teacher plans but the pupil *does*. From the kindergarten to the university, the educator so manages that a pupil discovers for himself, tells in his own words, and does things in his own way. Persons thus tutored become

independent thinkers, original writers, and self-reliant
actors. This law strikes at the roots of some of the
worst pedagogical evils.

VII. **Lead Learners to assimilate into Unity their
Acquisitions.**—Isolated ideas are not knowledge. All
things are related, and the universe is a unit. From
the kindergarten to the university the learner is led to
assimilate into unity his experiences. Even the child-
world is now wrought into unity. This is a law of the
new education, and it is absolutely revolutionary.

This unitizing process in our times is called *apperceiving*. It
requires many terms to fully express this very complex process.
Apperception stands for *psychic reaction, interpretation, conception,*
and *assimilation,* all taken together. This process involves the following elements: (1) A train of ideas already in the mind as a result
of experience; (2) a new idea which is brought into relation to this
train so as to be recognized through it, and (3) interpreted and explained by it; (4) this process resulting in a twofold result, namely,
a knowledge of the real existence of examples or individual instances of the idea in question; and (5) the subsumption of those
particular instances under a general concept and the recognition
that the individual perceived is only a special phase and not the
whole reality of the general idea.

VIII. **Train your Pupils to habitually do their best
in the Best Ways.**—This is the whole of method. Doing
one's best develops power; putting forth effort in the
best ways gives skill and culture. Men become great
and reach eminence by habitually doing their best.
Winship did his best in lifting two hundred pounds;
but day by day he lifted more and more until he could
lift three thousand pounds. Beecher told the students
that he owed his success to the habit of always doing
his best. Doing things feebly and bunglingly dwarfs.

We must expect great things of our pupils, and lead them habitually to make great efforts. This is the education that develops superior men and women.

IX. **Lead the Pupil through Right Ideas to Right Conduct.**—This is the crowning law of teaching. The pupil is rational, impulsive, free. Right ideas induce right impulses and right acts. *The teacher controls the pupil's ideas. Right ideas* are kept before the pupil until they become *right acts.* The pupil is led to repeat these acts until they become *habits.* Here you have the whole of *moral education* in a *nutshell.*

CHAPTER XXIX.

TEACHING PROCESSES.

THE teacher *must* have the pupil proceed in definite *ways* in order to learn. These ways are termed *teaching processes;* it is equally proper to call them *learning processes.* We group these processes thus:

TEACHING PROCESSES.

I.	{ Objective Process. { Subjective Process.	III.	{ Inductive Process. { Deductive Process.
II.	{ Analytic Process. { Synthetic Process.	IV.	{ Empirical Process. { Rational Process.

V. Apperceptive Process.

I. { Objective Process.
{ Subjective Process. These are the two ways of finding out. The first is the process of gaining particular ideas, and the second is the process of gaining general ideas.

1. *The objective process is the way we gain ideas directly from things.* Things, as here used, include material *objects*, mental *acts*, and necessary *realities*. At first the mental life is sensation. Through its sensa- tions we lead the child to gain ideas of material things, and we call these lessons *sense-object-lessons.* Later, the mental self is *awareness.* Through its awareness we lead the child to gain ideas of its mental acts, and we call these lessons *self-object-lessons.* Later, the mental life is *necessary-intuition.* Through its necessary-in- tuitions we lead the child to gain ideas of necessary- realities, and we call these lessons *necessary-reality object-lessons.*

2. *The subjective process is the way we gain general notions.* Things are related. We discern relations; we elaborate our percepts into concepts; we think our notions into truths; we make definitions and solve problems; we write essays and invent machines. We lead our pupils to *think* their notions into higher forms, and we call these lessons *subject-lessons.* Conceiving, judging, reasoning, are subjective processes.

The process of gaining ideas of things is *objective;* but the process of elaborating percepts into truths is *subjective.* When we study our- selves, self is both *object* and *subject.* The self studied is object; but the self that studies is subject. Objective knowledge is the basis of subjective knowledge. The objective and subjective processes go on together and continually re-enforce each other. The objective predominates in early life, but later the subjective predominates. "The mind ever rises from clear *individual* to distinct *general* no- tions."

II. { Analytic Process. Synthetic Process. } These are the two ways in which we must proceed in order to gain mastery. We divide to conquer, and unite to understand.

1. *The analytic process is the way we teach and learn by separating wholes into parts.* We are incapable of grasping complex wholes, so we divide them and master part by part. However we make the division, we call the process analytic whenever we separate wholes into parts in order to study the parts. Teaching is analytic when we lead our pupils to separate wholes into parts for detailed study.

2. *Synthetic process is the way we teach and learn by uniting parts into wholes.* The parts are considered in their relations to each other and in their relations to the whole. *Part* and *whole* are used in their widest sense. The earth is a part of the solar system, and oxygen is a part of water. The synthetic process includes all forms of combining parts into wholes. Teaching is synthetic when we lead our pupils to unitize their knowledge.

Analysis and Synthesis must go together.—They are always associated. Important as thoroughness of *analysis* is, it is worthless unless accompanied by a proper *synthesis*. Analysis is valuable only in its relation to unification. Unless the elements of analysis are *rightly* unified, they lose their importance. Synthesis is made more perfect by making analysis more complete; but when a proper synthesis is completed, there is no need for further analysis. Studies are termed *analytic* when the analytic process is most prominent, and *synthetic* when the synthetic process predominates.*

III. { Inductive Process. Deductive Process. } These are the two ways in which we investigate. We seek truth inductively and deductively.

1. *The inductive process* is the way we proceed in reaching generals through particulars. The child con-

* F. B. Palmer, in Science of Education.

tinually makes its easy inductions and thus finds out for itself. You lead your advancing pupils to make larger and still more important inductions. Thus they find out for themselves principles and laws.

2. *The deductive process* is the way we proceed in reaching particulars through generals. In this way we extend our knowledge as well as verify our conclusions. The child makes its little deductions as well as its inductions.

Induction and Deduction must go together.—Induction rises from particular truths to general truths, from fact to law; deduction descends from general truths to particular truths, from principles to consequences. Induction proceeds from parts to wholes; deduction proceeds from wholes to parts. Induction and deduction accompany each other and blend together so intimately that it is often difficult to sever them. Like analysis and synthesis, induction and deduction are always associated.

IV. { Empirical Process. Rational Process. We gain knowledge through experience and through inference.

1. *The empirical process* is the way we gain knowledge by experience. We find out by trying it that fire burns, and that the way of the transgressor is hard. We lead our pupils to gain knowledge by trying things, and we call this the *empirical* process of teaching. The pupil learns by experience that ice is cold and that wrong-doing brings remorse.

2. *The rational process* is the way we gain knowledge through inference. The universe is a unit. Laws express relations. We infer laws; we begin with our individual experiences and ascend through inference to a universe. The child *feels* its way, but the man finds how things *must* be.

The Empirical and the Rational must go together.—It is true that *experience* does not give *first truths*, but without experience we must remain ignorant of these truths. Insight into the essential unity of the experimental and philosophical processes goes far toward reconciling warring philosophers. Take chemistry, *the representative empirical science ;* even here the *rational* process conditions every step forward.

V. { **Apperceptive Process.** This process stands for unitizing our acquisitions. We generalize, we synthesize, we induct, we assimilate, we think into *oneness* our old and new experiences. Leading our pupils to thus assimilate and unitize their acquisitions is termed the *apperceptive* teaching process. The apperceptive process is the most comprehensive form of mental activity. It is the process of unifying mental data into related wholes.

Apperception supplements the other Processes.—"Apperception includes all of that activity of the self which identifies, recognizes, assimilates, and relates or connects the new in the object presented with what is old or known to us before, or felt to belong to us before I am inclined to think that the term apperception, as I understand it, includes or explains that activity of the mind which we term 'interest' and 'lively interest.' For just think of it, why is a person interested in a subject ? To feel an interest in a thing is to identify one's self with it. The object interests me because I think and feel it identical with me or mine. Is it not clear, therefore, that the very essence of 'interest' and 'lively interest' is apperception ? Does not apperception, therefore, furnish us the supreme category for education ? Education does not educate except so far as the pupil assimilates mental food which he takes. Not perception, as the followers of Pestalozzi proclaim loudly, but apperception, as the followers of Herbart announce, is to be the great word in educational psychology." *

* W T. Harris.

CHAPTER XXX.

HUMAN life, physiologically and psychologically, is divided into six periods—*childhood, boyhood, youth, young manhood, manhood,* and *old age.* We think of the self as a *child* up to the tenth year; as a *boy* or *girl* from the tenth to the fourteenth year; as a *youth* from the fourteenth to the eighteenth year; as a *young man* or *young woman* from the eighteenth to the twenty-fifth year; as a *man* or *woman* from the twenty-fifth to the sixty-third year; and as an *aged man* or *aged woman* from the sixty-third year to the end of life.

Mankind have recognized childhood, boy-and-girlhood, youth, and young manhood as the educational periods. The schools of the world are organized with reference to these periods, and methods of teaching are adapted to these stages of growth. The self, it is true, grows right on as the tree grows, and the development is continuous. But the educational periods named have well-defined characteristics. Our schools and our school work are arranged to meet the wants of these stages of growth.

I. The Kindergarten Period.—The self is an *infant* for six years. We call this the kindergarten educational period. During all the centuries the mother has been the kindergartner; but during the twentieth and succeeding centuries trained kindergartners will share with the mother the training of the child from the third to the sixth year. The work initiated by Froebel, now so rapidly spreading, will go on spreading until it fills the whole earth.

The Kindergarten.—(See map of infant growth, page 342.)—From the third to the sixth year the child attends the kindergarten and through *play* learns to *work*. These are precious years, for "as the twig is bent the tree inclines." Healthy, vigorous, physical growth is primary. Happy childhood must be realized and right habits must be cherished. The child is led to form the acquaintance of the beautiful world. Helpful emotions are tenderly fostered and hurtful feelings are gently repressed. The child is kept pure and sweet. Its feeble powers develop slowly, healthfully, gracefully.

II. **The Primary Period.**—The self is a *child* from the sixth to the tenth year. We call this the *primary* school period. The chief business of the child is to grow and be happy; but these are precious educational years. The child's restless activities must be rooted into right habits. Its acquaintance with nature must be greatly extended, and it must begin the mastery of the book-world.

The Primary.—(See map of child-growth, page 342, also 359.)— From the sixth to the tenth year the child attends the primary school. It now enters upon a larger and even happier life. In the kindergarten it could talk, but now it learns to read and write. The primary work of to-day in our best schools is a marvel of adaptability and efficiency. Nothing is left undone to promote the physical well-being of the child. Lines of kindergarten work are continued. Gentle manners and good morals are woven into the warp and woof of child-life. While all its powers develop healthfully, it is kept pure and sweet and graceful.

III. **The Intermediate Period.**—The self is a *boy* or *girl* from the tenth to the fourteenth year. As this stage of growth comes between childhood and youth, we call it the *intermediate* educational period. During these precious but difficult years mental growth and physical growth are equally fostered. The infant and the child have grown and grown. The weak infant powers have become stronger and stronger. What was hard for the child is easy for the boy. The pupil now enters upon a larger and even happier life. The worlds of animal and plant life are explored with absorbing interest; the wonder-worlds of history and literature begin to open. Self-control is now of paramount importance.

The Intermediate.—(See map of boy and girl-growth, pages 342 and 365.)—During these difficult years the faithful *intermediate teacher* co-operates with the parents to promote the healthy and vigorous physical, mental, and moral growth of the boys and girls. No Froebel has profoundly studied the growing self during this critical period. No master-educator has completely *adapted* intermediate work. This still remains the difficult and unsatisfactory educational period. The pupils are wayward and unstudious. Boys become rough and girls become giddy. A deeper insight into the growing self during this trying period, better arranged intermediate work, and better intermediate methods, are great educational needs. Too often our intermediate schools fail to carry forward efficiently and satisfactorily the work so well begun in our kindergarten and primary schools. But a brighter day is dawning.

The Ungraded School of the rural districts includes the *primary* and *intermediate*. The school is classified but not graded. One teacher does all the work. The course of study is the same as in the graded school. *Elementary schools* include all schools below the high-school.

IV. **High-School Period.**—The self is a *youth* from the fourteenth to the eighteenth year. These precarious years usually fix for weal or woe the career for life. Sex is now an important factor in education. In childhood sex is not considered, and the child is spoken of as " it." Boys and girls mutually repel each other, and boys associate with boys and girls with girls. In youth the sexes mutually attract each other. Coeducation now becomes a vital question. May it be so managed as to work the highest good of both sexes? It is firmly believed that it may. The logic of results has in a large measure given an affirmative answer to the question, though separate education is supported by strong physiological and psychological arguments.

The High-School.—(See map, page 342, and also page 367.)—The *pupil* now becomes a *student*, and *knowledge* becomes *science*. In the place of one teacher a faculty of *specialists* now conduct the work. The interests become wide and deep. Each power of the self is now highly active, and the youth is capable of great things. The high-school needs to be made as ubiquitous as our elementary schools, so as to place a high-school education within easy reach of every youth. The high-school is still the missing link in our educational evolution. The course of study needs to be arranged with the utmost care, so as to best prepare the youth for life and for college.

V. College and University Period.—The self is a *young man* or *young woman* from the eighteenth to the twenty-fifth year. This is the college and university educational period. These are the years of destiny. The student is at his best. The highest educational advantages are enjoyed and the highest stage of culture reached. The university, strictly, carries the highest culture over into the highest fields of achievement, and embraces special schools, such as law, medicine, divinity, pedagogy. The *college period* proper extends from the eighteenth to the twenty-second year, and the *university period* from the twenty-second to the twenty-fifth year.

Periods of Culture, not Years.—Some develop earlier than others. Girls develop earlier than boys. Some advance much more rapidly than others. Then the conditions are more or less favorable. Evidently our school systems must be made exceedingly flexible. Development and acquisitions, as well as years, must be considered.

CHAPTER XXXI.

PRIMARY METHODS OF TEACHING.

TEACHING methods are *lawful, systematic,* and *persistent* plans of teaching *adapted* to the several educational periods. We think of *teaching* methods as *kindergarten* methods, *primary* methods, *intermediate* methods, *high-school* methods, and *college* methods. As these have much in common, we study merely the distinctive characteristics of each. Primary methods are teaching plans adapted to childhood. What is the child? How does the child find out? What plans of teaching tend to promote child-growth? The primary teacher seeks satisfactory answers to these questions.

The Past.—The present looks to the past for instruction and inspiration. Each age has had its great teachers. From these gifted ones we have much to learn. The world's great teachers penetrated the mysteries of human nature and moved forward the dial of human progress. From these we may learn lessons of wisdom and gain inspiration; but from the "old *schoolmaster*" we have nothing to learn but to avoid his mistakes. Like the ancient mariner, he groped his way without chart or compass. Like his geography, *his* child was mapless. We look to the past for *warnings* as well as for *instruction* and *inspiration*.

I. **Map of Childhood.**—(See map of the mental powers, page 2; map of child-growth, page 342; and map

MAP OF CHILDHOOD.

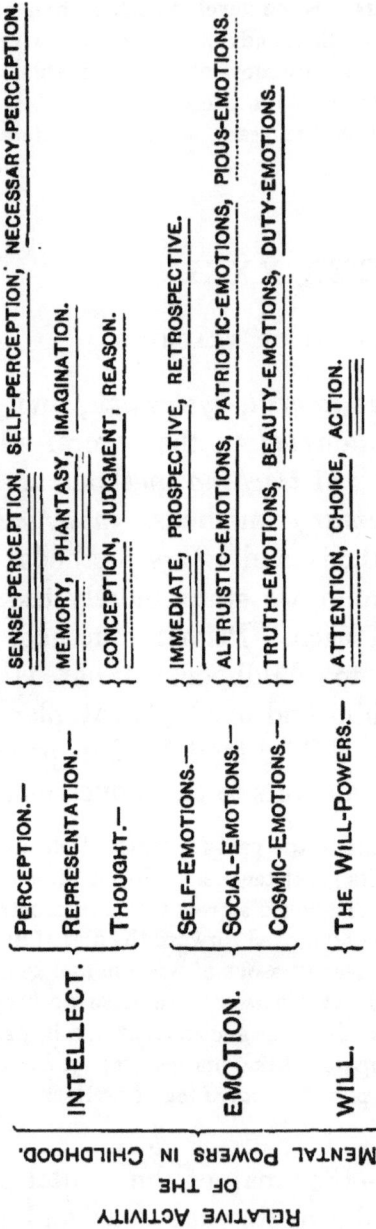

INTELLECT.	PERCEPTION.—	{ SENSE-PERCEPTION, SELF-PERCEPTION, NECESSARY-PERCEPTION.
	REPRESENTATION.—	{ MEMORY, PHANTASY, IMAGINATION.
	THOUGHT.—	{ CONCEPTION, JUDGMENT, REASON.
EMOTION.	SELF-EMOTIONS.—	{ IMMEDIATE, PROSPECTIVE, RETROSPECTIVE.
	SOCIAL-EMOTIONS.—	{ ALTRUISTIC-EMOTIONS, PATRIOTIC-EMOTIONS, PIOUS-EMOTIONS.
	COSMIC-EMOTIONS.—	{ TRUTH-EMOTIONS, BEAUTY-EMOTIONS, DUTY-EMOTIONS.
WILL.	THE WILL-POWERS.—	{ ATTENTION, CHOICE, ACTION.

RELATIVE ACTIVITY OF THE MENTAL POWERS IN CHILDHOOD.

Explanation.—The self is a child from the sixth to the tenth year. The relative activity of the child-powers is indicated by the lines underscored. The dotted line denotes *slight* activity; one line, *moderate activity;* two lines, *medium* activity; three lines, *high* activity. A dotted line added denotes greater activity.

The early activity of the innate powers of the infant self is a fact of science. That some of the native energies of the self develop earlier than others is a fundamental educational truth. The comparative growth of our capabilities is a most interesting and profitable study. [See map of mental growth, p. 342. See growth of sense-perception, 46; self-perception, 66; necessary-perception, 83; memory, 119; imagination, 129; conception, 175; judgment, 191; reason, 203; self-emotions, 231; social-emotions, 240; truth-emotions, 251; beauty-emotions, 257; duty-emotions, 269; attention, 297; choice, 312; action, 324.]

The map of childhood aims to represent the relative activity of the child's capabilities. To you it is merely suggestive. You will make your own map of childhood, representing the child as *you* view it. The very effort to do this will be invaluable to you.

of childhood, page 359.)—*"Know thyself"* expressed the wisdom of the *past.* *"Know yourself and know the child"* expresses the wisdom of the *present.* Froebel's rediscovery of childhood was his greatest work. Each primary teacher must make this discovery for herself. Go back to the scenes of *your* childhood " when fond recollection presents them to view." Live close to the living, loving, growing child. Ask the past and the present for light. *Your* maps of childhood and child-growth become replete with meaning. You feel a boundless interest in the child, for you see in it infinite possibilities.

II. **Primary Teaching Process.**—(See *Teaching Process,* Chapter XXIX, and *Teaching Periods,* Chapter XXX.)—The child *must* proceed in specific ways in order to acquire and grow. The processes we use in leading children in these ways are termed primary teaching processes.

Primary Teaching Processes.
{
I. **Objective Process ; Subjective Process.**

II. **Analytic Process ; Synthetic Process.**

III. **Inductive Process ; Deductive Process.**

IV. **Empirical Process ; Philosophical Process.**

V. **Apperceptive Process.**
}

Explanations.—The child processes are pre-eminently objective and experimental; this is denoted by the three lines under these processes. The child makes crude analyses and syntheses; this is indicated by one line under these processes. The child begins to apperceive; this is indicated by one line under the apperceptive process. The child induces, deduces, and philosophizes slightly; this is indicated by the dotted lines under these processes.

III. **Primary Methods of Culture.** — The musician so touches the keys of the instrument as to produce sweet music. The primary teacher so touches the keys of child-nature as to occasion the glad activity of all the child-powers. Sweeter harmony than the music of the spheres is the joyous activity and symmetrical development of childhood. As each stroke of the sculptor's chisel looks to the bringing out of the angel concealed in the marble, so each primary exercise looks to the harmonious development of child-capabilities.

Primary Culture Lessons. — We *can not* educate abstractions. We *can* cultivate this rose and this grape. We *can* cultivate our memory and our reason. We cultivate our minds when we cultivate our several activities. In the previous chapters we have studied plans for developing the powers of the child: *Sense-perception*, page 53; *Self-perception*, 71; *Memory*, 114; *Imagination*, 133; *Conception*, 178; *Self-emotions*, 233; *Social-emotions*, 243; *Beauty-emotions*, 259; *Conscience*, 272; *Attention*, 290; *Action*, 317. The primary teacher will restudy and co-ordinate these lessons.

IV. **Primary Methods of teaching the Branches.** — These include methods of teaching reading, language-lessons, science-lessons, information-lessons, arithmetic, vocal music, penmanship, drawing, manners, morals. *Your* methods are *your* plans for conducting the exercises. You are entitled to *all* you can gain from others, but you must *create* your own methods. You will read the choicest educational literature. You will provide yourself with the best *Manuals of Methods* for teaching each subject. I count these inexpensive helps, products of our times, of the highest value. You will find in these the best things. You will spend precious hours observing the work of superior primary teachers.

You will continually glean fresh suggestions from your educational journals. Each year you will find new inspiration at some good summer normal institute. All these are merely suggestive helps. You must create your own plans of work.

Primary Methods of teaching Reading, Arithmetic, etc.—Detailed methods of teaching the branches are considered out of place in a work of this kind. Some of our best works on pedagogy are thus cumbered. Separate manuals of methods prepared by experts are every way better. Here we seek insight into the mental economy, and into the laws and means and methods of promoting growth. We try to master the essentials.

CHAPTER XXXII.

INTERMEDIATE METHODS OF TEACHING.

These are plans of teaching adapted to boys and girls. In the primary, the work for the most part is necessarily oral. In the intermediate, book and oral work are about equal. The intermediate teacher studies to incite the self-activity of her pupils. She seeks to lead them into studious habits and train them to think. All her methods look to preparing boys and girls for complete living.

I. **Map of Boyhood and Girlhood.**—(See map of the mental powers, page 2; map of mental growth, page 342; and map of boyhood and girlhood, page 363.)— Know thoroughly your pupils. This is fundamental. Your own boyhood or girlhood is not remote. Surely you can live over again those marvelous years. Then you have lived very close to impulsive, wayward, prom-

MAP OF BOYHOOD AND GIRLHOOD.

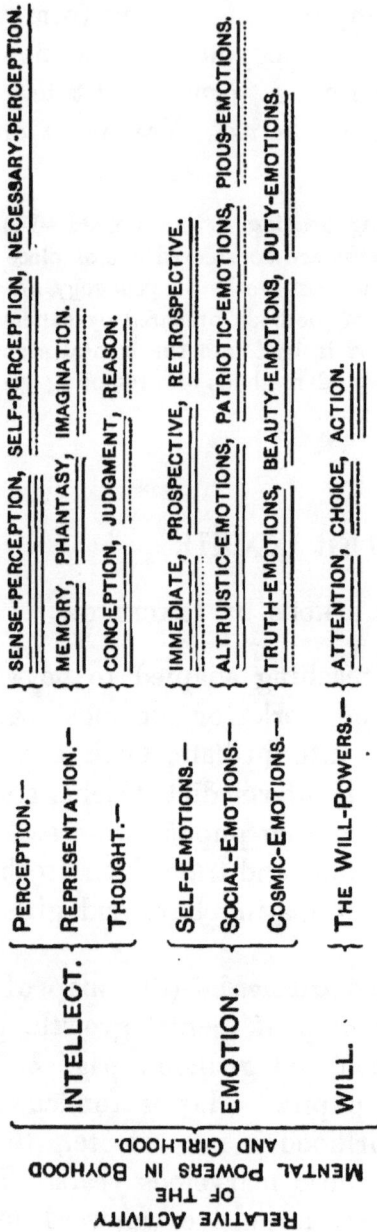

RELATIVE ACTIVITY OF THE MENTAL POWERS IN BOYHOOD AND GIRLHOOD.

INTELLECT.	PERCEPTION.—	SENSE-PERCEPTION, SELF-PERCEPTION, NECESSARY-PERCEPTION.
	REPRESENTATION.—	MEMORY, PHANTASY, IMAGINATION.
	THOUGHT.—	CONCEPTION, JUDGMENT, REASON.
EMOTION.	SELF-EMOTIONS.—	IMMEDIATE, PROSPECTIVE, RETROSPECTIVE.
	SOCIAL-EMOTIONS.—	ALTRUISTIC-EMOTIONS, PATRIOTIC-EMOTIONS, PIOUS-EMOTIONS.
	COSMIC-EMOTIONS.—	TRUTH-EMOTIONS, BEAUTY-EMOTIONS, DUTY-EMOTIONS.
WILL.	THE WILL-POWERS.—	ATTENTION, CHOICE, ACTION.

Explanation.—The self is a boy or girl from the tenth to the fourteenth year, and exerts with *more* or *less* vigor all his or her powers. The relative activity of the mental powers is indicated by lines underscored. The dotted line denotes *slight* activity or *slightly increased* activity. One line denotes *moderate* activity; two lines, *medium* activity; three lines, *high* activity.

The attempt to make a symbolical representation of the mental economy has its difficulties and its dangers. But Infinite Wisdom has so constituted us that we are compelled to struggle up to the unseen through the seen. Even in geometry we find the figures wonderfully helpful. The boy? The indefinite blank *stare* will not answer this question. You must explore the boy-world and girl-world. What do the boy and the girl mean to you? Keep in mind that the above crude map is meant to help you to make a better map, representing this period of mental growth as *you* understand it. You are a worker, not a dreamer. You must build on the rock.

ising boys and girls. You have learned what you could from others. You have gained a deep insight into their peculiarities. You now venture to represent as best you can the intermediate stage of mental growth. The maps in the old geographies were very imperfect, but they were vastly better than no maps. Your map of boyhood and girlhood may be crude, but it will nevertheless prove most helpful to you. It is so much better than the vague, shadowy views of teachers who make no attempt to grasp the mental economy.

II. **Intermediate Teaching Processes.**—(See *Teaching Processes*, Chapter XXIX, and *Teaching Periods*, Chapter XXX.)—Everything unfolds its meaning to its lover. Wisdom says, "*I love them that love me.*" You love the boys and girls, and they reveal to you their inmost selves You know their activities as the performer knows the keys of his instrument. Their predominant activities reveal to you the intermediate processes.

Intermediate
Teaching Processes.
{
I. Objective Process; Subjective Process.

II. Analytic Process; Synthetic Process.

III. Inductive Process; Deductive Process.

IV. Empirical Process; Philosophical Process.

V. Apperceptive Process.
}

The objective and empirical processes predominate in intermediate as in primary work. The analytic and synthetic processes are now prominent. It is not the exhaustive analysis and synthesis of later years, but the crude efforts of boys and girls. The apperceptive process is used more and more. The remaining processes are used moderately.

Teaching Processes are Tests.—You visit the primary or intermediate school; you observe that the teaching processes are subjective and philosophical rather than objective and empirical. It becomes clear to you at a glance that the teacher is ignorant of child-nature and child-processes. You detect erroneous methods of teaching almost as readily as you detect the mispronunciation of familiar words. Good teaching is as easily tested as good reading.

III. **Intermediate Methods of Culture.**—The development of power is primary in education. The feeble infant powers must grow into the mighty powers of the philosopher. You have attentively studied intermediate methods of promoting the growth of the several mental powers: *Sense-Perception*, page 55; *Self-Perception*, 71; *Memory*, 115; *Imagination*, 135; *Conception*, 179; *Judgment*, 196; *Reason*, 207; *Self-Emotions*, 233; *Social-Emotions*, 243; *Truth-Emotions*, 253; *Beauty-Emotions*, 259; *Conscience*, 274; *Attention*, 290; *Choice*, 300; *Action*, 317. You are now able to survey the entire mental economy. You study to lead your pupils to so put forth effort as to develop harmoniously all their capabilities.

IV. **Intermediate Methods of teaching the Branches.**—These are ways of leading our pupils to so put forth effort as to develop their capabilities by mastering the intermediate studies. Your methods must be your own. David could not fight in Saul's armor, nor can a teacher use efficiently another's methods. Gain everything possible from others, but make all your own. Procure the best manuals of intermediate methods of teaching reading, arithmetic, geography, and the other branches. Spend days in intermediate schools taught by able teachers. Gather information and inspiration from the best educational works. After all, you must *create* your own methods.

CHAPTER XXXIII.

HIGH-SCHOOL METHODS OF TEACHING.

THAT we may do intelligent teaching we must understand the plan of the subject taught as well as the plan of the mind. True teaching *fits* the subject to the stage of development of the learner. This adaptation of studies to periods of mental growth is what is understood by methods of teaching. High-school methods bring together youthful minds and elementary science.

" There is a method in the child and a method in the subject of study. A complete pedagogy brings these two elements into harmony—makes them complementary. The method in the subject at any stage exactly fits a corresponding stage of development. The development in the subject must be made at all stages to fit the development of the learner. In this view of pedagogy the office of the teacher is magnified." *

I. **Map of Youth.**—(See map of the mental powers, page 2; map of mental growth, page 342; and map of youth, page 367.)—From the fourteenth to the eighteenth year is a supremely interesting period of human life. Most of the intellectual powers act vigorously. The emotions are highly active. The will-powers are might-forces. The youth is capable of great

* Charles De Garmo, in Essentials of Method.

MAP OF YOUTH.

RELATIVE ACTIVITY OF THE MENTAL POWERS IN YOUTH.

INTELLECT.	PERCEPTION.	SENSE-PERCEPTION, SELF-PERCEPTION, NECESSARY-PERCEPTION.
	REPRESENTATION.	MEMORY, PHANTASY, IMAGINATION.
	THOUGHT.	CONCEPTION, JUDGMENT, REASON.
EMOTION.	SELF-EMOTIONS.	IMMEDIATE, PROSPECTIVE, RETROSPECTIVE.
	SOCIAL-EMOTIONS.	ALTRUISTIC-EMOTIONS, PATRIOTIC-EMOTIONS, PIOUS-EMOTIONS.
	COSMIC-EMOTIONS.	TRUTH-EMOTIONS, BEAUTY-EMOTIONS, DUTY-EMOTIONS.
WILL.	THE WILL-POWERS.	ATTENTION, CHOICE, ACTION.

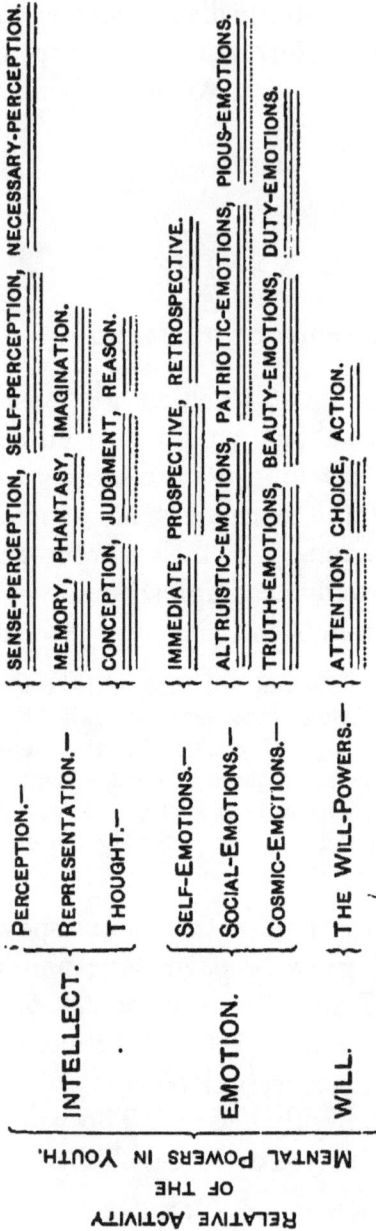

Explanation.—The self is a youth from the fourteenth to the eighteenth year. The self, in all his capabilities, is now active and highly active. But the youth puts forth effort with greater vigor in some directions than in others. This relative activity of the mental powers in youth is indicated by lines underscored. A dotted line denotes increased activity. One line denotes *moderate* activity; two lines, *medium* activity; three lines, *high* activity.

We may symbolize but we can not picture mental acts. No two persons have the same notion of the mental economy. Let each of a hundred teachers make a map of youth as understood; no two will be exactly alike, but there will be substantial agreement.

The youth? You have tried day and night to gain deep insight into youth-nature. You have traced the growth of each mental power from infancy to manhood. What does youth mean to you? You will represent in your map of youth your conception of the mental economy during this stage of growth. The map must be strictly *yours*; maps made by others are at best merely suggestive.

things. The great activity of self-perception indicates that the time has come for the systematic study of the self-world. The high activity of imagination and of the thought-powers tell us that the time has come for the mastery of elementary science and elementary mathematics and departments of history and literature. But, dear teacher, I leave the applications to you. I must not presume to do for you what you can better do for yourself. Your youth comes vividly to mind. You associate most intimately with youths; as you love them, they reveal to you their inmost selves. Literature is at its best when dealing with youth. In view of all, you will construct an original map of youth.

II. **High-School Teaching Processes.** — (See *High-School Period*, Chapter XXX, and *Teaching Processes*, Chapter XXIX.)—In high-school work we use all the processes, as all the mental powers are highly active. It must be true that the growth is continuous, but boys and girls seem to become youths with a leap.

	I. Objective Process; Subjective Process.
	II. Analytic Process; Synthetic Process.
High-School Teaching Processes.	III. Inductive Process; Deductive Process.
	IV. Empirical Process; Philosophical Process.
	V. Apperceptive Process.

Explanations.—Wide experiences have been accumulated, so that high-school pupils use the objective and empirical processes less and the subjective and philosophical processes more than during the previous periods. The analytic, synthetic, inductive, and deductive are now the dominant educational processes. Youths elaborate into higher forms their old and new experiences. The apperceptive process enters very largely into the high-school work. You will ponder these suggestions, but from your own insight you will make your map of high-school teaching processes.

III. **High-School Methods of Culture.**—The aim is increased energy. The purpose of each lesson is the development of greater power. Well-directed effort develops the capabilities and prepares the student for greater achievements. In the previous chapters we have considered high-school methods of educating each mental power : *Sense-Perception*, page 56 ; *Self-Perception*, 73 ; *Necessary-Perception*, 83 ; *Memory*, 115 ; *Imagination*, 138 ; *Conception*, 181 ; *Judgment*, 196 ; *Reason*, 208 ; *Egoistic Emotions*, 236 ; *Altruistic Emotions*, 245 ; *Truth-Emotions*, 252 ; *Æsthetic Emotions*, 260 ; *Conscience*, 276 ; *Attention*, 293 ; *Choice*, 303 ; *Action*, 320. You will often go back to these elementary lessons, but you now contemplate the mental economy as a whole. You think of the self as commanding all his powers in his efforts to achieve. You endeavor to so teach each lesson as to educate each activity.

IV. **High-School Methods of teaching the High-School Branches.**—The youth is a student and a science-maker. Investigation and systemization characterize high-school methods. The youth now learns the art of searching investigation. Through the facts, laws are discovered. The youth learns to build science. Central truths are discerned, and around these are arranged systematically the laws and the facts. Each study becomes to the youth an embryo science. The vernacular, heretofore an art, now becomes also a science. The knowledge of the matter-world, heretofore miscellaneous, is now dif-

24

fercntiated into the sciences. Each branch of study grows into a science.

Mistakes in High-School Methods.—Intermediate work grows into high-school work, and high-school work grows into college work. There must be no breaks. But high-school methods are well-defined plans of work adapted to the high-school period. Two grievous mistakes are made: (1) Many teachers fail to note the growth of boys and girls into youths, and so they carry intermediate methods over into the high-schools. (2) Many teachers carry college methods into the high-schools. They teach as they were taught in the colleges. These mistakes are fundamental and exceedingly hurtful.

V. **High-School Manuals of Methods.***—You will necessarily create your own methods. Still, you need all the help others can give you. I know some high-school teachers who do wretched work because of a foolish pride to be original. You may gain most valu_able help from books. Many high-school text-books are admirable teaching manuals. Besides these, we now have excellent hand-books prepared by able educators, full of helpful suggestions for teaching the several high-school branches. You will continue to study the best educational literature, you will continue to visit good high-schools, and you will continue to be an active worker in the associations of teachers.

* Methods of teaching Algebra and Geometry, by J. M. Greenwood; Methods of teaching History, by G. Stanley Hall, and similar works, are strongly commended.

CHAPTER XXXIV.

COLLEGE METHODS OF TEACHING.

COLLEGE professors of the twentieth century will look to their methods as well as to their matter. They will be great teachers as well as proficient scholars. The average professor in the past cherished a deep contempt for methods. He counted it presumption to call education a science and teaching an art. But a marvelous revolution is going on. All the great universities and colleges, before the close of the century, will have established departments of pedagogy. Students who elect teaching will be educated for their profession. The college professors of the future will be as noted for their great skill in teaching as for their great learning.

This work was planned to help kindergarten, primary, intermediate, and high-school teachers. The discussion of college work would be out of place here. But it is thought best to speak briefly .of college methods from the standpoint of the elementary teacher. Even the kindergartner needs to understand in some degree the college work. Every teacher should have a general knowledge of the educational work from the kindergarten to the university.

I. **Map of Early Manhood.**—(See map of the mental powers, page 2 ; map of mental growth, 342 ; and map of early manhood, 372.)—To trace from infancy to manhood the growth of each soul-energy is more fascinating than poetry or song. To the teacher it is meat and drink. From the eighteenth to the twenty-fifth year the self is a young man or young woman. Now all the powers are highly active. The maps given are designed to assist you in your efforts to gain a deeper insight

MAP OF EARLY MANHOOD.

INTELLECT.
- PERCEPTION.— { SENSE-PERCEPTION, SELF-PERCEPTION, NECESSARY-PERCEPTION.
- REPRESENTATION.— { MEMORY, PHANTASY, IMAGINATION.
- THOUGHT.— { CONCEPTION, JUDGMENT, REASON.

EMOTION.
- EGOISTIC-EMOTIONS.— { IMMEDIATE, PROSPECTIVE, RETROSPECTIVE.
- ALTRUISTIC-EMOTIONS.— { AFFECTIONS, PATRIOTIC-EMOTIONS, PIOUS-EMOTIONS,
- COSMIC-EMOTIONS.— { TRUTH-EMOTIONS, ÆSTHETIC-EMOTIONS, ETHICAL-EMOTIONS.

WILL.
- THE WILL-POWERS.— { ATTENTION, CHOICE, ACTION.

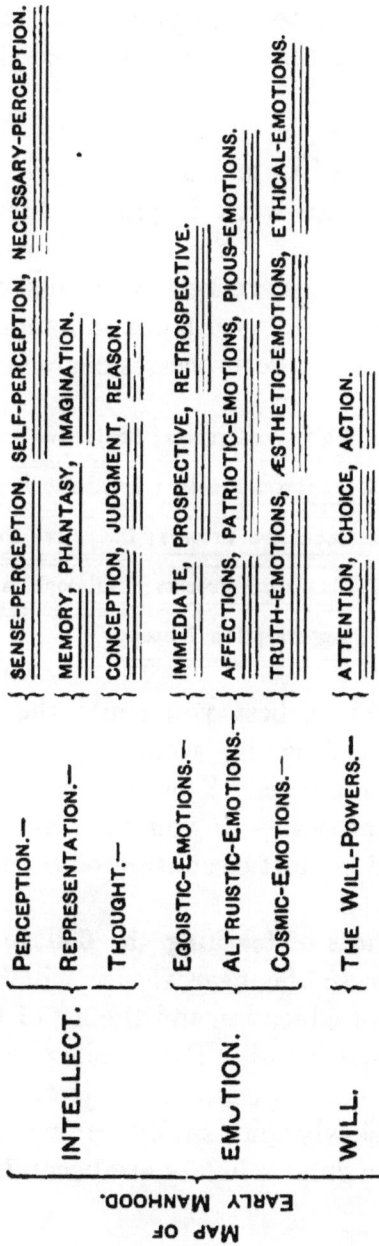

Explanation.—The infant self develops into the child, into the boy or girl, into the youth, into the young man or young woman, into the man or woman. We have studied as best we could these stages of growth. That we might better grasp the mental economy and mental growth, we have constructed these crude symbols. We think of the college student as powerful, with all his capabilities highly active. This grand period of growth is aimed to be represented by this map. While all the mental powers are now fully active, the self goes on growing, and it is in the school of life that a grand manhood is developed.

into early manhood, and to help you to construct for yourself maps truer to this educational period as you understand it.

II. **College Processes of Teaching.**—(See *Teaching Processes*, Chapter XXIX, and *Educational Periods*, Chapter XXX.)—College work is philosophical work. Each science now becomes a philosophy. The objective and experimental processes are relatively less used, but the remaining processes are used more and more. The philosophic and apperceptive processes characterize college methods.

College Teaching Processes.

I. **Objective Process; Subjective Process.**

II. **Analytic Process; Synthetic Process.**

III. **Inductive Process; Deductive Process.**

IV. **Empirical Process; Philosophical Process.**

V. **Apperceptive Process.**

You have studied as best you could the ways in which young men and young women proceed when they investigate and create. You will now make a map of the college processes as you understand them. The above presentation must be considered as suggestive but not as ultimate.

III. **College Methods of teaching the College Studies.** —College instructors in the near future will be proficient in the science of education and the art of teaching as well as in their specialties. Each college professor will be an educator. Antiquated and objectionable college methods are slowly but surely giving place to wiser methods. Our great scholars are becoming great teachers.

SYLLABUS
OF BALDWIN'S APPLIED PSYCHOLOGY.

*From the International Reading Circle Course of
Professional Study.*

Pages 1 to 43.

CHAPTER I.

1. The several departments of Pedagogy, as related to each other.
2. The elements of Psychology, as based upon study of self.
3. The Intellect, as having three modes of action or faculties.
4. The Feelings, as arising from three different sources of excitation.
5. The Will, as embracing three distinct kinds of effort.
6. Applied Psychology, as determining the right processes in the work of education.

CHAPTER II.

7. The physical organism through which the mind acts.
8. The relations of ganglia, nerves, and organs, constituting and connecting the sensorium and motorium.
9. The sensations produced by external or by internal sensor-excitation.
10. Sense-percept, an elementary knowledge derived from a material object through sensation.
11. Self-percept, an elementary knowledge derived from one's own mental act or state through consciousness.
12. Necessary-percept, an elementary knowledge arising from direct insight into realities and relations.

13. The powers, acts, and percepts of the mind, each determined by sense-relations, self-relations, or necessary-relations.

Pages 43 to 92.

CHAPTER III.

14. Education of sense-perception consists not in training the sense but in developing the power to interpret 'sense-percepts.

15. Education of this power fundamentally necessary to knowledge and to clear thought.

16. Only those branches of study that admit of objective work are of value in the education of sense-perception.

17. Primary lesson work should be objective in all the branches of study.

CHAPTER IV.

18. Education of self-perception essential, but must become specific later in the years of school life.

19. Constitutes the only means of interpreting character, literature, and the social sciences.

CHAPTER V.

20. Necessary-perception is to be developed by leading the mind from individual necessary relations to general relations.

CHAPTER VI.

21. The perceptive powers can be developed only by one's immediate experience.

22. Habits of exact observation are necessary to the right development of the powers of perception.

23. Apperception, or assimilation, is the essential step in acquiring knowledge through perception.

Pages 95 to 121.

CHAPTER VII.

24 Representative knowing occurs as memory, as phantasy, and as imagination.

25 Mere memory reproduces the ideas of our past experiences without any change.

26 The three steps in the memory process are: 1. Retaining. 2. Reproducing or representing. 3. Recognizing.

27 The laws of memory express the relations of association and suggestion.

28. Phantasy combines the products of memory in new relations.

29 Imagination combines the products of memory in new forms.

CHAPTER VIII.

30. Education of memory consists in acquiring ability to readily and accurately recall the ideas of past experiences.

31. Thought is possible only as memory supplies its materials.

32. Specific laws of memory development pertain to physical conditions and to mental activities.

33. In school work various subjects of study have different values as conducing to memory growth.

34. The value of a given study as conducing to memory culture will vary with the method of teaching.

Pages 122 to 151.

35. Phantasy uses the materials of experience, but combines them into new and purposeless forms.

36. Imagination differs from phantasy in being subject to the will.

37. The phantasy of childhood gradually passes over into the imagination of maturer years.
38. The power of imagination requires wise culture through well-chosen means.
39. Some subjects of study are of high value, some of low value, in the culture of imagination.
40. The method of work is more important than the subject-matter, as pertaining to the right development of this power.
41. Memory and imagination are the two re-presentative powers, as perception and assimilation are the two presentative powers to be cultivated.

Pages 155 to 171.

42. Thinking consists in seeing the relations between things.
43. Class-relations lead to concepts, truth-relations to judgments, and cause-relations to reasons.
44. Six several steps in the thought process of conception.
45. Distinction between synthetic and analytic judgments.
46. Informal reasoning may be expanded into full formal reasoning.
47. Deductive reasoning is secondary to inductive reasoning and is the converse of it.
48. The three terms and the three propositions involved in every complete process of formal reasoning.

Pages 171 to 218.

49. The education of conception is the development of the power to form general notions from the individual percepts that come to the mind through experience or imagination.

50. Breadth and vigor of thinking depend upon the power to form concepts.
51. The conceptive power manifests different characteristics during the several periods of growth from childhood to manhood.
52. The three general laws of effort, means and method have their special application in the education of conception.
53. The characteristics of the several periods of mental growth call for methods in education.
54. Most errors in conception-culture are due to anticipating results before taking the steps that properly lead to those results.
55. Education of judgment is the development of the power to see true relations between things.
56. The several periods of mental growth determine the particular application of general laws in the education of judgment.
57. Self-activity of the learner's mind is the essential characteristic of right method in the education of judgment.
58. Work too easy, or too difficult, or poorly graded, is not conducive to right development of the power of judgment.
59. Education of reason is the development of the power to see the relation of cause and result, or of premise and conclusion.
60. The prime value of knowledge is in the material it supplies for the activities of reason.
61. Good teaching consists in the intelligent directing of the self-activities of the child's mind so as to secure full development of the several powers of right thinking, and hence of right action.

Pages 219 to 249.

62. The emotions differ from sensations in being occasioned by ideas, not by affections of the body.
63. The emotions are classified according to the nature of the ideas awakening them.
64. It is the duty of the teacher to stimulate the emotional nature into right activity.
65. The egoistic emotions lead the individual to make the best of himself.
66. The emotions must be carried over into resolves and acts or their force is wasted.
67. Self-respect, and the elements of a good disposition and of manliness, should be cultivated in school life.
68. Culture of the altruistic emotions elevates human society and increases human happiness.
69. The altruistic emotions produce kind acts, and these in turn develop the altruistic emotions.
70. Literature for the young should present right ideas in relation to the egoistic and altruistic emotions.

Pages 249 to 281.

71. The truth-emotions are awakened by our recognition of reality in facts and in relations.
72. The education of the truth-emotions is essential in the development of noble character.
73. Right teaching involves the presentation of knowledge in such manner as to awaken the active enjoyment of acquiring.
74. The æsthetic emotions constitute the elements of taste.
75. Æsthetic culture is closely related to the development of character in matters of truth and right.

76. Kindergarten work furnishes the best means for awakening the æsthetic emotions.

77. The spirit of the kindergarten should permeate all the later teaching in elementary and higher grades.

78. The ethical emotions underlie conscience and impel to right action. ·

79. Conscience is cultivated by training in intelligent right action.

80. Enforced obedience may be, and if necessary should be, the precursor of voluntary right doing.

Pages 285 to 339.

81. Will is the power of *self* to put forth voluntary effort in the three forms of attention, choice, and action.

82. Nonvoluntary or attracted attention prevails in the period of childhood, and education develops it into the voluntary attention of matured will-power.

83. Choice is the act of determining what course to pursue in view of conflicting desires or motives.

84. Action results from choice, and is the final effort of self in the manifestation of will-power.

85. The ability to so educate the attention as to concentrate all the energies upon a given work determines a fundamental principle in pedagogy.

86. The basis of right teaching rests in the development of the power and habit of attention.

87. True attention must be secured through awakened interest, not by compulsory requirement.

88. The power of choice, or of self-determination, is the fundamental element of strength of character.

89. School discipline should aim not merely to restrain evil tendencies but to develop self-restraint and right choice.

90. The power and habit of prompt and vigorous action characterize the person of efficient executive power.

91. Pupils should be trained to do as well as to know.

92. Will-culture along the three lines of attention, choice, and action constitutes character-training.

Pages 343 to 373.

93. Teaching is an art, based upon a science, and having its laws, processes, periods, and methods.

94. The central idea in the science of education is growth through lawful self-activity, and teaching is the art of promoting this growth by inducing the appropriate self-activity.

95. The laws of teaching are the ways in which the teacher may secure the right self-effort on the part of the learner.

96. The teaching processes are the definite ways in which the teacher must have the pupil proceed in order to learn.

97. Each of the teaching periods—childhood, boyhood, youth, and early manhood—has its special characteristics, and requires its special applications of the teaching laws and processes.

INDEX.

25

THE END.

*F*ROEBEL'S EDUCATIONAL LAWS FOR ALL TEACHERS. By JAMES L. HUGHES, Inspector of Schools, Toronto. Price, $1.50.

This book is a real contribution to the Froebelian literature. It is a clear and comprehensive statement of Froebel's principles adapted to the work of everyone engaged in the education and training of humanity in the kindergarten, the school, the university, or the home. Froebel aimed to make as radical changes in the university as in the primary school. The book not only explains but applies Froebel's ideals in regard to Unity, Self-activity, Apperception, Correlation, Individuality, Co-operation, Evolution, Nature Study, Object Teaching, Manual Training, The Educational Value of Play, The Harmony between Control and Spontaneity, and Ethical Training. It is the most comprehensive exposition of the fundamental principles of the New Education as revealed by Froebel.

*T*HE PSYCHOLOGY OF NUMBER, and its application to Methods of Teaching Arithmetic. By JAMES A. McLELLAN, M.A., LL.D., Principal of the Ontario School of Pedagogy, Toronto, and JOHN DEWEY, Ph. D., Head Professor of Philosophy in the University of Chicago. Price, $1.50.

This book is both philosophical and practical. It gives for the first time a sound and systematic presentation of the real nature and origin of number, and so clearly that the youngest teacher or student cannot fail to master the subject. It discusses the definition, aspects, and factors of numerical ideas, and shows their application to common-sense methods of teaching. It divests fractions of their mystery, showing that they are contained in the fundamental ideas of all number. In the practical part it shows how to give first lessons in number in a rational way, and how to arouse and maintain the child's interest in number. It is a *vade mecum* for every student and teacher of arithmetic, and for every student of rational pedagogy.

*T*HE SCHOOL SYSTEM OF ONTARIO, CANADA. Its History and Distinctive Features. By HON. GEORGE W. Ross, LL.D., Minister of Education for the Province of Ontario. 12mo. Cloth, $1.00.

This volume contains an outline of the history of the School System of Ontario, Canada, from the passage of the first Act of Parliament respecting schools, in 1837, down to the present time. It treats of the organization of the Public School System of the Province—how established, how maintained, and how inspected; together with a discussion of kindergartens and their value to the Public School System. It gives also the history of high schools and their relation to the university, modes of examination, inspection, etc. The qualifications for matriculation into the Provincial University, and the place which it serves in the training of teachers are fully set forth. A chapter is devoted to each of the following subjects: Normal College, Denominational Schools, and Schools and Public Libraries.

Though the work shows the evolution of the School System of Ontario, its main purpose, however, is to supply information with regard to the organization and management of the different departments of the system, and the means which have been provided for promoting its efficiency through uniform examinations, the training of teachers in both public and high schools.

Toronto : GEORGE N. MORANG, 63 Yonge St.

*T*EACHING THE LANGUAGE-ARTS. *Speech, Reading, Composition.* By B. A. HINSDALE, Ph.D., LL.D., Professor of Science and the Art of Teaching in the University of Michigan. 12mo. Cloth, $1.00.

This work is not a collection of "Exercises" and "Composition Lessons," but a clear and full discussion of the principles which underlie the acquisition of the language-art in its oral and written forms. The book is addressed to teachers, and will prove a valuable aid to them in an important branch of their educational work.

*T*HE EDUCATION OF THE GREEK PEOPLE, *and its influence on Civilization.* By THOMAS DAVIDSON. 12mo. Cloth, $1.50.

" This work is not intended for scholars or specialists, but for the large body of teachers throughout the country who are trying to do their duty, but are suffering from that want of enthusiasm which necessarily comes from being unable clearly to see the end and purpose of their labors, or to invest any end with sublime import. I have sought to show them that the end of their work is the redemption of humanity, an essential part of that process by which it is being gradually elevated to moral freedom, and to suggest to them the direction in which they ought to turn their chief efforts. If I can make even a few of them feel the consecration that comes from single-minded devotion to a great end, I shall hold that this book has accomplished its purpose."—*Author's Preface.*

*T*HE SONGS AND MUSIC OF FROEBEL'S MOTHER PLAY. Prepared and arranged by SUSAN E. BLOW. Fully illustrated. 12mo. Cloth, $1.50.

This is the second and concluding volume of Miss Blow's version of Froebel's noted work which laid the foundation for that important branch of early education, the kindergarten. The first volume, "The Mottoes and Commentaries," may be designated as the Teacher s or Mother's book, and "The Songs and Music," the present volume, as the Children's book. In the latter, many of the pictures have been enlarged in parts to bring out the details more distinctly. New translations are made of the songs, eliminating the crudities of poetic composition that have appeared in the litera-imitations of Froebel, and new music is substituted where the original has been disl carded.

*T*HE MOTTOES AND COMMENTARIES OF FRIEDRICH FROEBEL'S MOTHER PLAY. " Mother Communings and Mottoes" rendered into English verse by HENRIETTA R. ELIOT, and "Prose Commentaries" translated by SUSAN E. BLOW. With 48 full-page illustrations. 12mo. Cloth, $1.50.

The increased interest in kindergarten work, and the demand for a clearer exposition of Froebel's philosophy than has heretofore appeared, have made a new version of the "Mother Play" an imperative necessity. No one is better equipped for such a work than Miss Blow, as her late book, " Symbolic Education," has attested. It is an attractive volume of a convenient size, and a book of specific value to mothers, as well as to teachers of every grade. It will be followed shortly by another volume, containing the songs and games.

Toronto : GEORGE N. MORANG, 63 Yonge St.

www.ingramcontent.com/pod-product-compliance
Lightning Source LLC
Chambersburg PA
CBHW032315280326
41932CB00009B/821